The changing situation in South Africa and Eastern Europe prompts Charles Villa-Vicencio to investigate the implications of transforming liberation theology into a theology of reconstruction and nation-building. Such a transformation, he argues, requires theology to become an unambiguously inter-disciplinary study.

This book explores the encounter between theology, on the one hand, and constitutional writing, law-making, human rights, economics, and the freedom of conscience on the other. Locating his discussion in the context of the South African struggle, the author compares this situation to that in Eastern Europe, and the challenge of what is happening in these situations is identified for contexts where 'the empire has not yet crumbled'.

A THEOLOGY OF RECONSTRUCTION

CAMBRIDGE STUDIES IN IDEOLOGY AND RELIGION

General Editors: DUNCAN FORRESTER *and* ALISTAIR KEE

Editorial Board: JOSÉ MÍGUEZ BONINO, REBECCA S. CHOPP, JOHN DE GRUCHY, GRAHAM HOWES, YEOW CHOO LAK, DAVID MCLELLAN, KENNETH MEDHURST, RAYMOND PLANT, CHRISTOPHER ROWLAND, ELISABETH SCHÜSSLER-FIORENZA, CHARLES VILLA-VICENCIO, HADDON WILLMER

Religion increasingly is seen as a renewed force, and is recognised as an important factor in the modern world in all aspects of life – cultural, economic, and political. It is no longer a matter of surprise to find religious factors at work in areas and situations of political tension. However, our information about these situations has tended to come from two main sources. The news-gathering agencies are well-placed to convey information, but are hampered by the fact that their representatives are not equipped to provide analysis of the religious forces involved. Alternatively, the movements generate their own accounts, which understandably seem less than objective to outside observers. There is no lack of information or factual material, but a real need for sound academic analysis. 'Cambridge Studies in Ideology and Religion' will meet this need. It will give an objective, balanced, and programmatic coverage to issues which – while of wide potential interest – have been largely neglected by analytical investigation, apart from the appearance of sporadic individual studies. Intended to enable debate to proceed at a higher level, the series should lead to a new phase in our understanding of the relationship between ideology and religion.

A THEOLOGY OF RECONSTRUCTION

Nation-building and human rights

CHARLES VILLA-VICENCIO

Professor of Religion and Society,
University of Cape Town

CAMBRIDGE
UNIVERSITY PRESS

Published by the Press Syndicate of the University of Cambridge
The Pitt Building, Trumpington Street, Cambridge CB2 1RP
40 West 20th Street, New York, NY 10011–4211, USA
10 Stamford Road, Oakleigh, Victoria 3166, Australia

First published 1992

Printed in Great Britain at the University Press, Cambridge

A catalogue record for this book is available from the British Library

Library of Congress cataloguing in publication data

Villa-Vicencio, Charles.
A theology of reconstruction: nation-building and human rights /
by Charles Villa-Vicencio.
p.   cm. – (Cambridge studies in ideology and religion)
Includes bibliography references and index.
ISBN 0-521-41625-6. – ISBN 0-521-42628-6 (pbk.)
1. Christianity and politics. 2. Human rights – Religious aspects – Christianity
3. Economics – Religious aspects – Christianity.
4. Law and ethics.   I. *Title.*   II. *Series.*
BR 115.P7V55   1992
261.7–dc20   91-30793 CIP

ISBN 0521 41625 6 hardback
ISBN 0521 42628 6 paperback

SE

Contents

Dedicated to Frank Chikane

General editors' preface

Only twenty years ago it was widely assumed that religion had lost its previous place in western culture and that this pattern would spread throughout the world. Since then religion has become a renewed force, recognised as an important factor in the modern world in all aspects of life, cultural, economic and political. This is true not only of the Third World, but in Europe East and West, and in North America. It is no longer a surprise to find a religious factor at work in areas of political tension.

Religion and ideology form a mixture which can be of interest to the observer, but in practice dangerous and explosive. Our information about such matters comes for the most part from three types of sources. The first is the media which understandably tend to concentrate on newsworthy events, without taking the time to deal with the underlying issues of which they are but symptoms. The second source comprises studies by social scientists who often adopt a functionalist and reductionist view of the faith and beliefs which motivate those directly involved in such situations. Finally, there are the statements and writings of those committed to the religious or ideological movements themselves. We seldom lack information, but there is a need – often an urgent need – for sound objective analyses which can make use of the best contemporary approaches to both politics and religion. 'Cambridge Studies in Ideology and Religion' is designed to meet this need.

The subject matter is global and this will be reflected in the choice both of topics and of authors. The initial volumes will be concerned primarily with movements involving the Christian religion, but as the series becomes established movements involving other world religions will be subjected to the same objective critical analysis. In all cases it is our intention that an accurate and sensitive account of religion should be informed by an objective and sophisticated application of perspectives from the social sciences.

Theologies of liberation, struggle and protest have made a major contribution to today's theological debate. They have had considerable impact in Latin America and many other parts of the Third World, and are by no means examples of 'arm-chair' theology. But there comes a time when theology must address a rather different agenda, not neglecting, but building upon, the concerns of liberation theology. This pioneering study by a leading South African theologian opens up the issues of theological responsibility for nation-building in post-apartheid South Africa. But its relevance to other situations and its significance as a work of constructive interdisciplinary theology are considerable. It is sure to stimulate widespread discussion.

DUNCAN FORRESTER AND ALISTAIR KEE
New College, University of Edinburgh

Acknowledgements

This book is largely the fruits of a sabbatical year spent at Georgetown University in Washington DC in 1990. During this year as Visiting Fellow at Woodstock Theological Center and Visiting Scholar at the Kennedy Institute of Ethics, both on the Georgetown Campus. I enjoyed access to the vast facilities of the university. Jack DeGioia, dean of students, was the person who on behalf of the university 'put it all together'. My first word of sincere appreciation goes to Jack. Without his support and enthusiastic assistance at numerous different levels, the research that resulted in this manuscript would not have happened. The time of personal enrichment for us as a family in the United States is a legacy that we cherish.

The financial and other forms of assistance received from Georgetown University is gratefully acknowledged. The sabbatical and research leave which enabled me to be absent from my responsibilities in the Department of Religious Studies at the University of Cape Town is appreciated. The financial assistance of the Institute for Research Development towards the research which resulted in this book is also acknowledged. The opinions expressed in the book, and conclusions arrived at, are those of the author and should not necessarily be attributed to the Institute of Research Development. Chapters 1 and 2 appeared in different forms in the *Journal of Church and State* (32, Autumn, 1990) and the *Emory Law Journal* (40:1, Winter, 1991) respectively.

Given the interdisciplinary nature of the research that has gone into the writing of this book, I am necessarily indebted to a number of scholarly experts in a range of academic fields who have given of their time to read, discuss and comment on various aspects of my work. Some were generous enough to read the entire manuscript in its penultimate form. Their observations, corrections and questions have contributed greatly to what now appears between these two covers. It is customary to exonerate such people of all responsibility for errors in fact or judgment that may have made their way into the pages that follow. This I readily do. Some have directly contributed to, and helped shape, opinion expressed in the book. Others do not agree with all the opinions and judgments I have expressed. All have nevertheless generously engaged me in dialogue, and I am extremely grateful to them for this process. These include: Jim Connor, John Langan and Terry Pinkard at Georgetown University; Eugene Klaaren at Wesleyan University; Kadar Asmal, Pieter le Roux and Dullah Omar at the University of the Western Cape, Laurie Ackermann and Bernard Lategan at Stellenbosch University; and Sean Archer, Mike de Klerk, Johan Maree and John de Gruchy at the University of Cape Town. Colleagues in the Institute of Contextual Theology, Smangaliso Mkhatshwa and Albert Nolan have also contributed to this project in discussion and debate, as have Paul Germond, Robin Petersen and Molefe Tsele, South African doctoral students presently studying in the United States. Ed Huenemann, George Hunsinger, Rosemary Ruether and many others were, in turn, generous enough to give time to discuss aspects of my work. Lindiwe Mabuza, Madoda Hlatshwayo, Tladi Ditshego and Nenzi Plaatje, South African exiles in Washington DC, each in different ways contributed to the research and publication of this book. I am most thankful to them.

No manuscript sees the light of day, even in the days of word processors, without secretarial assistance. My usual most sincere appreciative gratitude goes to Pat Lawrence. And then one's family pays the inevitable price associated with a writing project. Eileen, Heidi and Tanya have all assisted me greatly.

My most sincere 'acknowledgement' is for the privilege of having lived my days in the troubled land of my birth, South Africa. Context shapes perceptions, ideas and ideals. In the struggle for a new South Africa I have gained such strength that I have. In despair and hope I have been empowered. And now in anticipation of a new age of struggle and realisation I reach forward to the emergence of a society built on the strong foundation of justice, non-racism, non-sexism and democracy.

The quest for things that are new has been shaped in this land by many people, both within and without the church. I dedicate this book to one such person whose costly, formative influence in both church and society is very significant – Frank Chikane, General Secretary of the South African Council of Churches.

Cape Town

Introduction

Winds of change are blowing across large sections of the globe, with the political crises in Eastern Europe, the Soviet Union and South Africa presenting a new challenge for theology. Hitherto the task of liberation theologians has essentially been to say 'No' to all forms of oppression. The prophetic 'No' must, of course, continue to be part of a liberating theology. As the enduring struggle for democracy in some parts of the world begins to manifest itself in differing degrees of success, however, so the prophetic task of the church must include a thoughtful and creative 'Yes' to options for political and social renewal.

Crisis fatigue and political indifference on the part of those removed from the anguish of oppression, together with a relentless longing to break down and destroy by those who have suffered most over generations of authoritarian rule, is slowly giving way to a measure of cautious optimism in South Africa. It is an optimism inter-mingled with a fear that the winds of change might become simply another whirlwind, without the promise of anything decisively new. This would result in further polarisation, conflict, violence and human defeat – a possibility with which society is always obliged to contend.

In the wake of these developments seers, prophets and political pundits are eager to make pronouncements, offer predictions and project utopian solutions. Commenting within a lesser climate of expectations some years back, British historian E.P. Thompson observed: 'watch . . . for a century or two before you cut your hedges down!'[1] His words are sobering and come as

---

[1] E.P. Thompson, *Whigs and Hunters: The Origin of the Black Act* (New York: Pantheon Books, 1975), p. 266.

I

sound advice for those engaged in important global and regional struggles for qualitative change. There is at the same time an *urgent* need to seize the moment, in shaping a new age.

Unlike many political situations around the world, within which there is no obvious end to entrenched oppression and political captivity in sight, in Eastern Europe, the Soviet Union and South Africa it can be said, 'the old *is* dying' even though 'the new is not yet born', and there is no clear indication what form the new society might take.[2] The suggestion behind the pages that follow is that if there be anything new under the political sun it is likely to be manifest in situations of genuine crisis, where the context *demands* creativity and change as the only reasonable basis for just and peaceful co-existence. Renewal occurs, as suggested in what follows (without insinuat-ing that there is any 'quick fix' solution), not where empires endure and power reigns, but where ideologies crumble and failure is acknowledged. The lessons learned in areas of conflict are at the same time lessons worth learning in relation to more stable situations where inequality, racism, sexism and class division also abound, even though the political and economic infra-structures in these situations still hold.

The task of the church, whose theological responsibility it is to restore justice and affirm human dignity within the context of God's impending reign, is to join with others to ensure that the 'new' which emerges in those regions where renewal now seems possible, is a qualitative improvement on the 'old'. It is to ensure that in the process of reconstruction nations are able to turn away from greed, domination and exploitation, in whatever clothes they may appear, to an age of communal sharing *and* personal fulfilment. The quest for human rights and the struggle for just law-making within these contexts provides, at the level of both theory and praxis, an opportunity for renewal among all the nations of the world – not least the dominant nations of the West that gloat over the collapse of eastern bloc countries.

The South African debate on human rights, given the demographic, racist, sexist, economic and political contradic-tions within which it is located, constitutes an important global

---

[2] Antonio Gramsci, *Selections from the Prison Notebooks*, edited by Q. Hoare (London: G. Nowell Smith, 1971), p. 276.

focus with implications well beyond its own borders. This is what makes the present study more than a book on South Africa. The issues involved have significance for the wider international community, at the centre of which is the political and theological imperative to balance individual freedom and communal justice.

The study is unambiguously inter-disciplinary. It is written at the nexus of theological, political, economic, philosophical and legal debate, with a focus on human rights in a struggle for the creation of a more equitable and just society. There is an implicit theology operative even within the non-theological sections of the book. Indeed, without what Horkheimer called a 'theological moment' – the space for critique, openness and renewal within secular debate – 'no matter how skilful, [politics] in the last analysis is mere business'.[3] This is a category of politics which simply cannot be afforded if a new kind of society is to emerge where oppression is dominant today. The more obvious theological sections of the book, on the other hand, are written in dialogue with and in response to theoretical issues and problems raised by contemporary legal and political philosophers and economic theorists. As such every effort is made to acknowledge and define the existing secular debate on the topics under consideration, as basis for enquiry and debate.

CONTEXTUAL DEMANDS

The particular challenge in this regard obviously differs from one social context to another. Kyril, the Archbishop of Smolensk and Kaliningrad has, for example, spoken of the implications which the process of *perestroika* has presented for the church in the Soviet Union:

For the first time in decades society is opening up and finding the opportunity to hear the voice of the church. This signifies that the church is recovering the opportunity to realise her pastoral ministry in all its fullness, and to act as a personal and societal standard. The new situation offers the church new challenges; society now wants to know the church's position on issues of individual and social morality,

---

[3] M. Horkheimer, 'Die Sehnsucht nach dem ganz Andern: ein interview mit Kommentaar von Helmut Gumnoir', (Hamburg: Furche, 1975), p. 60.

politics, economics, ecology, culture, education, international relations, the rearing of children, marriage and much more. Naturally the
church's response must bear a pastoral character, and be founded
upon serious theological assessment. It must be geared first of all to the
members of the church, but not only to them. For without the
cooperative efforts of believers and non believers it will be impossible to
surmount the problems faced by society today. Therefore the response
of the church must be formulated in language which is understandable
not only to Christians . . . Is it not acceptable for the church to refrain
from participation in law-making and from the opportunity to
influence the political process, where not only the church's own future
but the future of the entire country is dependent upon laws and
political decisions?

Despite the difference in social context with which the church is
confronted in the Soviet Union and certain Eastern European
countries on the one hand and South Africa on the other, the
Archbishop's words go a long way to providing an agenda for the
church generally. In situations where the church's voice has long
been silenced in the political arena, people may well 'want to
know' what the church has to say on a variety of political and
socio-economic issues. In the West the situation is different. Here
the church has often failed to express any ideas significantly
different to those of the dominant classes, and certainly failed in
praxis to show itself to have an identity readily distinguishable
from that of dominant society. Unless the church is able in these
situations to translate the values of the *gospel* into practice, and
proclaim its beliefs in a language that makes sense even to those
who are no longer interested in its views, it may well have no
significant role at all to play in the period of reconstruction. This
means that unless the church's theological values make sense to
those beyond its own membership, and are given expression
through secular debate in a language understandable to a broad
constituency of people (without any attempt to draw attention
to itself), it may not be heard at all.

GIVING LIFE TO PALE THEORY

Whether the overt crises in Eastern Europe, the Soviet Union
and South Africa can become the cradles of new global socio-

political and economic formation and intellectual renewal only time will tell. What, however, is often sterile discussion on social theory, dry theological debate and abstract philosophical reflection has already acquired a new urgency in, and in relation to, these situations. Latent ideas, long buried in ancient doctrines and theories are being activated in new ways, and people who have traditionally espoused (or simply been trapped in) one or another secular or religious philosophy of life are being drawn beyond any point that they ever thought they would be prepared to go – opening up new possibilities for the new social, political and economic syntheses to occur.

The consideration of philosophical, economic and legal ideas in what follows is limited and modest. The author is a theologian. This much will become clear from the sections dealing with non-theological subjects. The realisation that a theology of reconstruction cannot be written in isolation from a range of social disciplines is, however, hopefully enough to justify the theological reaching into politics, economics and law-making which follows, with every attempt being made to lift this exercise above mere meddling. The attempt is to address *theological* issues which emerge from debate within the areas to which reference has been made.

As such there is no intent to become engaged in all the specialised academic problems encountered *en route*, nor to follow each ethical problem to its logical conclusion. It is rather to use the existing philosophical, economic and legal debate as a basis for setting a limited current inter-disciplinary agenda for a *theological* consideration of human rights.

The point of departure is *liberal* theory, primarily because of the importance this tradition has played regarding the rule of law and the human rights debate. Turning to the radical critical tradition, influenced as it is by Marxian thought, the highest ideals of liberalism and socialism are weighed and tested in an attempt to respond to the demands of an historically unequal and radically pluralistic society.

John Keats once commented on seeing Benjamin West's *Death on a Pale Horse*: 'It is a wonderful picture . . . but there is nothing to be intense upon; no woman one feels mad to kiss, no face swelling into reality.'[4] Social theory, whether of political, legal, theological or economic ilk, removed from a renewing context which gives passion and life to the 'pale horse', can be little more than a form of escapism from the realities of injustice, loneliness and conflict which destroy the human spirit. To the extent that theory, on the other hand, emerges from the context of struggle and is developed in relation to struggle, it is part of the struggle for renewal.

Most South Africans are aware that something different *must* be born if the country is not to be torn apart by competing ideologies. As the struggle in South Africa intensifies, there is also a cautious but growing hope that something new and important *can* be born here. It needs to transcend the limitations of the aggressive individualism without social concern which dominates so many western countries, as well as the sterility and submission to that brand of socialism without democracy or individual responsibility associated (until recently) with Eastern Europe.

The various contextual theologies that have over the years emerged from within the South African struggle have constituted an important part of resistance within this country. This same struggle, now in a decisively new phase, is contributing to further theological turmoil and renewal as the process of political reconstruction and nation-building unfolds. One consequence manifests itself in the theological quest for liberation (formally grounded almost exclusively in the biblical theme of the exodus) now in the shape of a theology of nation-building, drawing on different biblical metaphors. These include the *wilderness* experience before entering the promised land, the *exile* prior to rebuilding Jerusalem and the return of the Babylonian exiles in the *post-exilic* period. Seriously to anticipate a post-apartheid South Africa and realistically to share in the process of creating a liberating and healing culture of human rights in South Africa, requires that the reality of the past and the pathos of the present specifically inform all that is undertaken in an attempt to create a new future. In other words,

---

[4] *Letters of John Keats*, edited by Maurice Forman (London: Oxford University Press, 1952), p. 70.

in looking forward to possibilities of justice, we are obliged to do so retroactively, remembering past failures and mistakes and present challenges. Because South Africa is in so many ways a microcosm of global problems, the opportunities inherent to this exercise could have global implications which other nations of the world can scarcely afford to ignore.

In this context, debate on and the search for political, moral, legal and theological solutions is more than an exciting academic exercise. It has to do with the creation of social structures, with which people will be obliged to live for generations to come. The life and death of millions of people is dependent on the outcome of this search.

A THEOLOGY OF RECONSTRUCTION

The banning and restricting of political leaders and organisations in South Africa prior to 2 February 1990 had confronted the church with a challenge to fill the political vacuum, in providing a social and political space for resistance to continue. Many within the church managed to rise to this challenge only with great difficulty. Others did so with more purpose, while a few helped lead the charge in saying 'No' to the atrocities of the apartheid regime.[5]

The challenge now facing the church is different. The complex options for a new South Africa require more than resistance. The church is obliged to begin the difficult task of saying 'Yes' to the unfolding process of what could culminate in a democratic, just and kinder social order.

The kind of theology of reconstruction demanded by this challenge is in every sense a post-exilic theology. It addresses a situation within which political exiles are quite literally returning home, having left the country in steady streams since the banning of the African National Congress and the Pan Africanist Congress in 1960. It involves the important task of breaking-down prejudices of race, class and sexism, and the difficult task of creating an all-inclusive (non-racial and

---

[5] See, C. Villa-Vicencio, *Trapped in Apartheid: A Socio-Theological History of the English-Speaking Churches* (Maryknoll: Orbis. Cape Town: David Philip, 1987).

democratic) society built on the very values denied the majority of people under apartheid. As this challenge is met, *it could mean the birth of a different kind of liberatory theology*. As already suggested it would need to be of a radically interdisciplinary nature, emerging at the interface between theology and law, economics, political science and related disciplines. This constitutes a decisive methodological challenge facing theology in the decades ahead.

It is a task that will involve the theological wisdom of the ages and the discerning creativity of contextual decision-making. It has to do with bridging the gap between the ideals of a people who have in their long exile (without and within the country) dreamed utopian dreams of a new South Africa, and the realities of a land torn apart by generations of race, gender and class division. It will at the same time need to be developed within a context marked by an apartheid ravaged economy. Utopian visions created by prophets, preachers and poets are important ingredients in the process of reconstruction. Ultimately, how-ever, these visions need to be translated into social practice and laws operative in the here and now. This practice and these laws will necessarily fall short of the projected vision, but must provide the basis and vision for the long walk to social and economic freedom beyond political liberation.

Here the life-giving power and incentive of theological and other visions must be integrated into the stubborn realities of everyday life. The social demands of the gospel must never be reduced to the social realism of a given time and place. Bonhoeffer's words need to remain central to a theology of reconstruction:

[When] the message is trimmed and cropped until it fits the frame for which it has been decided, the result is that the eagle (with clipped wings) can no longer rise and fly away to its true element but be pointed out as a special showpiece among the animals.[6]

To quote the revered Afrikaner theologian Andrew Murray, 'the danger always exists that the voice of blood, the voice of passion, of partisanship, of group interest will overpower the

[6] Dietrich Bonhoeffer, *No Rusty Swords* (New York: Harper and Row, 1965), p. 309.

voice of the gospel'.[7] The gospel vision, which demands more than a given society can offer, needs to function as a source of continuing social vision and renewal.

The immediate task of an ethic of reconstruction involves placing certain values and structures in position to *begin* the process of social renewal. A neglected ethical device designed to serve this need emerged from the work of J.H. Oldham in 1937, as he faced the social crisis that ultimately engulfed the world in war. Speaking at the Oxford Conference on Life and Work, he referred to the urgent need for the creation of 'middle axioms' to facilitate social construction.[8] He saw these axioms as 'not binding for all time', but rather as 'provisional definitions' of the kind of society required to meet the challenges of the time. John Bennett suggested they constitute 'the next steps that our own generation must take'.[9] A theology of reconstruction in the 1990s in situations of social revolution is required to address a situation similar to that where the church (and indeed all social and political institutions) failed prior to World War II. John Bennett's challenge to the church after the war is also a challenge which a contemporary theology of reconstruction needs to take seriously.

It is at the same time always important to locate the 'middle axioms' of society under the renewing power of the gospel which demands more than a society can deliver at a particular time. To fail to do so could result in a form of civil religion which is sometimes used merely to legitimate the existing social order.

THEOLOGY AND LAW

Concerned to emphasise the tentative and changing nature of 'middle axioms', Oldham saw them to be less rigid than fixed laws or moral codes. They were, for him, *evolving principles*. Constantly being reshaped by the eschatological vision of the

---

[7] Quoted in Andre Hugo, 'Christelik-Nasionaal in Suid Afrika', *Pro Veritate*, May, 1968).

[8] W.A. Visser 't Hooft and J.H. Oldham, *The Church and its Function in Society* (Chicago: Willet, Clarke and Co, 1937), p. 210.

[9] John Bennett, *Christian Ethics and Social Policy* (New York: Charles Scribner's Sons, 1946), pp. 76–7.

gospel, middle axioms function as a lure, drawing society beyond values to which it holds at any particular time of its history, while specifically addressing the challenges of the time. As such they constituted a theological incentive to a society in perpetual growth, while seeking to provide specific content for a specific context.

Thomas Jefferson sought to incorporate a similar incentive into the law-making process in the eighteenth century. He affirmed certain truths, which constitute the basis of all laws, to be self-evident:

That all men are created equal, that they are endowed by their Creator with certain inalienable rights, among these are life, liberty, and the pursuit of happiness.

At the same time he realised that the renewal and transformation of all values was the responsibility of each new generation. (Little did he realise that this responsibility would include the need to transform sexually exclusive language!)

I am not an advocate for frequent changes in laws and constitutions (he wrote to a friend), but laws and institutions must go hand in hand with progress of the human mind. As that becomes more developed, more enlightened, as new discoveries are made, new truths discovered and manners and opinions change, with the change of circumstances, institutions must advance also to keep pace with the times. We might as well require a man to wear still the coat which fitted him when a boy, as civilized society to remain ever under the regimen of barbarous ancestors.[10]

Recognising the importance of the sanctity and stability of law, Harold Berman in *The Interaction of Law and Religion*, recognises the need for law to function 'as an active, living human process' which 'involves . . . man's whole being, including his dreams, his passions, his ultimate concerns'.[11] 'Law', he argues, 'through its stability limits the future; religion through its sense of the holy challenges all existing social

---

[10] See the inscriptions on the walls of the Thomas Jefferson Memorial in Washington DC.

[11] Harold J. Berman, *The Interaction of Law and Religion* (Nashville: Abingdon Press, 1974), p. 31.

structures'.[12] These two emphases need to be held in creative tension.

Theology, it will be argued in a later chapter, requires law to provide a life-giving sense of order and purpose to society. It is at the same time, correctly understood, an incentive to transform law. 'Grace', said Barth, 'is the enemy of everything, even of the most indispensable "interim ethic". Grace is the axe laid at the root of the good conscience which the politician and civil servant always wish to enjoy.'[13] As such grace is for Barth the source of a God-given restlessness located at the heart of social construction.[14] It is the source of what Paul Lehmann has called Barth's theology of 'permanent revolution', giving rise to a political incentive which powerfully militates against the absolutisation of any human revolution or set of social values. The loss of a sense of the biblical notion of the *eschaton* which always demands more than any particular society can offer is, for Barth, the beginning of social atrophy and the institutionalisation of oppression.[15]

The need for continuing social renewal is central to Berman's perception of law as the 'living . . . functional *process* of allocating rights and duties, of resolving conflicts, of creating forms and channels of cooperation'. 'Religion', he suggests 'is a shared intuition of and collective concern for the ultimate meaning and purpose of life'.[16] Developing the importance of the dialectic between law and religion, John Witte, emphasises that the relationship between the two should never be reduced to either 'dualistic antinomy nor monistic unity'. 'Law', he suggests, 'helps to give society the structure, the order, the predictability it needs to survive. Religion helps to give society the faith, the vision, the *telos* it needs to move forward.'

---

[12] *Ibid.*, p. 24.
[13] Karl Barth, *The Epistle to the Romans* (London: Oxford University Press, 1960), p. 430.
[14] *Ibid.*, pp. 475–502; Karl Barth, *The Word of God and the Word of Man* (New York: Harper and Row, 1975, p. 299. See also my 'Karl Barth's Revolution of God: Quietism or Anarchy?' in C. Villa-Vicencio (ed.), *On Reading Karl Barth in South Africa* (Grand Rapids: Eerdmans, 1988), pp. 45–58.
[15] Paul Lehmann, 'Karl Barth, The Theologian of Permanent Revolution', *Union Seminary Quarterly Review*, 28 (1972).
[16] Berman, *The Interaction* p. 24. Italics are added.

Without religion, (Witte argues) law decays into empty formalism. Without law, religion decays into shallow spiritualism. Part of the crisis of our law today is that it has become formalistic, dispirited, undirected, lacking in vision. It has lost its religious dimension. Part of the crisis of our religion is that it has become spiritualistic, disorganized, diluted, lacking in discipline. It has lost its legal dimension.[17]

At the centre of a post-exilic theology of reconstruction is an encounter between theology and jurisprudence. 'Religion and law' could become the next vital point at which theological growth should take place. Bonhoeffer's concern to affirm the renewing presence of God at the centre of life and to discern the presence of God in the 'ordinary' has long haunted theology. 'God', he said, 'is the beyond in the midst of life.' To acknowledge this God is to acknowledge a sense of openness beyond the dogma and ideology of any human revolution.[18] It is the challenge of our times, Bonhoeffer thought, to speak of this presence in a *religionless* way. The church, he said, was obliged 'to lose its life . . . in its service to and through the world'.[19] In secular parlance this has something to do with promoting the rule of law and facilitating liberatory law-making as a basis for social transformation.

To acknowledge the presence of God at the centre of life has to do with the proclamation of the public meaning of the gospel. To do so in a religionless way is to be prepared to promote this meaning without drawing attention to the church. It has to do with affirming a liberating reality at the centre of the political arena which challenges and transcends what the political elite may regard 'liberation', 'national identity' or 'political realism' to mean at any given time, while recognising that specific, concrete and realistic steps are required to attain this goal in the here and now. Politics, suggested Bonhoeffer, is about the penultimate. It has to do with the shaping of society before the dawning of the kingdom. As a penultimate he suggests politics must be taken very seriously. At the same time it is *not* to be taken

[17] John Witte, 'The Study of Law and Religion: An Apologia and Agenda', *Ministry and Mission*, 14:4 (Fall, 1988).
[18] Dietrich Bonhoeffer, *Letters and Papers From Prison* (London: Fontana Books, 1964), p. 155.   [19] *Ibid.* p. 91.

seriously, in the sense that social vision is what is most important.

This in a nutshell is the essence of the theological contribution to social reconstruction. It is a theology committed to enthusiastic participation in the constitutional debate, the establishment of a society governed by the rule of law, the affirmation of human rights and the creation of laws designed to produce justice *now*. The church, in other words is obliged, in the words of John Bennett, to promote 'the next steps that our generation must take' in order to attain social justice.[20] It must also keep alive a social vision of what society ought to become. As such it is a theology which must continually subject even the most essential (self-evident) truths enshrined within the instruments of statecraft to review, renewal and the process of reshaping in response to the 'revolution of God'.

LEARNING FROM THE PAST

The quest is for a new kind of liberating theology to meet a new kind of challenge. It is at the same time important to draw on the experience of past attempts to theologically share in social reconstruction. The notion of middle axioms emerged as Oldham, Bennett and others struggled to make sense of the European crisis of the 1930s and 40s. Karl Barth, whose thought is returned to in later sections of this study, wrote explicitly in relation to Hitler's Germany, and later within the context of European reconstruction after 1945. Bonhoeffer anticipated the role of the church in modernity with a skill shared perhaps by none. Others before them – Calvin in Geneva, the Nonconformists in Britain and evangelicals in revolutionary America all addressed the complexities of political reconstruction, endeavouring to enable the church to collapse neither into Constantinian conformity nor to be the agent for cataclysmic revolution. The Wesleyan revival in eighteenth-century Britain, and the Social Gospel Movement in the United States and elsewhere, addressed social renewal with a sense of vigour that can scarcely be ignored in present attempts to address nation-building from a theological perspective. The important study, *Christian Participa-*

[20] See footnote number 6.

tion in Nation-Building in India, under the direction of M.M. Thomas and P.D. Devanandan, in turn, provides invaluable insights for a contemporary theology of reconstruction.[21]

Certainly not all that emerged from these initiatives served the process of serious social renewal, and much played directly into the hands of the dominant classes. The tragedy is, however, that the salutary voices of decisive theological responsibility and renewal that *do* constitute part of the Christian tradition have frequently been ignored by the institutional church in its capitulation to social and other pressures during periods of political reconstruction.

In articulating a theology of reconstruction in response to the momentous events of the 1990s, the lessons of social renewal in earlier times need to be remembered and taken into the dialogue with the present. As such the United Nations' Declaration of Human Rights drafted in the wake of the devastation of Hitler's pillage and destruction, as well as related international and regional human rights documents need to form part of this process. The theological response of the churches to nation-building in Africa and in other Third World situations provides further material for reassessment as the church faces the challenge of social renewal.

The issues confronting places of contemporary renewal – hope, expectation, realism, power and greed are the issues that others have faced both politically and theologically. There is not much new under the political sun. We would do well to learn from the partial successes and dismal failures of those who have travelled this road before.

The sober (and moderate) character of the reconstruction debate in South Africa is partly in response to this realisation. It has emerged in response to generations of shattered dreams and persistent struggle. This less than romantic state of affairs comes, of course, as a disappointment to some within the 'old world' who long for the exotic and different as a basis for responding to their own social and theological captivity. The contradictions of

---

[21] *Christian Participation in Nation-Building: The Summing Up of a Corporate Study on Rapid Social Change*, compiled by M.M. Thomas (Bangalore: National Christian Council of India and Christian Institute for the Study of Religion and Society, 1960).

the existing structures, social and economic systems and the theological ideas in South Africa are at the same time being stretched to breaking point. Indigenous values are being introduced as a basis for 'new' (and yet 'old') answers to the stubborn challenges of our time. The continuity between First and Third World debates, together with the realisation that problems faced in Pretoria, Moscow, Gdansk and in the eastern part of a united Germany are not vastly different from those latent in Washington, Paris, London and Bonn, in turn, emphasise the irreversibility of the inter-related, global character of contemporary political debate and struggle.

This suggests that the more or less comfortable divide between First and Third World theologies that has in recent years simply come to be accepted by theologians on both sides of the divide, needs to be challenged and overcome with a new sense of urgency. There are lessons which each needs to learn from the other.

GENDER AND RACE

A theology of reconstruction is essentially a remedial and compensatory theology. It has a special responsibility to put right past wrongs and old abuses. This makes affirmative action a central ingredient to a constructive nation-building process, requiring that the topics to be dealt with in the present study – constitutionalism, human rights, questions of political economy and the freedom of conscience – be assessed and promoted with a view to showing a priority concern for those marginalised by past discriminatory laws and practices. In the South African situation this requires affirmative action regarding blacks and also women.

Affirmative action (including the complex notion of human equality before the law) and gender and race are not, however, dealt with as separate issues in the pages that follow. These issues are assumed to stand central to each of the topics under consideration. This methodological approach is obviously open to criticism. Accepting that the time must come when there will be no reason for special comment on the rights of people who are women and/or black, some would argue (with good cause) that the continued disadvantaged status of people by virtue of gender or race necessitates separate comment in a book of this kind. The chapter entitled 'Judges and Gender: The Constitutional Rights of Women in Post-Apartheid South Africa', in Albie Sach's *Protecting Human Rights in a New South Africa*, points to the kind of discussion that could well have brought an emphasis to this book that is lacking.[22] The alternative argument is that human rights and socio-economic liberation, which includes a rider on the rights of women and black people, implies that women and blacks be dealt with *differently* from the rest of the human race. In reality males constitute only half the human population, and ruling-class males perhaps as little as 5 per cent of the entire global population. The plight of women, black people and other exploited groups, forming the overwhelming majority of people on earth and discriminated against by successive ruling-classes in most societies (not least South Africa), ought to inform *every* aspect of planning for a new era. Differently stated, exploited people should form the *norm*, not the exception to a human rights agenda. Theology, compelled by a biblical imperative to show a special preference for the poor, oppressed, marginalised and excluded sections of society, has a special obligation never to lose sight of this requirement.

Convention on the Elimination of All Forms of Discrimination Against Women (The Women's Charter) of the United Nations, which came into force in September 1981, is a comprehensive and widely acclaimed international instrument on women's rights. It, *inter alia*, urges states to 'take all appropriate measures, including legislation, to modify or abolish existing laws, regulations, customs and practices which constitute discrimination against women'; not simply to prevent discrimination but to 'ensure the full development and achievement of women and . . . in particular in the political, social, economic and cultural fields . . . guaranteeing them the exercise and enjoyment of human rights and fundamental freedoms on a basis of equality with men'.[23]

---

[22] Albie Sachs, *Protecting Human Rights in a New South Africa* (Cape Town: Oxford University Press, 1990), pp. 53–63.

[23] *Convention on the Elimination of All Form of Discrimination Against Women*, 18 December 1979, 34 UN GOAR Supp. (No. 21) (A/34/46).

Discrimination against women continues, however, to persist. This is a stubborn reality which no advocate of human rights – simply no decent person – can afford to ignore.

Discrimination against women in South Africa is older than the colonially imposed scourge of apartheid, and it may well be more difficult to eradicate than racism. The ground swell of claims and expectations in a new South Africa are, at the same time, likely to include the demands of women for their rights. At the forefront of this struggle will be black women – the most oppressed of all the oppressed. The problem is not, however, peculiar to Africa. If language be a measure of culture, it is blatantly clear that sexism is as much part of the culture of the English-speaking world as is racism. Any author who deals with historical (and contemporary) documents and literature is faced with the question what to do about sexually exclusive language. In order to avoid the ubiquitous use of '*sic*' every time the male gender dominates a quotation, these are cited without comment or alteration. To the sensitive reader the discordant note will serve as a reminder of the extent to which language has plagued our struggle for a discrimination-free culture.

THE BOOK IN OUTLINE

In *Chapter 1* the theological presuppositions already identified in this Introduction are developed in relation to the church's responsibility regarding nation-building and law-making.

In *Chapter 2* the historical context is discussed, within which this theological quest for renewal is located. For the purposes of this study it is grounded in the history of constitutionalism and law-making in South Africa. This is necessary because theologians (and other theoreticians) all too often ignore the historical pathos involved in the issues under discussion.

In *Chapter 3* the theoretical debate on human rights in social theory and legal philosophy is discussed. Theologians are notorious for answering questions that not too many other people are asking, or alternatively not appreciating the full implications of the difficult questions that are asked. The interdisciplinary nature of the present study requires that theological debate be integrated into the existing debate in cognate disciplines.

In *Chapters 4 and 5* a broad-based theology of human rights is provided in response to the historical and theoretical agenda set by the discussion in the previous chapters. In so doing a theoretical basis for individual, socio-economic and ecological rights is developed.

In *Chapters 6 and 7* human rights concerns are developed as they apply to economic questions, these being an essential part of a Christian understanding of human worth and dignity.

In *Chapter 8* the freedom of conscience and religion is discussed as a pre-requisite for democracy and continuing social renewal.

In *Chapter 9* the foregoing debate is drawn together in a methodological proposal for a theology of reconstruction.

CHAPTER I

Theology and nation-building

A theology of nation-building raises the pertinent question: Are we not repeating the same mistake all over again? Critics of theology and critical theologians alike, draw attention to a range of theological debacles within which national ideologies have been theologically legitimated to the frequent destruction of the people whose destinies they seek to promote. The mission of those burdened with what they imagine to be a divine mantle cast across their shoulders, has invariably violated their own moral integrity and destroyed their chosen victims.

The history of Christian crusaders in the 'old' world, conquistadors in the 'new' and the sense of manifest destiny among North American settlers are different manifestations of a similar theologised mission of conquest. Each is closely related to a theology of empire or nation-building. In more recent times, the missionary arm of British imperialism came close to totally destroying the cultural and religious identity of millions of colonised people. Theological support for Hitler's Third Reich contributed to the annihilation of 6 million Jews. And, most recently, theological support for Afrikaner nationalism has resulted in a cauldron of chauvinistic white supremacy and black resistance that has ultimately brought the richest and most technologically advanced country in Africa to its knees. Whatever the complexity of events which may or may not have contributed to this particular venture – a heretical, doctrinaire theology of apartheid has been the inevitable outcome.

All of this is slowly becoming a part of past history as the world enters the last decade of the twentieth century. For some it is an anachronism to even speak of a nation-building theology. In an

increasingly pluralistic world, the only hope for peaceful co-
existence, it could be argued, is secular politics – leaving the
affairs of state to the elected officials, and having theologians
confine their concerns to matters of the soul and the metaphysical complexities of reality. To leave politics to the politicians, it is
argued in what follows, is as inherently dangerous as it is to
reduce theology to a specific political ideology that ultimately
results in a marriage between church and state. The role of the
church not only in nations facing reconstruction, but also in
nations engaged in the process of continuing renewal and
reform, is of significant theological and political importance.
This is not least the case in nations where Christianity has
historically influenced popular culture, as it has in parts of
Eastern Europe, through Eastern Orthodoxy in the Soviet
Union and as a result of missionary activity in South Africa.

There is a sense in which the Edict of Milan is to be revisited.
Even to suggest this much, is heady stuff. The invitation by the
Emperor Constantine in 312CE to the church, hitherto persecuted and prevented from having any direct political influence,
to operate from *within* the power structures of the state resulted in
the church's capitulation to imperial demands. Constantine
'achieved by kindness', it has been suggested, 'what his
predecessors had not been able to achieve by force'.[1] The
Christian religion was transformed into a new imperial cult.
Despite the theological opportunity to begin anew that has come
with every major political or ecclesial revolution, the church has
never succeeded in exercising a positive, liberating and prophetic role within the structures of power. It has been either
essentially excluded from the political decision-making process,
or used as an instrument of ideological self-legitimation.

The abuse of theology for sectarian political purposes is
universal and widespread. The history of the church is shot-
through with examples of theologically legitimatised political
triumphalism and economic greed. Biblical scholars have
discerned a theological propensity to legitimate political domi-

---

[1] Alistair Kee *Constantine Versus Christ* (London: SCM Press, 1982), p. 154.

nation ever since the time of the Hebrew monarchy.[2] And a theology of political submission can readily be identified in the New Testament.[3] When Constantine managed to grab the imperial throne from his political rivals, Christians showed little resistance in rewriting their theology to support the new-found political opportunity which came in the wake of the emperor's efforts to open up the political sphere to Christians who had hitherto been regarded as politically undesirable. Medieval Europe was conquered in the name of Christ, and the Protestant Reformation was as much a theologised struggle of national independence among German princes and dissident groups in other parts of Europe as it was a religious movement. Columbus colonised the Americas bearing the cross and the sword, and the conquistadors, blessed by the church, slaughtered the Aztecs, Mayas, Incas and other indigenous nations. Kaiser Wilhelm sent his troops into battle with 'Gott mit Uns' inscribed on their buttons. 'German Christians' promoted the ideals of Nazism. British soldiers fought and died 'for God, queen and country' in British colonies scattered across the globe, and Christian symbolism is today still part of the United States of America's ideology of global conquest. These and similar abuses have convinced even those who have been theologically inspired in their resistance against oppression to acknowledge that theology has a bad track-record in the history of nation-building. Bluntly stated, theology works well in combating political abuse, but can become a dangerous device in the arena of power. This concern has legitimately resulted in a hesitation by theologians to move beyond what they regard as legitimate forms of *liberation theology* to a *theology of nation-building*.

Others have seen resistance theology as inherently ill-equipped to take this step for different reasons. Paul Tillich has, for example, insisted that while 'a mighty weapon in warfare' theologies of resistance are often 'an inconvenient tool for use in

---

[2] *Inter alia*, Walter Brueggemann, 'Trajectories in Old Testament Literature and the Sociology of Ancient Israel', in Norman K. Gottwald (ed.), *The Bible and Liberation: Political and Social Hermeneutics* (Maryknoll: Orbis, 1983), pp. 307–33.

[3] See, C.E.B. Cranfield, *The Service of God* (London: Epworth Press, 1965).

the building trade'.[4] His concern was with Barth's insistence that the most important theological contribution to be made, not only in oppressive regimes, but in *all* political situations, was to say 'No' to all political endeavour that could give rise to a sense of human pride and achievement. Reflecting on reconstruction in Europe after World War I and the failure of the 1918 Russian Revolution to realise what he and many European socialists had expected, Barth feared that a theological 'Yes' could be the first step on the slippery slope to political triumphalism and tyranny. The point has already been made. 'Grace', said Barth 'is the axe laid at the root of the good conscience which the politician and the civil servant always wish to enjoy . . . '[5] 'God's revolution', he thought, condemns not only the tyranny of unjust rulers, it also demands more than what even the most socially responsible governments can offer.[6] It is the source of what Paul Lehmann has called Barth's theology of 'permanent revolution', giving rise to a political incentive which powerfully militates against the sacralisation and/or absolutisation of any political ideology.

This kind of theology was an important political incentive in oppressive situations, such as Nazi Germany, within which Barth wrote. It has also been a powerful ingredient in theological resistance in South Africa. It furthermore has a significant contribution to make in situations of political stability, militating against political complacency where the danger always exists of the nation being elevated to the level of an absolute. National security ideologies, which dominate in many First and Third World situations, locating the state 'beyond the reach of judicial norms, beyond good and evil', are a stark vindication of Barth's theology of radical critique.[7] In emerging nations and situations of reconstruction, however, often plagued by internal divisions and suffering in the

[4] Paul Tillich, 'What is Wrong with Dialectical Theology?' *Journal of Religion*, Volume 15 (1935), p. 135.
[5] Karl Barth, *The Epistle to the Romans* (London: Oxford University Press, 1960), p. 430.
[6] *Ibid.*, pp. 475–502. Also my 'Karl Barth's Revolution of God: Quietism or Anarchy?' in C. Villa-Vicencio (ed.), *On Reading Karl Barth in South Africa* (Grand Rapids: Eerdmans, 1988), pp. 45–58.
[7] *Pro Mundi Vita Bulletin: The Churches of Latin America in Confrontation with the State and the Ideology of National Security*, No. 71, March-April, 1978, p. 7. Also Jose Comblin, *The Church and the National Security State* (Maryknoll: Orbis Books, 1979), p. 72.

aftermath of prolonged and exacting war, the primary theological task is often a different one. Here the church is frequently required to share in the creation of a culture of national unity, given to tolerance, compromise and moderation. History suggests that in this situation resistance theology more often than not surrenders its prophetic task, becoming yet another legitimating theology. Alternatively, being an 'inconvenient tool in the building trade' (Tillich) it destabilises the emerging new society, and sometimes becomes an instrument in the hands of reactionary forces. In many oppressive situations right-wing religious movements are fuelled by selectively drawing on the remnants of what were once vital religions of resistance in Nazi Germany and elsewhere. In Nicaragua, for example, this kind of theology was used as a basis to persuade some Christians to oppose the Sandinista government, and in South Africa a distorted theology of this kind has been used for condemning the forces of resistance.

In summation: Theology has, overtly and by default, often through its long history legitimated the status quo in different parts of the world. At times it has fuelled resistance and revolution, but rarely has it contributed seriously to the difficult programme of nation-building and political reconstruction. The question is whether the church is theologically capable of contributing to the establishment of good government (reducible in classical theology to promotion of the 'common good'), or whether this responsibility is better left to secular forces.

THE POST-EXILIC CHURCH

Theology is an attempt to understand 'human existence as . . . interpreted through the symbols of the Christian tradition'.[8] More specifically, it is an attempt to understand the human quest for *wholeness* in all its possible dimensions, in terms of the Judeo-Christian tradition. In this particular study, an attempt is made to make sense, in terms of this tradition, of the history of

---

[8] Langdon Gilkey, 'Theology as the Interpretation of Faith for Church and World', in Theodore Jennings (ed.), *The Vocation of the Theologian* (Philadelphia: Fortress Press, 1988), p. 90.

struggle for socio-economic, political and cultural liberation and national reconstruction within the South African context – identifying the implications of this for a political theology of a more universal kind.

Despite the complexity of the Judeo-Christian tradition (and it contains many conflicting elements and internal contradictions), a central element concerns the quest by oppressed people to break out of their captivity in response to an innate, God-given will to be free. This is a hermeneutic present within a range of Bible stories extending from those of Abraham and Sarah, through the Exodus, the Hebrew prophets and the Exile to the story of the poor man of Nazareth. St Augustine spoke of theology as a response to a restlessness located within the essence of what it means to be human. 'Do not you believe', he asked, 'that there is in [the human person] a "deep" so profound as to be hidden even to that person in whom it is.'[9] Different academic disciplines and cultures have interpreted this human restlessness differently. In each case, however, whether understood psychologically, socially or theologically, it is articulated in relation to the need to transcend the real or imaginary limits imposed on the individual or the community as a whole. The Christian tradition is primarily concerned with the interpretation of this restlessness, the quest for wholeness and the cry for emancipation from captivity (both at a communal and an individual level), in terms of what it identifies as a liberatory reality located within history and attributable to the presence of God.

The contemporary quests for liberation and reconstruction in various parts of the world are interpreted in a variety of different ways and responded to in terms of language and behaviour originating in different cultures and traditions. *Theologically* it is not the primary task of the church to impose a theological interpretation on this process. Its task is rather to assist those who do interpret life theologically to understand current developments, while encouraging those who do not interpret life theologically to respond to the liberatory struggle in other ways.

The biblical tradition tells of a people who learned little by

---

[9] St Augustine, *Expositions on the Book of Psalms*, vol. II (Oxford: A Library of the Fathers, 1848), p. 194.

little, usually only with difficulty and often reluctantly, who or what the notion of God meant. Eventually, through struggle, the Hebrew people came to associate the liberatory events of their history with a reality which they named 'God'. In other words, the reality and meaning of the Hebrew notion of God was part and parcel of the Hebrew history of liberation. God came to be understood 'as an ever new and always surprising recognition of a liberating presence'.[10] This means, God was *experienced* and *acknowledged* within history, rather than metaphysically or abstractly defined. Indeed, so sacred was the name of God that it was not even mentioned by the pious believer. To do theology in accordance with this understanding of God, is to rediscover a dynamic liberatory interpretation of God. It suggests that the most important theological task is not (evangelically) to insist that the event of liberation be named and promoted in terms of ecclesial symbols and culture, but that liberation (which is biblically understood as a manifestation of the presence of God) be celebrated and acknowledged by all people in accordance with their own culture and symbol-structure. In terms of Bonhoeffer's vision, part of the challenge of the church is to proclaim the presence of God in a secular or religionless way.[11] It is to enable people (all kinds of different people), to find unity in action as they respond to the liberatory events of life by drawing on a variety of different cultures, speaking a variety of different languages and by employing many different interpretative frameworks.

Recognising the influence of theology on the culture of many grassroots people in the West and East (including many black and white South Africans), and the role of religion (positive and negative) in the contemporary quest for liberation and reconstruction, a *theological* framework is provided in this chapter in relation to which the remaining chapters are to be understood. In so doing, the distinguishing mark of the liberation theology debate is taken as a point of departure, in affirming the *liberatory event* as the fundamentally mediating mechanism of the Chris-

[10] Cornelius Van Peursen, *It's Him Again!* (Richmond, John Knox Press, 1969), p. 106.
[11] See *Introduction*, footnote number 15. Dietrich Bonhoeffer, *Letters and Papers from Prison* (London: Fontana Books, 1964), p. 91.

tian faith – a position which is in direct continuity with the biblical revelation of God. It is a theology which insists that *event precedes word and interpretation*. The tribes of Yahweh learned who Yahweh was in response to the events of encounter and liberation which came to characterise their history. It is this realisation which motivates Christians today, struggling to understand who and where God is in the contemporary liberatory events of history.

In order to do so, the events of contemporary history need to be weighed and critiqued against biblical history, where Christians believe there is evidence to be found of the way in which God acts in history. Given the complexity of trends within the biblical and Christian tradition, however, the biblical tradition itself needs to be weighed and measured against each new experience of liberation. Not all in the Bible and Christian tradition is 'of God' in the sense of being liberatory and redemptive. A clear distinction needs to be made between the residue of oppression within the Christian tradition and that part which points to, and symbolises, the true message of liberation. This involves an exercise in discerning what Protestants define as the Word of God *within* the biblical and Christian tradition. No one would today, for example, accept biblical teaching on slavery as normative. Feminist theologians have transformed the Christian tradition to include a vision which supports the full personhood of women, and black theologians have criticised and corrected the Christian tradition from the perspective of the black struggle for liberation. James Cone speaks for many engaged in the struggle for human emancipation when he writes that black theology 'is only concerned with that tradition of Christianity which is usable in the black liberation struggle'.[12] In so doing Cone has reminded us that, if God is indeed a God of liberation, that part of the Christian tradition which is not 'usable' in the quest for liberation is perhaps little more than a cultural accretion or oppressive residue which might provide little more than an interesting comment on the history of religions. And yet, when

---

[12] James Cone, *A Black Liberation Theology* (New York: Lippincott, 1970), pp. 65 and 74.

exegeted within their own socio-historical context, even some of the most obscure and seemingly irrelevant texts acquire a new level of meaning within the contemporary situation. This debate aside, Rosemary Radford Ruether suggestively notes that each 'new liberatory experience is empowered to write new stories, new parables, new *midrashim* on old stories'.[13] Ancient texts acquire new meaning in new situations. The hermeneutical relationship between past and present is a dynamic liberating exercise. Employing this kind of hermeneutic, black and feminist have shown how seemingly 'unusable' parts of the Bible are pregnant with meaning, to be used as a basis for correcting and promoting the struggle for a better world.

The notion of the 'post-exile church' is employed hermeneutically in this way. From the perspective of liberation theology, not all within the exilic and post-exilic period and literature, immediately offers itself for appropriation. The home-coming for the Jews was largely a restrictive and oppressive event, resulting in isolation from other nations. And yet, metaphor is 'pure adventure'.[14] The post-exilic metaphor is used as a tentative, open-ended symbol which draws on the liberative spirit of hope located alongside all else within the exilic period and the return of the exiles. 'A metaphor that works', suggests Sallie McFague,' is sufficiently unconventional and shocking so that we instinctively say no as well as yes to it.'[15]

A post-exilic biblical theology has not been fully developed by biblical scholars.[16] The dichotomy suggested by some scholars between doom, judgment and law in the pre-exilic period over against hope, salvation and grace in the post-exilic period is an oversimplification of the more complex biblical shift in emphasis at the time of the return from exile. Prophetic and priestly

[13] Rosemary Radford Ruether, *Womanguides: Readings Toward a Feminist Theology* (Boston: Beacon Press, 1985), pp. xii, 247.
[14] J. Dickey, *Metaphor as Pure Adventure*. A lecture delivered at the Library of Congress, 4 December 1967.
[15] Sallie McFague, *Metaphorical Theology: Models of God in Religious Language* (Philadelphia: Fortress Press, 1982), p. 38.
[16] See R. Klein, *Israel in Exile* (Minneapolis: Fortress, 1979); T Raitt, *A Theology of Exile* (Minneapolis: Augsburg, 1977); the relevant chapter in John H. Hayes and J. Maxwell Miller (eds), *Israelite and Judean History* (Philadelphia: Trinity Press International, 1990).

themes, for example, tended towards a closer synthesis, with the prophets Haggai and Zechariah calling for the rebuilding of the temple, while in the Third Isaiah, especially chapter 56, there is a blend of cultic and ethical concerns. In brief there is renewed emphasis on worship *and* social justice. Brueggemann nevertheless talks of the exile and post-exilic period as 'an inversion of the traditions, so that the Mosaic theme is in crisis and is apparently less germane, while the promissory royal tradition now becomes the dominant theological mode for Israel'.[17] Differently stated, there are energising resources within the biblical literature of this period which give credence to the use of the post-exilic metaphor as a basis for a theology of prophetic reconstruction and political stability rather than revolution.

Post-exilic theology at the same time incorporates the contradictions and conflicts inherent to most theologies. It includes the moralisms of Deuteronomy, the passionate rebellion of Job against these impositions, the prophetic judgment and suffering of Jeremiah, Ezekiel's theology of renewal and the hope and anticipated home-coming of Deutero-Isaiah. After the return these contradictions continued in the ideological conflicts inherent to Nehemiah, Ezra and other reconstructionists, counter-balanced against the apocalyptic dreams of Zechariah and Joel. The exile was a period of 'theological inventiveness', says Brueggemann, but ultimately a return to the 'royal-creation-promise tradition with its social conservatism, the very truth which the "new truth" of (the Mosaic-liberatory tradition) challenged'.[18] The question is whether theology needs to remain indefinitely trapped between these options. The long season of exilic and post-exilic discontent contains within it the promise of something 'new' to be realised through the suffering of the Servant of Yahweh. The contextual theological implications of this promise are investigated in the pages that follow.

The post-exilic metaphor as used here is built on the emphasis of Gerhard von Rad who identifies the poetry of Jeremiah, Ezekiel and Deutero-Isaiah as an important turning point in the traditions of the Old Testament. It is this that causes him to

[17] Walter Brueggemann, 'Trajectories', in *The Bible and Liberation*, p. 318.
[18] *Ibid*, p. 321.

make Isaiah 43:18–19 the hinge between the two volumes of his *Old Testament Theology*:

> Do not remember former things.
> Behold, I am doing a new thing.

Prior to this time in the history of Israel the prophets and poets looked back to former times and old traditions. Then come the exilic poets, no longer appealing to the continuing power of the old tradition, but enunciating new actions of God that are discontinuous with the old traditions.[19] The promise of the old tends to give way to the new. It is this shifting emphasis that is employed in what follows in the metaphorical use of post-exilic theology as a theology of reconstruction and nation-building.

The history of neo-colonialism on the African continent and elsewhere is enough to caution against complacency in this regard. Utopian dreams are important, but not enough to create something that is qualitatively different from the structures of oppression. Oppressive practices and ideologies dominant in one age have a way of stubbornly enduring periods of social reconstruction, economic upheavals and political revolution. For the dreams of the oppressed to become a reality they are to be translated into political programmes and law-making that benefit those who have longed for, and fought for, the new age, while protecting the new society against the abuses which marked past oppression. This ultimately is what a liberatory theology of reconstruction is all about.

There are many historical instances of the Christian religion being little more than the opium of the oppressed masses. It has also given rise to visions of justice and peace, although frequently underestimating the structures of power which militate against the realisation of these visions. Some (but notably *not* the poor themselves) have romanticised powerlessness and poverty, holding up a vision of the early church which suggests that it is not the business of Christians to seek power. Others have

---

[19] Gerhard von Rad, *Old Testament Theology* (New York: Harper and Row, 1965). See also Walter Brueggemann, *Hopeful Imagination: Prophetic Voices in Exile* (Philadelphia: Fortress Press, 1986), p. 2; Walther Zimmerli, 'Prophetic Proclamation and Reinterpretation', in *Tradition and Theology in the Old Testament*, D.A. Knight (ed.), (Philadelphia: Fortress Press, 1977), pp. 69–100.

resorted to theocratic models, and themselves expoused visions of society every bit as restrictive and oppressive as those societies that need to be dismantled. Mark Ellis, the Jewish liberation theologian, addressing the Israeli–Palestinian conflict, is correct: 'The desire to remain a victim is evidence of disease; yet to become a conqueror after a victim is a recipe for moral suicide.'[20] To forget the lessons learned in the bitter years of suffering and oppression is to perpetuate the cycle of hatred and repression. Power can be used to create and maintain justice and peace in society. It can also destroy it, inviting resistance and revolution. Responsible nation-building theology can afford neither.

LOCATING THE CHURCH

The church is obliged by the demands of the biblical tradition, but also by the exigencies of political reality, consciously to live at the nexus of powerlessness and power. Even when located 'on the side' of rulers and in ministering to a government that seeks to promote social justice, it is to do so in solidarity with those who suffer most in society.

The church which is faithful to the prophetic biblical vision can never allow itself to become trapped within the limits of what the dominant forces of any society insist is realistically possible. It is theologically and morally obliged to resist obsolete First World visions of economic development, which result in the economic development of the few at the expense of the many, the cities at the expense of the rural areas, and dominant nations at the expense of dependent nations.

Utopian dreams are what great nations are made of. To this the most casual reading of the Bible and/or Marxian literature testifies. A vision of God's Kingdom on earth is a vision of a society at peace because it is a society within which justice reigns. If the church loses that vision, allowing that the prevailing order at any given time is essentially all that can be hoped for, it neglects an essential eschatological contribution to society. Religion is ultimately about vision. It has to do with transcend-

[20] Mark Ellis, *Toward a Jewish Theology of Liberation* (Maryknoll: Orbis Books, 1987), p. 25.

ing seemingly impregnable barriers and enabling people to reach toward what some regard as impossible dreams. It has to do with the affirmation of a God who calls people ever forward to a new, better and transformed society.

Yet, if these theological ideals cannot be translated into programmes of action which, although not immediately realising all that is theologically envisaged, convincingly affirm the immediate and reasonable demands of the poor which constitute a proleptic ingredient of the greater ideals, then religion is no more than the opium of the people. Differently stated, prophetic biblical teaching shows that the essential requirements for a decent human living (housing, a living wage, education, human and political rights) are an essential part of the more inclusive vision of God's rule on earth. This means that the highest and most utopian ideals of the Christian faith can never be affirmed in isolation from, or used as an excuse to neglect, the hard work of political struggle and nation-building.

Responsible political theology *must* be utopian and priests are *obliged* to be turbulent and (annoyingly) visionary in even the most socially responsible societies. And yet, the church must *also* be realistically committed to what is attainable *here* and *now* as part of a greater vision. A theologically responsible notion of what is possible and realisable at any time must, however, always be assessed from the perspective of the poor and marginalised of society. This is because the church, biblically understood, is obliged to counteract the bias in favour of the powerful which undergirds most political societies. To neglect this obligation is for the church to neglect its most fundamental political role in society.

For theologians peace always includes an eschatological dimension, but the vision of God's ultimate peace can never be used as an excuse not to work for maximum proximate peace in every political situation. In the wake of the fall of Rome in 410, St Augustine sensed this responsibility when he suggested that civil peace was more than the absence of war, it was the ordered harmony of its citizens, 'well ordered concord'.[21] It is the

---

[21] St Augustine, *The City of God*, translated by Marcus Dods (New York: The Modern Library, 1950), Book XIX, Chapter 13, p. 690.

obligation of the Christian, he insisted, to bring the earthly city into as much conformity to the heavenly city as possible. But ultimately he argued that politically no more could be hoped for than 'the peace of Babylon', tempering his theological vision with a realism that legitimated the imperial interests that struggled to survive against competing political forces.[22] When faced with the resistance of the Donatists (in what threatened to erupt into a full-scale peasants' revolt in the North African church) Augustine relied on the imperial army to prevent the emergence of an alternative vision for church and society on the African continent.[23] Rosemary Ruether's critique is a telling one: 'When faced with the test of a non-Roman identity, Augustine, as much as Eusebius, proved that his catholicity was a closed universe, bounded by the Greco-Roman oecumene.'[24] It is this captivity, born in Eusebius' celebration of Constantine as the 'friend of God' and systematically, although with more nuances, incorporated into the identity of the church by Augustine and subsequent establishment theologians, that has been so explicitly exposed by the different types of liberation theology in the past few decades. The response of liberation theology to a church on the side of oppressive regimes has been part of the hope and the promise of people and a church in exile. It must now be translated into a theology of home-coming and nation-building.

A NEW THEOLOGICAL RESPONSIBILITY

The call for the church to share theologically in the nation-building process as the old order begins to collapse, is of course nothing new. Churches in situations of radical change around the globe have also demonstrated how difficult it is to adjust to the new role. The church in Germany took a step in this

---

[22] See T.J. Bigham and A.T. Mollegan, 'The Christian Ethic', in R.W. Battenhouse (ed.), *A Companion to the Study of St. Augustine* (Grand Rapids: Baker, 1979), pp. 388–95.

[23] Peter Brown, *Augustine of Hippo* (Berkeley: University of California Press, 1969), p. 289.

[24] Rosemary Radford Ruether, 'Augustine and Christian Political Theology', *Interpretation*, 29, 1975, p. 258.

direction with the *Stuttgart Confession of Guilt* in 1945, while members of the Confessing Church took a much more decisive step towards reconstruction in the *Darmstadter Confession*.[25] Hans Jochem Margull's iconoclastic reference to the Confessing Church in Germany as 'a conglomerate of heterogeneous individuals bound together primarily by a need to counter a common enemy' at the same time serves to underline the dilemma facing the church required to move beyond resistance to nation-building. 'When Hitler no longer rendered the church this service', he added, 'it collapsed and was absorbed into the all-encompassing structures of a new brand of liberal Christianity not easily distinguishable from the dominant culture of post-war Germany.'[26] The complexity of the persecution and control of the church in Eastern Europe and the Soviet Union in the wake of the institutional church's restraint and quietism in the face of some of the worst violations of human rights in modern history, in turn, points to a different kind of ecclesial non-involvement in the political struggle for human emancipation.

The long and painful journey travelled by the church in Cuba after the *fidelista* victory in 1959 tells a different story of the church failing to rise to the challenge of revolutionary change. Having for so long ignored the excesses of the Batista dictatorship and the demands of the majority of the Cuban people, it became part of the counter-revolutionary process with which the new regime was obliged to deal. As such it surrendered the moral right to provide a prophetic critique of the new society. It took a long time for serious dialogue to emerge between the church and Cuban government, with the *Final Document of the National Encounter of the Cuban Church*, published in 1986 marking the beginning of an important turning point in this regard. Msgr. Adolfo Rodriguez, President of the Cuban Episcopal Conference observed: 'A church that wishes to be a sign of communion is to be part of the people, otherwise it would be an "opium of the masses" and cease to be the church . . . The

---

[25] Franklin H. Littell, 'From Barmen (1934) to Stuttgart (1945): The Path of the Confessing Church in Germany', *Journal of Church and State*, 1, May, 1961. Martin Greschat (ed.), *Im Zeichen der Schuld. 40 Jahre Stuttgarter Schuldbekenntnis: Eine Dokumentation* (Neukirchener-Vluyn: Neukirchener Verlag, 1985).

[26] In conversation with the author in Hamburg in 1979.

Cuban church is to be the church of openness and dialogue, with
our hands extended and our doors open.' The document
includes a crucial self-critique of the church's historical and
pastoral role in Cuba, it accepts the broad social goals of the
revolution and provides constructive criticism of Cuba's present
social problems.[27] The tragedy is that it has taken the church so
long officially to express seriously the desire to share propheti-
cally and democratically in the reconstruction process.

The story of the role of the institutional church before and
after the successful Sandinista revolution in Nicaragua in 1979
portrays similar difficulties.[28] While many Christians identified
with the struggle to rebuild the nation, the dominant institutional churches in many instances sided with counter-revolutionary forces. These situations underscore the thesis already
described. A theology useful in resistance does not easily become
a useful instrument in the period of reconstruction.

The church in Africa discovered this theological reality in the
1960s when the euphoria of independence was sweeping across
the continent. World War II had been used by imperial powers
to cajole Africans into defending 'democratic freedom' and 'self-
determination' among the nations of North Africa and Europe.
Africans fought and died alongside their colonial masters, and
returned home fired with a desire for a freedom of their own.[29]
When independence came to nations claimed by colonial
powers during the last century in the scramble for Africa, the call
was for the church to share in a nation-building process.

A new era had dawned for the church in Africa. The colonial
task of the missionary (and not all missionaries succumbed with
the same level of intensity) had simply been to persuade African
converts to concentrate on spiritual concerns and remain
indifferent to politics. The result was that many African

---

[27] *Documento Final, Encuentro Nacional Cubano* (Havana: Mimeo, 1986) is discussed in John
M Kirk, 'The Church in Revolutionary Cuba', *The Ecumenist*, 26:6, September-
October, 1988. See also John M. Kirk, *Between God and the Party: Religion and Politics in
Revolutionary Cuba* (Tampa: University of South Florida Press, 1989.

[28] Guilio Girardi, *Faith and Revolution in Nicaragua* (Maryknoll: Orbis, 1989).

[29] Gabriel Setiloane, 'The Ecumenical Movement in Africa: From Mission Church to
Moratorium', in C. Villa-Vicencio and J.W. de Gruchy (eds.), *Resistance and Hope:
South African Essays in Honour of Beyers Naude* (Cape Town: David Philip. Grand
Rapids: Eerdmans, 1985), p. 139

Christians saw no connection between religion and political liberation. Some African Christians collaborated with their imperialist overlords. Others were driven out of the church because of their political commitment, but perhaps most were confused as to how religion and politics were *supposed* to be related.

Ultimately, however, there was always a latent resistance present in the church.[30] Shula Marks speaks of the 'ambiguity of dependence' that characterises all colonised societies.[31] Indeed, no exploited people known to historians, suggests E.P. Thompson, have ever been deprived of their land without finding some way of fighting back.[32] The first general secretary of the All African Council of Churches (AACC), Donald M'Timkulu, in 1962 sought to incorporate this resistance – the will to freedom and a grassroots desire to rebuild Africa into the post-colonial African church. 'African Christians', he warned, 'are growing impatient with so-called non-participation in politics . . . Freedom from colonialism means the freedom and obligation of all nationals to participate in the nation's political life.' It meant, he said, being 'involved on the ground floor in the task of nation-building'.[33]

Yet soon the euphoric expectation that political independence would herald a new age of socio-economic development and political democracy, radically improving the quality of life of all Africans, was shattered. Colonial nations and super-powers were not prepared to surrender ideological and political influence in the former colonies, and neo-colonialism, corruption and political opportunism turned the dream of independence into the nightmare of new forms of oppression for many African nations. The dominant nations in the West refused to loosen their strangle-hold on the world economy and African

---

[30] See A. Hastings, *A History of African Christianity: 1950–1975* (Cambridge: Cambridge University Press, 1979).

[31] Shula Marks, 'Ambiguities of Dependence: John L. Dube of Natal', *Journal of Southern Africa Studies*, 1:2, 1975, pp. 162–80.

[32] E.P. Thompson, *The Poverty of Theory and Other Essays* (London: Merlin Publishers, 1978), pp. 345–6.

[33] D. M'Timkulu, *Africa in Transition: The Challenge and the Christian Response* (Geneva: AACC and WCC, 1962), pp. 15–27.

nations were plunged into debt, becoming trapped in the cycle of spiralling interest rates. To this was added the devastation of drought and famine, and the economic divide between themselves and their former colonial masters increased.

There are African nations, of course, that have made remarkable progress since independence, despite these obstacles. At a continental level, however, it is not an exaggeration to speak of the 'failure of Africa'. King Moshoeshoe II (who is himself now in exile), in his address to the Lesotho Council of Churches in 1988, for example, observed that 'after more than thirty years of so-called development . . . millions of Africans are still constantly hungry, millions still live in entirely inadequate conditions and have grossly insufficient access to education, to health care and many basic necessities for decent living'. There is 'ample evidence', he suggests, 'to confirm that abject poverty in Africa has grown in proportions never experienced before'.[34] A great deal of responsibility for this must be laid at the doors of generations of colonialism and the determination of neo-colonial powers to continue to dominate this continent. But not all the blame can be placed here.

Africa would be most irresponsible to suggest that it bears no responsibility for its plight. To do so would be to mimic the trivial excuses of former colonial dictators who insisted that it was the 'communists' and a few anarchical agitators who were responsible for the tyranny with which they were obliged to rule. At the 1984 Vancouver Assembly of the World Council of Churches, Archbishop Desmond Tutu called African delegates to that assembly to a special meeting, reporting that he had witnessed the violation of basic human rights in Africa that reminded him of what he had seen in South Africa. 'Why have you been silent?' he asked the African church leaders. 'While Africa is guilty of violating human rights', he continued, 'our task in South Africa is made that much more difficult.'

Moral blame aside, Africa is to shoulder the responsibility of her own burdens, and the great leaders of this continent (Julius Nyerere, Kenneth Kaunda, Robert Mugabe and others) are on record as saying precisely this. 'This awareness', said King

[34] King Moshoeshoe II, 'Key Note Address', 12 August 1988, Mazenod Conference Centre, Lesotho.

Moshoeshoe II, '. . . has caused us to look to our own resources, to search the realms of our own culture, history and traditional religion, our own politics and economics, as well as our own "African" Christian faith.'[35]

For African solutions to structural African problems to become a reality, however, two fundamental institutional and structural global changes must take place: (i) The structures of the western economy (and notably the World Bank and International Monetary Fund) need to give way to a new and more just international economic order. (ii) Apartheid (in its present and all its 'reformed' guises) needs to be destroyed, ensuring that every root, branch and seed of this evil scourge is eradicated from the African continent. The price paid by Africa, and more especially the front-line states in Africa, for opposing apartheid will perhaps never be fully told. It is a price exacted in the form of military aggression, economic impoverishment and political destabilisation.

For a whole range of reasons (both legitimate and questionable), including the focus of world attention on South Africa, African churches have never focussed their fullest attention on nation-building in their own countries. And perhaps not until South Africa is completely free, will churches in Africa and elsewhere be able to translate the vision of nation-building first articulated by the AACC in 1962 into serious theology and a viable programme.

Today South Africa stands on the brink of a new society, if only in the sense that a new phase in the history of struggle has begun. Reconstruction is anticipated at a number of different levels, and the time is overdue to identify the essential characteristics of a theology of nation-building. It could have implications for what it means to be the church in other parts of the world.

THE POLITICAL TASK OF THEOLOGY

Christians in places where transition and renewal are happening need not, and probably *should not*, follow the theological models of the First World any more than they need to follow their

[35] *Ibid.*

political, economic and social inventions. The existence of African, black and other contextual theologies in South Africa, together with Third World and liberation theologies elsewhere suggests that the break with classical theology has already taken place. In struggling to discover what it means to be theo-politically responsible at a time of political transition, Christians in these situations would, however, do well to learn from the insights and mistakes of others who have grappled with similar programmes of theological and political reconstruction in earlier times.

Reference has already been made to Barth's theology of the 'permanent revolution'. It is important that a theological imperative of continuing social renewal be kept alive in a nation-building theology. It is equally important, however, for the church to accept that if theology is to be taken seriously within the political arena (and more especially during a period of political reconstruction) it has to contribute to the process of producing concrete proposals to deal with complex political and economic problems. The Christian realism of Reinhold Niebuhr addressed precisely this need. He insisted that in the real world of politics certain calculated political compromises are required – and argued that political theology needs to be done within the context of this conviction.[36]

The outcome of Niebuhr's 'compromises' was a brand of Christian realism that was slowly absorbed into the American dream. It is this that motivated John Coleman to refer to the understanding of 'Christian realism' as 'imperialistic realism' and feminists, blacks and other marginalised groups to reject his notion of what is 'realistic' and 'possible' as shaped by dominant white, bourgeois and male-dominated realism.[37]

Niebuhr's brand of political realism is unacceptable in Africa and other Third World situations for precisely these reasons. The Third World requires a nation-building theology of a

---

[36] Reinhold Niebuhr, 'Ten Years That Shook My World', in Loren Baritz (ed.), *Sources of the American Mind* (New York: John Wiley and Sons, 1966), pp. 317–25.

[37] John Coleman, 'Reinhold Niebuhr's Political Theology', *The Ecumenist*, 24:6, September-October, 1986, p. 85. Also Beverley Wildung Harrison, in Carol Robb (ed.), *Making the Connections: Essays in Feminist Social Ethics* (Boston: Beacon Press, 1985), pp. 22–40.

different kind. The 'calculated' political compromises required in the Third World and other situations of transition are not intended to preserve or reform the existing order, but radically to transform it. Herein lies the importance of liberation theology for situations emerging from structural and colonial oppression.

In these situations the need is for a theology that preserves neither the global status quo nor the neo-colonial structures left over from colonial days. The need is for a theology which promotes such material and ideological resources as are necessary to facilitate the transfer of resources and power from the *few* (the rich and the powerful) to the *many* (the poor and the powerless).

TOWARDS A NATION-BUILDING THEOLOGY

The two poles to be avoided in a nation-building theology are clear from what has already been said. The one is the absolutising of relative political systems and ideologies, which suggests that God can be exclusively identified with a particular political option. The other is the use of divine absolutes to reduce all political systems and ideologies to the *same* level of inadequacy and sinfulness, allowing the Christian to remain *theologically* indifferent to specific political choices.

The detail of a particular theology of nation-building is dependent on the detail of the social context within which it is located. Such detail is, however, to be developed in relation to certain basic theological tasks considered here as items to be placed on the church's agenda for nation-building. This agenda has many prophetic, pastoral and ethical implications. In subsequent chapters only one dimension of this agenda will be explored, namely the obligation of the church to share in law-making and the affirmation of human rights, understood in a broad and inclusive sense. 'The church', suggested Karl Rahner in seeking to provide a theology of ministry in a different situation, 'can be wide of the mark in such imperatives and directives', and 'more palpably [so] than in theoretical declarations'. 'But this', he warned, 'is a risk that must be taken if the church is not to seem pedantic, to be living in a world of pure theory, remote from life, making pronouncements that do not touch the stubborn concreteness of real life.'[38] If an agenda of nation-building does not take the church beyond debate into the actual process of shaping the character of society, the church will again have failed to demonstrate that its pronouncements on social justice ought in any way to be taken seriously by those whose concern it is to reconstruct society in the wake of the devastation left behind by dying and dead societies of corruption.

Social analysis

A theology which fails to address the most urgent questions asked by ordinary people (and given the bias of the church in favour of the marginalised people, *especially* their questions) is not theology at all. It is little more than an academic exercise in uncovering archaic or dying religious beliefs and reified doctrines about God. Ultimately it is an escape from the challenge of discerning the liberating presence of God in the midst of the struggle for a better world. It is a false theology.[39] False because theology has the critical and permanent task of promoting liberation from every form of captivity in each new age.

For this to happen theology's first task is to probe and understand 'the meaning of the time' (Luke 12:56) at any particular point in history. Closely related to such an exercise is social analysis, the separating of the different components of a policy or political programme, with a view to uncovering its true intent and actual consequences. It involves uncovering the causes of suffering and exploitation in society, as well as identifying the signs of new birth that reside within the community – as a basis for both confronting the state and encouraging programmes of hope and renewal.

Important in this regard is that the church heed the warning not to judge by outward appearances. Things are not always what they appear to be. Jesus warned that the leaders may 'look

---

[38] Karl Rahner, *The Shape of the Church to Come* (London: SPCK, 1974), p. 79.
[39] Gustavo Gutierrez, *A Theology of Liberation* (London: SCM Press, 1974), p. 13.

fine on the outside but are full of bones and decaying corpses on the inside' (Matt. 23:27). When the prophet Samuel was sent to search for a new King of Israel the Lord warned 'I do not judge as people judge. People look at the outward appearance, but I look at the heart' (I Sam. 16:7). To 'discern the signs of the times' is to 'see deep', it involves hard-nosed and critical analysis. Marx warned: 'Whilst in ordinary life every shopkeeper is very well able to distinguish between what somebody professes to be and what he really is, our historians [read *theologians*] have not yet won even this trivial insight.'[40] The church has too often allowed itself to be persuaded by nice words and simple explanations. Called to be as gentle as a dove, the church is also called to be as wise as a serpent.

A theology of reconstruction is pre-eminently a contextual theology. It explicitly addresses the present needs of a particular society. It is at the same time a retroactive theology, seeking to correct the causes of previous suffering and conflict in society. The critical analysis of past and present structures is an essential ingredient of the theological task. Nation-building theology must emerge in relation to posing tough and uncomfortable questions about the economy, international alliances, national development programmes and such local issues that affect the lives of ordinary people at a material and spiritual level. For this to happen, church leaders and theologians continually need to be exposed to the insights of critical economists, social scientists and political analysts. Theology and ministry outside of this encounter is at best simply irrelevant. At worst, wittingly or unwittingly, it can become part of a national lie.

In any political situation the most important political task of the church is simply 'to tell the truth'. It is to reach behind what rulers and others profess to be, in making known the actual effects of their policies and what it is they really stand for. It is to analyse political policy, to expose its consequences for the poor and anticipate its long-term effects on society as a whole. In response to this obligation, in 1989 Christians in South Africa

---

[40] Karl Marx, 'The German Ideology' Quoted in Anthony Gibbon, *Capitalism and Modern Social Theory: An Analysis of the Writings of Marx, Durkheim and Weber* (London: Cambridge University Press, 1972), p. 42.

joined in a nation-wide Defiance Campaign against unjust laws under the banner of the *Standing for the Truth Campaign*. This resulted in thousands of Christians being beaten by the police, brutalised, arrested and imprisoned for insisting that a government that does not face the truth about its policies of exploitation and serve the common good is theologically and morally illegitimate.

In a post-apartheid situation (hopefully) under a government committed to promoting national reconstruction, truth-telling is likely to make different demands on the church. As a participant in the nation-building process it will, however, continue to be the task of the church to look critically, and yet to make positive proposals concerning reconstruction at the level of the constitutionalism and law-making for nations in transition. This is a task addressed in later chapters.

Cultural empowerment

Located at the heart of constitutional debate and law-making, however, is the creation of social values. It is this that persuades Johan Degenaar that, given the level of ideological diversity and social turmoil in South Africa, a more appropriate starting point than the promotion of one or another grandiose nation-building scheme is the establishment of a genuine democratic culture which respects the dignity of people, the right to dissent and meaningful political participation.[41]

Whatever else the church may be, it is required to be a value-generating community committed to such values that facilitate and enable people to live together in mutual respect. Theologically, it is a community within which people are taught to love one another, to forgive one another and to bear one another's burdens. Specifically it is a culture which elevates those who have previously been marginalised or excluded from the fullest participation in the community. As such it is obliged to address the specific challenge of racial and sexual discrimination. This requires the challenging of social prejudices, and the empower-

[41] Johan Degenaar, 'Nation-Building: An Example of Outdated Thinking?' *Democracy in Action*, June-July 1990.

ing of black people who have, as a result of generations of oppression internalised negative self-perceptions, to demand their rights. It also involves enabling women, who have been socially conditioned to live in submission to males, to claim their rightful place in society.

Theological cultural empowerment moreover concerns the anticipation of the year of the Lord (Luke 4: 18–19) within which injustices will be reversed, and to celebrate jubilee year within which the land taken from peasants by landowners will be restored (Lev. 25). As such it is a theology with a special bias in favour of a form of economic reconstruction which benefits the most impoverished sections of the community. This is a task addressed in chapters 6 and 7.

Nation-building theology has a special obligation to enable and empower the nation to realise the highest ideals which may be enshrined within a new society. And, given its theological bias in favour of the poor and dispossessed, it is to facilitate the emergence of a social force that specifically empowers the poor and marginalised people of society. For this to happen those who are oppressed are, without being parochial or isolationist, obliged to look to their own resources and discern the Spirit of the Lord within their own culture, history and identity.

This concern has, of course, implications for the integration of indigenous values into the dominant culture of the nation. Theologically this has implications for the continuing debate between African cultural theology (dominant in many parts of Africa), South African black theology and other forms of contextual thought. An important question is whether the empowering and liberating resources being sought as a basis for renewal are to be found in mining cultural resources hidden within native or pre-colonial traditions, or within the more contemporary culture of struggle for socio-economic and political change.[42] (The question, of course, has implications for the encounter between indigenous religions and the Christian church in North America, Asia and elsewhere.) Leaving aside the details of this debate it is worth noting the observation of

---

[42] Kwesi Dickson, *Theology in Africa* (London; Darton, Longman and Todd. Maryknoll: Orbis, 1984), pp. 124–40.

Archbishop Desmond Tutu concerning this debate in South Africa:

African theology has failed to produce a sufficiently sharp cutting edge ... very little has been offered that is pertinent to the theology of power in the face of the epidemic of coups and military rule, about development, about poverty and disease and other equally urgent present-day issues. I believe this is where the abrasive black theology may have a few lessons for African theology.[43]

Traditional symbols continue to be powerful ingredients in African and similar cultures. Black and other liberation theologies recognise, however, that human identity embraces more than culture. It also fundamentally embraces political and economic identity. If indigenous theologies do not address *these* sources of alienation, they do not address the hard reality of actual deprivation and oppression. On the other hand, only to the extent that contemporary liberation theologies develop a spirituality that speaks to the soul of grassroots people in Africa, the Americas or elsewhere will it mobilise and empower the sons and daughters of these continents.

A theologically liberating African spirituality is still in the process of being born. African culture refuses to separate the sacred and the secular and it is here that a theology which empowers the poor must begin. When Africans celebrate their religion, says John Mbiti, 'they dance it, they sing it, they act it'.[44] In the South African context the *itoyi-toyi* is as much part of religion as it is of political resistance. Resistance culture in South Africa has incorporated that part of the church that understands the political struggle in South Africa to be part of its God-given mission, and this kind of religion has enriched and empowered the struggle against apartheid.

Given the nation-building task of the church, however, it is also its responsibility to heal and restore as a contribution to national unity. In South Africa's apartheid history there are few resources available and waiting to be appropriated in a culture

[43] Desmond Tutu, 'Black Theology/African Theology: Soul Mates or Antagonists', *Journal of Religious Thought*, Fall/Winter, 1975, pp. 32–3.

[44] John S. Mbiti, *An Introduction to African Religion* (London: Heinemann, 1975), p. 126.

of national unity. Hidden within the long history of black resistance there are at the same time memories of non-racism, democracy and struggles for human values and rights. These are resources to be uncovered and celebrated as a basis for a new-found unity.

The role of the church in the formation and development of culture is, of course, fraught with problems. The history of the church in Eastern Europe, the Soviet Union, South Africa and elsewhere earlier in this century suggests that ecclesial involvement in the building of a national culture has resulted in the entrapment of the church on the side of dominant and oppressive classes. And yet it is only to the extent that the church successfully engages in the cultural struggle against oppression that it is likely effectively to be able to share in the process of the reconstruction of culture. The creation of a culture which motivates and enables people to realise their highest moral ideals and sense of communal duty is perhaps the most important function awaiting the church in the period of reconstruction. Considering this challenge within the context of reconstruction in the Soviet Union, the Archbishop of Smolensk and Kaliningrad writes:

The ministry of the church today must include the cultivation in her flock of a sense of duty to the common good, as well as the surmounting of personal and collective egoism . . . In other words, the understanding of culture is closely related to the spiritual essence of man and therefore with the ethical condition of existence . . . Authentic culture must uplift man intellectually and aesthetically, encouraging personal spiritual/ethical growth. Man's spiritualisation signifies his ability to govern himself (that is, control his instincts and passions), to achieve inner integrity, to keep his flesh in submission to its spiritual foundation. If culture does not serve this end, it becomes *anticulture* which whether in a decent or indecent incarnation, can wield a dangerous destructive power.[45]

For the church to fail to share in the creation of a new culture is for the church to fail to address its liberating obligation to society. It is to marginalise itself from the task of reconstruction.

[45] Kyril, Archbishop of Smolensk and Kaliningrad, 'The Church in Relation to Society Under "Perestroika".'

Liberation

This kind of liberating culture can only emerge as existing culture is brought into creative tension with the gospel. H. Richard Niebuhr's formative study, *Christ and Culture*, is a tried and tested thesis.[46] It cannot be addressed here, except to recognise that *Christ* or the *gospel*, has never been an entity separate from, or above, culture. The gospel was first dressed in Hebrew and Greco-Roman garb, and for the past few centuries has worn the clothing of every colonial nation to wander through Africa. So entrapped within these cultures has been the liberating message of Jesus that some have come to mistake cultural impositions for the gospel itself.

The point has already been made. These impositions are to be eradicated from society and the Christian tradition. A nation-building theology has the important task of relativising all cultural prejudices before the unqualified gospel incentive that all of God's people might always become free in all situations. The task of the church in political transition and the emerging new society is to promote the destruction of all forms of cultural oppression and exploitation, whether located in the church or in society, to a similar critique. There is no place for racism, sexism or classism in the gospel of Jesus Christ. The church, therefore, cannot rest content until all structural and residual forms, of these basic violations of the rights of people created in the image of God, are eradicated from the statute books, as well as from the basic fabric of society.

Democratisation

A nation-building theology which takes the liberatory incentive of the gospel seriously is necessarily a theology which supports and promotes democracy at every level of society. It operates from the assumption that the best and most effective way to ensure human rights and to promote the eradication of racism, sexism and classism in society is to enable the full and

<hr />

[46] H. Richard Niebuhr, *Christ and Culture* (New York: Harper Torchbooks, 1951).

unqualified participation of people of all races, all sexes and all classes in all aspects of society.

Imposed 'answers'to the complex questions of reconstruction are never accepted with the same enthusiasm as those programmes of reconstruction which emerge from the grass-roots of the community. Recognising this, and facing the enormous challenges of nation-building in India immediately after independence, Jawaharial Nehru insisted that 'democracy may be slow to start but will be faster in the longer run'.[47] This emphasis became the very foundation of the church's proposed nation-building theology in India at the time.[48]

For the church authentically to promote democracy it is, of course, obliged to democratise its own structures. One of the consequences of the alliance between the historic Constantinian alliance between church and state has been the emergence of a hierarchy of control in the church similar to that which exists within the state. Indeed, in many situations the church is today more authoritarian, more hierarchical, more oppressive and less democratic, less participatory and less liberating than the state.

Judgment begins with the household of God. Today there is a revolution sweeping through the church. A new theological vision of the church's place in society is emerging from among ordinary, often oppressed and frequently alienated Christians. Church leadership and theologians are to listen and learn afresh from such people, who are challenging ecclesial sexism, racism and classism.

A pertinent question is whether the new wine of God's liberatory presence that is sweeping across the globe can be contained within the old wine-skins of institutional church structures designed for a colonial age. Differently stated, it is not only society, but also the church that requires renewal if in the post-exilic age we are not going to recreate the same monster all over again. It cannot be legislated that people in society love one another, but, as Martin Luther King once observed, the law can prevent people from being lynched. In proclaiming a gospel of love, the church also has a responsibility to ensure that, at

[47] M.M. Thomas, *Christian Participation in Nation-Building*, p. 6.   [48] *Ibid.*

minimum, people learn to treat one another in the best possible way. This is why law-making is so important.

BEHOLD, A NEW THING

It has earlier been suggested that inherent to the metaphor of a post-exilic theology is the expectation of the emergence of something new. Biblically the renewing poems of Jeremiah, Ezekiel and Deutero-Isaiah constitute a reorientation of prophetic literature within which God's promise is not found by looking back, but by anticipating the future. The exilic prophets also knew, however, that the new age is born in present struggle. It was in obedience to God and in solidarity with one another that the new society would be born. The kind of society that will prevail in different parts of the world tomorrow is being forged on the anvil of struggle today. The church of tomorrow is also in the process of being born today.

It is not an exaggeration to say that there are forces at work within the church in many transitionary situations today that are perhaps as powerful as those that rocked the church in Europe at the time of the Protestant and Catholic Reformations. Unless these forces are creatively responded to by the institutional church, Christians who are committed to discovering the significance of God's liberatory message in society might well look elsewhere for institutions through which to strive for a more just, more sustainable, more participatory and more human society.

At the beginning of this chapter it was suggested that the Constantinian proposal be reconsidered. Historically the church capitulated before Constantine's invitation to participate within the power structure, finding itself trapped in a new kind of Babylonian exile. The only alternative was to not refuse to participate, while clinging to a persecuted status, but to participate in a *different* way. Abstract theological agendas as to what this means can be little more than 'pale theory' until given life and content in praxis. As already suggested in the introduction, this is the task being thrust on the church in different parts of the world, where the 'old' is giving way to the 'new'. It is also the task addressed in the pages that follow.

CHAPTER 2

The weight of dead generations

The quest for something qualitatively new, which is the pulse-beat of exilic hope and a contextual theology of liberatory nation-building, can only succeed to the extent that history is taken seriously. The biblical story is the story of a people who anticipated the future by remembering the journey they had already travelled. If we ignore history we are not only condemned to become its victims, but also fail realistically to assess the resources available from which to create a new future. Karl Marx's observation in this regard needs to indelibly inform the struggle for a new age:

[People] make their history . . . not under circumstances chosen by themselves but under circumstances directly encountered, given and transmitted from the past. The tradition of all dead generations weighs like a nightmare on the brain of the living.[1]

To fail to understand the history of law in South Africa as an instrument of exploitation and oppression is to fail to understand the suspicion with which debate on the rule of law and proposals concerning a Bill of Rights is greeted by oppressed people. This can only lead those who have not been the victims of apartheid to assume a naïve and unrealistic nation-building process. The legacy of past oppression cannot be ignored, neither can it simply be swept under the carpet as though it had never happened. It is to be acknowledged, repented of spiritually, and dealt with politically.

Frank Chikane, the General Secretary of the South African Council of Churches, vividly makes the point concerning the

---

[1] K. Marx and F. Engels, *Selected Works: The Eighteenth Brumaire of Louis Bonaparte* (Moscow: Progress Press, 1968), p. 95.

burden of oppression and the rejection of all laws by many black people, in referring to black youths refusing to pay the prescribed fare when boarding trains between Soweto to Johannesburg – arguing that they have no obligation to contribute (even at this level) to a system of laws designed to exploit and repress them. 'The question', asks Chikane, 'is whether these young people will pay train fares in the new society?' The effects of capricious law and law-breaking are likely to be carried in the wounds and scars of the nation for generations to come.

Organised resistance in South Africa has nevertheless over generations (as a rule) been a *disciplined* struggle, without suggesting that any revolution has ever been without its indiscriminate and morally indefensible events. Strikes have been co-ordinated, consumer boycotts basically disciplined, civil-disobedience well-planned and armed struggle (with a few exceptions) carried out with a limited loss of civilian life. It is here that the possibility of law becoming a liberatory and transforming reality in society needs to be investigated and developed. The positive dimensions of the present legal system, long buried under layers of oppressive legislation, constitute a further factor likely to help shape the future. Throughout the struggle for a new South Africa this dimension of the rule of law has been affirmed by apartheid's strongest opponents. In the rejection of oppressive laws there has been the affirmation of values of both restraint and liberation that have functioned among oppressed people as a kind of latent alternative legal system.

The devastating outbreaks of violence internal to the black community since the beginning of 1990 (whether fuelled by right-wing or government or not) have at the same time raised the very fear of the kind of lawlessness which Chikane feared most. Constituting the gravest concern, it is at the same time to be recognised that a country as ridden with oppression and generations of structural violence as South Africa, is unlikely to accomplish its nation-building task without still further wanton violence before the task is accomplished. The fearful and sobering agreement between Karl Barth and Reinhold Niebuhr that the United States did not, and could not, become a nation without its terribly bloody Civil War, is an observation which should not be lost sight of in assessing the morality of the South African struggle. This much said, it must be recognised that the blood of South Africans has already flowed in excess, and a further spiral of violence must be avoided at almost any cost.

Within the South African struggle there resides not only the rejection of oppression and violence, but also the affirmation of renewal and good order, on which the nation-building task feeds as it engages the future. Religion and law cannot be written in isolation from this history. Yet, suggests James Gustafson, ethicists and theologians have traditionally done their work with 'a strong inclination to neglect history'.[2] This leaves theology (and other forms of theory) all too often entrenched in the ideas of the dominant classes. As such it fails to explore the promise of renewal which resides within the revolutionary aspirations of the oppressed.

LAW-MAKING AND NATION-BUILDING

The kind of socio-political order that will emerge from the chaos of South Africa's long history of oppression cannot be predicted. There are simply too many variables at stake. Whatever the character of the new society, unless it degenerates into (and perpetuates) arbitrary rule by decree, which has (despite some recent reforms) characterised political rule in South Africa at least since 1948, it must be shaped by law and law-making. This is what makes the encounter between theology and law such a vital ingredient of a theology of reconstruction.

Theologically understood, the law-making process can and must be an instrument of restitution and justice. 'Law', suggests Paul Lehmann, '[ought to] bend the things which have been towards the things which are to come.'[3] Karl Barth described God's law for Israel in a similar way.

---

[2] James M. Gustafson, 'The Relevance of Historical Understanding', in Paul Deats, Jr. (ed.), *Toward a Discipline of Social Ethics: Essays in Honor of Walter George Muelder* (Boston: Boston University Press, 1972), p. 42.

[3] Quoted in Milner S. Ball, *Lying Down Together: Law, Metaphor and Theology* (Madison: University of Wisconsin Press, 1985).

And in content each of the commands reflects and confirms the fact that Israel is . . . the people created and maintained by these very acts [commands] of God. *Thou* shalt! means Israel shall! and everything that Israel shall is only an imperative transcription of what Israel *is*, repeating in some sense only what Israel has become by God, and what it must always be with God.[4]

Inherent to this theology is a notion of law not as a negative and/ or oppressive reality, but as a positive incentive which reveals the presence of God in society enabling and drawing a people forward to what they ought to be. Milner Ball draws on Shakespeare's *Hamlet* to show that 'the purpose of playing was and is, to hold, as 'twere, the mirror up to nature'. Law, he suggests, is not to picture people as they are, but as 'nature' intended them to be – as they *ought* to be. The law (and more specifically constitutional law) in South Africa must provide a new image of what a post-apartheid South Africa can become.[5] Restitution in a just and orderly manner constitutes the greatest challenge to be worked within this process.

A nation's constitution is a social vision of what that nation understands itself to be. In the words of human rights scholar Louis Henkin, constitutionalism bridges the 'chasm between natural and positive law by converting natural human rights into positive legal rights'.[6] Because theology has to do with the creation of a society that conforms to the Reign of God, nation-building theology is to be defined in relation to the constitutional process. Theologically stated, constitutionalism has to do with relating the ideals of what it is believed a society ought to be to the specific needs of a given society. Yet more than this is needed. Theology has an obligation to contribute towards the creation of a culture and praxis within which the state aspires towards these ideals and honours its own constitution.

The essential failure of the Russian revolution was that the human rights clauses enshrined in the various constitutions of the Soviet Union since 1918 were unenforceable against the

---

[4] K. Barth, *Church Dogmatics* (Edinburgh: T. and T. Clark, 1957), II/2, p. 572.
[5] Milner S. Ball, *The Promise of American Law: A Theological Humanistic View of Legal Process* (Athens: The University of Georgia Press, 1981), p. 64.
[6] Louis Henkin, *The Rights of Man Today* (New York: The Center for the Study of Human Rights, Columbia University, 1988), p. 19.

dictatorship of the state. A constitutional vision is, at the same time, a vital first step in the reconstruction process. 'There is nothing more futile', argues Hannah Arendt, 'than rebellion and liberation unless they are followed by the constitution of the newly won freedom.' She rightly reminds us that revolution in and of itself is no guarantee of freedom and that often there is 'very little in form or content of new revolutionary constitutions which [is] even new, let alone revolutionary'.[7]

A consideration of law as a liberatory and recreative dynamic in society is undertaken in Chapter 3. What follows here is an outline of the historical framework within which this debate occurs in South Africa. It is a history frequently neglected by politicians and too often forgotten by scholars who prefer the realm of ideas to the stubborn reality of the existing order.

THE MORAL BURDEN OF LAW

The history of oppressive law in South Africa reaches back to the earliest days of colonisation, beginning with the imposition of arbitrary laws by the Dutch East India Company on the Khoi-Khoi in 1652. It includes the rough-and-ready frontier rule imposed by trekboers on the northern and eastern frontiers of the white colony. But primarily it was the ruthless efficiency of British colonial rule that set the framework for law as the institutionalisation of oppression in South Africa.

The British also introduced the *rule of law* (with its insistence on access to the courts of law and reputed 'equality' before the law) to South Africa.[8] In addition, British imperialism brought *parliamentary sovereignty* to the region, which was later abused by the successive rulers and governments as a basis for arbitrary and exploitative rule.

To hold the British responsible for all South Africa's legal and political woes, would nevertheless be a serious error. Law in South Africa has long been a composition of Roman, Dutch and

---

[7] Hannah Arendt, *On Revolution* (New York: Viking Press, 1965), p. 141. Also p. 111.
[8] T.R.H. Davenport, 'The Consolidation of a New Society: The Cape Colony', in Monica Wilson and Leonard Thompson (eds.), *The Oxford History of South Africa* (Oxford: Oxford University Press, 1969), pp. 297–311.

English influences decidedly shaped and reconstituted to conform to the political needs of successive undemocratic and racist governments in South Africa. In this sense it is *South African* law.

It is scarcely an exaggeration, suggests Albie Sachs, to suggest that South African political and legal structures have come to include the worst of all the traditions on which they draw, while ignoring the safeguards against the abuse of power inherent to those traditions.[9] John Dugard in affirming the liberal tradition in South African law-making, in turn, argues that 'if faith is to be restored in the South African legal system *while there is yet time* sweeping changes will need to be made to the entire edifice of law'. This, he argues, involves the affirmation of such principles (often neglected) within South Africa's legal heritage which 'recognises the intersection of law and moral values'.[10]

The liberating and justice-giving elements of law, which are inherent and latent to the South African legal tradition as identified by Sachs, Dugard and many other lawyers and judges in South Africa (including Gandhi, Schreiner, Seme, Fischer, Rose-Innes, Nokwe, Kahn, Mandela, Tambo, Slovo, Kentridge, Ishmael Mohamed, and others) constitute the promise of what law can and ought to be in a new society.

When Mandela [writes Sachs] made his famous denunciation of South African justice at his first trial after his capture, he did so with an elegance that enriched the patrimony of English usage in South Africa, and, utilising the principles and procedures of South African law to the full, he turned Roman–Dutch law into a weapon of attack. His basic critique against the legal system was not that it was Roman–Dutch but that is was racist. Thus, he did not object to having courts with trained judges, to written laws, to defence and prosecution lawyers doing battle with each other according to defined procedures, but to the fact that he felt he was a black person in a white person's court; the laws were made by the whites and administered by the whites in a courtroom that breathed the atmosphere of white domination, and this should not be so. He should be a South African in a South African

---

[9] Albie Sachs, *Protecting Human Rights in a New South Africa* (Cape Town: Oxford University Press, 1990), p. 94.

[10] John Dugard, *Human Rights and the South African Legal Order* (Princeton: Princeton University Press, 1978), p. 398.

court, he declared, and not someone subjected to a system whereby the guilty dragged the innocent before them.[11]

Inherent to revolution is the desire to start again, a time to rewrite, reconceive and restructure the basis of society, and there is much to be discarded in South African law if the intersection between law and moral value is to be rediscovered. Realism and the history of post-independence in Africa and elsewhere in the world suggests, however, that rather than re-invent the wheel, the legal instruments at hand (which are not inconsistent with a post-revolutionary Constitution) can be cleansed and developed to serve the interests of the entire population. For this to happen the sickness of South African political and legal history is to be discerned and defined – both with a view to excising the disease and ensuring that it does not reappear at any time in the future.

THE BRITISH PARLIAMENTARY HERITAGE

This is a disease that grew and developed from what was effective government in Britain, given to the hard-won affirmation of individual rights, into a monster that ultimately devoured justice itself when transplanted into colonial South Africa. It is a monster with two limbs: the *unrestrained supremacy of parliament* and the *constitutional denial of democracy*, which resulted in an all-powerful white racist rule.

Sir William Blackstone's famous affirmation of the supremacy of parliament in his 1765 publication, the *Commentaries on the Laws of England*, was to leave an indelible mark throughout the British Empire. 'If the legislature positively enacts a thing to be done which is unreasonable', he wrote, 'I know of no power in the ordinary forms of the constitution, that is vested with authority to control it.' Parliament can 'do everything that is not naturally impossible'. Its power is 'absolute and without control'.[12] 'To set the judicial power above that of the

---

[11] Sachs, *Protecting Human Rights*, p. 4. See also Nelson Mandela, 'Black Man in a White Court – First Court Statement', in *The Struggle is My Life* (London: International Defence and Aid Fund, 1986), pp. 133–60.

[12] Quoted in John Dugard *Human Rights*, p. 16.

56 *A theology of reconstruction*

legislature', insisted Blackstone, 'would be subversive of all government.'[13]

Raoul Berger, insisting on the importance of judicial review of parliamentary law, suggests that Blackstone's statement is refuted by the history of American government.[14] It is enough for our purposes to note that in the American colonies, during the latter part of the eighteenth century, it was the unbridled power of the British parliament within which the colonists had no representation that needed to be restrained. And as the framers of the constitution sought to structure the future of an independent America, they were concerned never again to suffer arbitrariness, *even at the hands of their own elected parliament*. Despite this, slavery was tolerated until 1865 and the Civil Rights Act only passed in 1964.

In England the Glorious Revolution of 1688 took place in a different context. It was the King's arbitrary power that needed to be curtailed. Parliamentary democracy was seen as the way to accomplish this, and when James II (the last of the notorious Stuarts) was removed from the throne and replaced by William and Mary, they were obliged to sign the Bill of Rights, limiting the power of the monarchy and guaranteeing parliamentary supremacy. Writing almost 100 years later, Blackstone was adamant that this hard won parliamentary democracy should never again be compromised.[15] There was, however, no attempt by him to ignore or disregard the most fundamental moral and democratic values of the British parliamentary tradition – one

[13] Quoted in Raoul Berger, 'Doctor Bonham's Case: Statutory Construction or Constitutional Theory?' *University of Pennsylvania Law Review*, 117, February 1969, p. 524.
[14] *Ibid.*, p. 522. For a discussion of the rule of law in Britain and the United States of America see A.E. Dick Howard *The Road from Runnymede: Magna Carta and Constitutionalism in America* (Charlottesville: The University Press of Virginia, 1968).
[15] Raoul Berger's article shows how Sir Edward Coke's rejection of any Act of Parliament which is 'against common right and reason' in the case between Dr Bonham and the Royal College of Physicians (which did not in itself address matters of constitutional law) was seized on by American colonists for political and eventually constitutional, ends. 'When the Colonists', he writes, 'concluded that Parliament was intolerably abusing its power, they not unjustifiably took Coke's words, which meanwhile had been repeated respectfully by judges and in the *Abridgments* for 150 years, at face value.' 'Dr Bonham's Case' (p. 545).

which came to show respect for constitutional conventions and political compromise. Its affirmation of liberty was strong enough to form an effective barrier against arbitrary action by the government of the day. Separated from this tradition, parliamentary supremacy in Britain loses its identity as an instrument designed to end political tyranny. In other words, it cannot be understood and must not be assessed apart from a strong sense of the rule of law earned through the history of legal and parliamentary reform in Britain.

Blackstone showed no concern that parliament would ever want to act against the interests of the people or the 'fundamental law' contained in Magna Carta (signed by King John in 1215), the Bill of Rights (signed by William and Mary in 1689) and related legislation. His confidence in parliamentary supremacy further needs to be viewed against the views of Chief Justice Edward Coke, which constituted the dominant legal tradition prior to the acceptance of Blackstone's creed. Dismissed by James I in 1616 for refusing to obey royal instructions, a hundred years later Coke's understanding of law came to be celebrated by American colonists for his insistence that both king and parliament are bound by the 'fundamental law' of reason and justice. 'The common law', Coke said, 'will control Acts of Parliament, and sometimes adjudge them to be utterly void: for when an Act of Parliament is against common right and reason . . . the common law will judge it, and adjudge such Act to be void.'[16] Blackstone's teaching is a direct rejection of the judicial testing of parliamentary laws as conceived by Coke. Blackstone's writings are nevertheless supportive of the ethical reforms and restraints which are part of the British tradition. He further acknowledged Coke's concern to protect these rights with 'great veneration and respect'.[17]

When Blackstone's affirmation of parliamentary supremacy is located within this historic context, it is clear that, although for Blackstone 'parliament is supreme, it would be misleading and indeed inaccurate to characterise the powers of the British

---

[16] Quoted in Dugard, *Human Rights*, p. 14. See also Berger, 'Dr Bonham's Case', pp. 521–2.   [17] Raoul Berger, *ibid.*, pp. 523 and 535–6.

parliament as an instance of the absolute unlimited sovereignty of statute'.[18] This lesson the white South African parliament never learned in turning parliamentary supremacy into an instrument to exploit the disenfranchised black majority. The fact that the British parliament has conducted itself with less integrity in colonial and foreign policy than it has on the domestic front, as witnessed in the American colonies, in India, Africa and other parts of the Empire is, in turn, enough to establish beyond all dispute the importance of direct representation in parliamentary government.

Debate on specific options for law-making in South Africa, given its lack of democratic custom and practice, and the place of judicial review within the Rule of Law must wait for Chapter 3. Suffice it to say for the present, it is in relation to these options that the decisive constitutional debate in South Africa is likely to occur. The appeal of unbridled parliamentary supremacy to the black majority in South Africa is immense, and not easily turned away from.

The attack on majoritarianism, which underlies many arguments in favor of a Bill of Rights, is manifestly racist, since South Africa has been governed without a Bill of Rights and in accordance with the principles of majority rule [for the minority!] since the Union of South Africa was created in 1910. It is only now that the majority promises to be black, that constitutional doubts and the need for checks and balances suddenly become allegedly self-evident.[19]

The present debate on the virtue (or otherwise) of a Bill of Rights and the judicial review of law is intense and likely to continue well into the new South African society. In appealing for 'a new way of thinking about law', John Dugard, at the end of his important book, *Human Rights and the South African Legal Order*, suggests 'it is fascinating to speculate on what would have happened had South Africa, like America, been colonized by Britain in the seventeenth century [prior to the advent of Blackstone's creed]'. 'Would it', he asks, 'today have a rigid

---

[18] J.D. van der Vyver, 'Depriving Westminster of Its Moral Constraints: A Survey of Constitutional Developments in South Africa', *Harvard Civil Rights-Civil Liberties Law Review*, 20:2 (Summer, 1985), p. 300.

[19] Albie Sachs, 'Towards a Bill of Rights for a Democratic South Africa', *The Hastings International and Comparative Law Review*, 12:2 (Winter 1989), p. 294.

Constitution with a Bill of Rights and judicial review?'[20] More important is whether this would have made a fundamental difference to the unfolding of events in South Africa? The American constitution continued to allow for slavery and failed to prevent the exploitation of native Americans in the name of 'federal Indian law'. 'Congress', writes Milner Ball, 'has worked its will upon the tribes in whatever way it has wished, even when its actions have wholly lacked a constitutional basis or have obviously violated tribes.'[21] Women have been exploited in America in the presence of a constitution affirming the unalienable rights of 'man' (language *is* important), and blacks had to wait until the Civil Rights struggle in the 1960s for the rights of the Constitution to be extended to them.

In South Africa, the so-called 'independent homelands' of the Ciskei and Bophuthatswana each have a 'Bill of Rights' and 'independent judiciary', that were proudly celebrated at the time of 'independence'. Yet ironically Bantustan rule has turned out to be *the* most overtly corrupt and violently repressive manifestation of apartheid rule in the country. Constitutions *per se* are not enough to ensure just government. Furthermore, such indiscriminate advocacy of 'judicial review' in relation to a Bill of Rights, coming as it does from those who had hitherto resolutely turned away from the very thought of a Bill of Rights, is not by definition the *only* solution to South Africa's problems, but clearly one seriously to be considered.

In the chapters that follow I will argue *for* a Bill of Rights on theological and political grounds. In so doing consideration will be given essentially to the fact that it is primarily the rights of those whose rights have systematically been denied throughout South African history that need to be promoted in a future Bill of Rights, although clearly these rights will extend to all South Africans. It must be assured that no future government be allowed to act against its own citizens, as have past South African governments. In addition to protecting the rights of individuals in a new society, a Bill of Rights must protect the state against itself. Is there, given the long history of the abuse of

[20] Dugard, *Human Rights*, p. 394.
[21] Milner Ball, 'Stories of Origin and Constitutional Possibilities', *Michigan Law Review* (August, 1989), p. 2297.

human rights, a national-will to affirm this option? Can such a will and commitment to human rights be culturally generated? What is the role of theology in this regard? These are questions which are returned to in later chapters. For the present, attention is given to the history which weighs on the present quest for renewal.

British parliamentary supremacy, emerging from a long history of struggle against the arbitrary rule of the King and later that of the nobility, gave rise to a tradition of equality before the law and, in time, to universal suffrage. The consequence is a homogeneous common law of democratic values to which parliament is expected to adhere. On occasions the British parliament has violated its most basic values (for example, on matters of race in the United Kingdom and Rhodesia's unilateral declaration of independence), in much the same way that the United States Congress has violated its constitution. In South Africa, however, parliamentary supremacy has operated *without* affirming either a British sense of the rule of law or a sense of American unalienable rights. This 'double fault' constitutes the vulnerable context within which political reconstruction in South Africa must take place.

To contours of this history we now turn. It is a history within which all entrenched clauses in the various constitutions which, at one time or another influenced or shaped contemporary South Africa, were deliberately removed. The only exception to this practice being the continued entrenchment of Afrikaans and English as official languages. To fail to understand this history is to fail to appreciate the pathos of contemporary constitutional debate in South Africa. More important, it undercuts an empathetic appreciation for the suspicion with which many black people and other sincere democrats respond to the recent (and uncharacteristic) moves by the white establishment to investigate the entrenchment of certain individual and group 'rights' in a new constitution.

SOUTH AFRICAN LAW-MAKING

The Achilles heel of parliamentary rule in South Africa has always been the lack of universal suffrage. In the nineteenth century franchise in the British ruled Cape Colony was extended to all adult males, irrespective of race, who met certain educational and economic requirements. Then, as the numbers of African voters increased, the qualifications were raised. When Natal was occupied by the British a similar procedure was adopted, although here the political rights of blacks were effectively restricted to the point where in 1907 out of 23,480 registered voters, only 150 were Indian, 50 'coloured' and 6 African![22] Yet even these limited rights afforded to black people were more than Boers in these regions were prepared to accept. They trekked north to establish the Orange Free State and South African Republic in the Transvaal.

Parliamentary supremacy

The framers of the Orange Free State constitution were strongly influenced by American constitutionalism. They turned away from parliamentary supremacy and entrenched certain individual rights under the protection of a Superior Court.[23] In reality, however, the court never saw fit to over-rule the actions of the *Volksraad* (parliament) and the guarantee of rights was extended only to 'citizens' – and, according to the customs of Boer ideology, this excluded blacks![24]

Constitutionalism in the Transvaal was a more involved process. When a constitution was finally agreed on, 'it was not clear whether the *Grondwet* [constitution] created fundamental law and whether the constitution was superior to the legislature, although there were several articles that seemed to point to the sovereignty of the people, not the *Volksraad*.'[25] This ambiguity was soon, however, eliminated. In 1895 Chief Justice J.G. Kotze found certain *besluiten* (informal decisions) by the *Volksraad* to be contrary to the *Grondwet*. Some (including the prominent Orange Free State judge and a future Prime Minister of the

---

[22] L.M. Thompson, *The Unification of South Africa: 1902–1910* (Oxford: The Clarendon Press, 1960), p. 111.

[23] H.R. Hahlo and Ellison Kahn (eds.), *The Union of South Africa: The Development of Its Laws and Constitution*, volume 5 in George W. Keeton (gen. ed.) *The British Commonwealth: The Development of Its Laws and Constitution* (London: Stevens and Sons. Cape Town: Juta and Company, 1960), pp. 77–8.

[24] Dugard, *Human Rights*, p. 19. For discussion on the Orange Free State Constitution see Hahlo and Kahn, pp. 72–83.   [25] Dugard, *ibid.*, p. 20.

Union of South Africa, J.M.B. Hertzog) supported his right to 'test' legislation, but J.C. Smuts, a future attorney general in the Transvaal republic (later also to be a Prime Minister of the Union of South Africa), argued in favour of 'British parliamentary practice' and supported President Paul Kruger in his confrontation with the judiciary.[26]

Kotze was dismissed from his post and, at the swearing-in ceremony of Chief Justice R. Gregorowski as Kotze's successor, Kruger insisted that 'the testing right is a principle of the devil'.[27] The independence of the Boer nation was seen as part of the providence of God, and the constitution an instrument that located sovereignty in the hands of a legislature whose task it was to ensure white hegemony in a land demographically dominated by blacks. In varying religious and secular forms this philosophy would influence South African politics for generations to come.

When the Union of South Africa was established in 1910 in the wake of the Anglo-Boer War, it was this version of parliamentary supremacy that was imprinted on its Constitution. Limitations on the legislature were seen as a sign of political subordination.[28] Only one person fought publicly for a rigid Constitution, and that was former Chief Justice J.G. Kotze, who had been assigned to a post in the Eastern Districts Courts of the Cape Colony since his fall from grace in the Transvaal. His concern was for a new political beginning, and his fear was that unrestrained actions of parliament could militate against this.

Kotze's plea was largely disregarded. The Constitution of the Union of South Africa was an overtly racist document. Despite the representations to the British Government by a non-racial delegation led (at the request of the South African Native Convention and 'coloured' people's African Political Organisa-

---

[26] Legal debate and the quest for political compromise was extensive. Lord de Villiers who was Chief Justice of the Cape Colony, for example, unsuccessfully intervened to establish a compromise between the President and the Judiciary. See Eric A. Walker, *Lord de Villiers and His Times: South Africa 1842–1914* (London: Constable and Co., 1925), pp. 293–4. Also J.W. Gordon, *Law Quarterly Review*, 343 and 365 (1898), quoted in Dugard, *Human Rights*, p. 23.   [27] Dugard; *Human Rights*, p. 24.

[28] Leonard Thompson comments: 'Full flexibility was a mark of national autonomy, so that a flexible constitution seemed to be the proper national ideal.' This, he suggests, was 'a confusion of thought which has persisted in South Africa to the present day'. Thompson, *The Unification of South Africa*, p. 100.

tion) by former Prime Minister of the Cape Colony W.P. Schreiner, the Constitution was approved by the British parliament and Union declared on 31 May 1910.

It contained three entrenched clauses: Section 35 provided that no persons registered or capable of registering as voters in the Cape according to the pre-Union qualifications could be deprived of their vote by reason of race or colour, while section 137 entrenched English and Afrikaans as official languages. Section 152 stipulated that a two-thirds majority vote at the joint sitting of both Houses of Parliament (the Senate and House of Assembly) was required to amend either of the entrenched clauses.

In effect, as a consequence of the 1865 Colonial Laws Validity Act, any attempt by the South African parliament to amend the entrenched clauses also required the approval of the British parliament. When the Statute of Westminster Act, however, became law in 1931 (providing that no Act of the British parliament would extend to a Dominion without the consent of that Dominion) South Africa was freed from any external controls. In 1936 the Representation of Natives Act was passed with the necessary two-thirds majority vote, removing African voters from the common voters' roll. When challenged in Court the Appellate Division ruled:

Parliament . . . can adopt any procedure it thinks fit; the procedure express or applied in the South Africa Act so far as Courts of Law are concerned is at the mercy of Parliament like everything else . . . Parliament's will . . . as expressed in an Act of Parliament cannot now in this country, as it cannot in England, be questioned by a Court of Law, whose function it is to enforce that will not to question it.[29]

The ghost of Kruger had returned. Kotze was vindicated but it was too late. The wording of the ruling in favour of parliamentary action was seen to place the entrenched clauses at the mercy of a parliamentary majority. Some, in fact, interpreted the ruling to mean that the two-thirds majority in a *joint-sitting* of the two houses of parliament as having lapsed with the Statute of Westminster. When the National Party was elected to

---

[29] Appellate Division Report, 1937. Quoted in Dugard, *Human Rights*, p. 29.

power in 1948 it acted on this assumption and set about removing 'coloureds' from the common voters' roll. The Separate Representation of Voters' Act was approved in both houses of parliament, *sitting separately* – but rejected by a unanimous decision of the Appellate Division. The court held that parliament was obliged to comply with the unicameral procedure laid down in the Constitution when dealing with entrenched clauses. The Government responded by enacting the High Court of Parliament Act (in the normal bicameral way) insisting that decisions of the Appellate Division concerning parliament were to be reviewed by parliament itself, forming itself into a High Court of Parliament. The Prime Minister, Dr D.F. Malan, reiterated the position of Paul Kruger:

Neither Parliament nor the people of South Africa will be prepared to acquiesce in a position where the legal sovereignty of the lawfully and democratically elected representatives of the people is denied, and where appointed judicial authority assumes the testing right.[30]

Dr T.E. Donges, the Minister of the Interior who presented the High Court of Parliament Act in parliament, in turn, observed that the choice was between 'judicial supremacy as you have in the United States' and 'parliamentary supremacy as you have in the United Kingdom'.[31] The Appellate Division refused to be intimidated, ruling that the High Court of Parliament was essentially parliament in disguise, insisting that the entrenched clauses required judicial protection.

The government, still unable to obtain a two-thirds majority at a joint sitting of both houses of parliament was not ready to concede defeat. It increased the size of the Appellate Division from 5 to 11 judges. It also increased the size of the senate, while changing the method of electing senators. The outcome was a sympathetic Appellate Division and the necessary two-thirds National Party majority in a joint sitting of both houses of parliament. The South Africa Act Amendment Act, 1956, was passed with the necessary unicameral majority and the Separate Representation of Voters Act revalidated. 'Coloureds' were

removed from the common voters' roll.[32] The Act also removed
the clause concerning voters in the Cape Province from the scope
of the entrenchment procedure of the 1910 Constitution. It
further stated, in order to remove all confusion:

No court of law shall be competent to enquire into or to pronounce
upon the validity of any law passed by Parliament other than a law
which alters or repeals or purports to alter or repeal the provisions of
sections 137 or 152 of the South African Act, 1909.[33]

The Act was challenged before the newly constituted Appellate Division, but upheld by a 10 to 1 majority. British
parliamentary supremacy had been abused in isolation from the
history out of which it was born, and needless to say, without
regard for universal suffrage as the only possible justification for
parliamentary supremacy.

When white South Africans elected to become a Republic and
a new Constitution was enacted in 1961, described in its
preamble as one 'best suited to the traditions and history of our
land', it was not necessary to institute any further major changes
to the law-making process in South Africa.[34] The supremacy of
the legislature had been asserted beyond all doubt in the 1950s.
The 1961 Constitution simply needed to affirm:

Parliament shall be the sovereign legislative authority in and over the
Republic, and shall have full power to make laws for the peace, order
and good government of the Republic . . .
No court of law shall be competent to enquire into or pronounce upon
the validity of any Act passed by Parliament, other than an Act which
repeals or amends or purports to repeal or amend the provisions of
section one hundred and eight or one hundred and eighteen. [These
provisions entrench Afrikaans and English as official languages.][35]

In so doing the testing right of the judiciary was confined strictly
to the language question. When the 1983 Constitution was

---

[32] Initially 'coloured' people were given limited separate representation in parliament
by being allowed to elect white representatives, but this too was abolished in 1968. An
attempt was then made to channel 'coloured' politics into the Coloured Representative Council, but this body predictably collapsed in 1980.   [33] *Ibid.*, p. 31.

[34] See Appendix 11, Ellison Kahn, *The New Constitution: Being a Supplement to South Africa:
The Development of Its Laws and Constitution* (London: Stevens and Sons. Cape Town:
Juta and Co., 1962), p. 39.   [35] *Ibid.*, p. 52.

introduced, allowing for the appointment of an executive State President, it again restricted the judiciary to law enforcement rather than testing, while locating many of the powers hitherto located in parliament in the hands of the executive branch of government. Before turning to this development it is helpful, however, to be reminded of the extent to which an unrestrained parliament was used to deprive people of their most basic human rights, and to criminalise what in most western nations would be regarded as democratic politics – the right to protest and resist.

Law as repression

The South African version of parliamentary supremacy cannot be fully understood apart from the legal repression to which it has given rise. Parliament and related legislative structures were used to create laws, reshape existing legislation and engineer black oppression and exploitation from the time this form of rule was introduced into South African soil.

The roots of black impoverishment go back to the arrival of whites in the area. It was, however, essentially British colonialism and the discovery of diamonds and gold that created the legal structures of dispossession with which South Africa lives today. In the words of mine owner, Cape politician and imperialist *par excellence*, Cecil John Rhodes, this legislation 'removed natives from a life of sloth and laziness, teaching them the dignity of labour, made them contribute to the prosperity of the state, and made them give some return for our wise and good government'.[36]

After the defeat of the Boer republics in the Anglo-Boer war, Lord Alfred Milner's colonial government introduced legislation which imposed controls over every aspect of African life.[37] Pass laws were more strictly imposed, legal procedures developed to deal with a breach of contract, a register of finger-prints was introduced, a non-competitive mechanism of hiring black labour was legalised and a new understanding between mine

---

[36] Eddie Webster, 'Background of the Supply and Control of Labour in the Gold Mines', in *Essays in Southern African Labour History* (Johannesburg: Ravan Press, 1983), p. 10.
[37] Julius Lewin, *Politics and Law in South Africa* (London: Merlin Press, 1963), pp. 90f.

owners and the government was established. The outcome was a
set of legal restraints on black participation in society which was,
in the words of British historian Thomas Pakenham, 'applied
with an efficiency the Boers had never been able to muster'.[38]

It has already been shown that the 1910 Constitution of the
Union of South Africa excluded the majority of blacks from the
vote, and that before long all black South Africans were
disenfranchised. The 1913 Land Act designated 13 per cent of
the land 'native reserves', leaving the rest to whites who made up
less than 20 per cent of the population, and a range of related
oppressive legislation followed. By the time the ruling National
Party came to power in 1948, the process of dispossession was
almost complete. The National Party inherited a situation
which had ensured that 'white domination . . . [was] firmly
entrenched in South African law'.[39]

With renewed vigour, however, the new government saw to it
that white domination was perfected and apartheid legally
entrenched at every level of social, political and economic
existence. This legislation has been documented and explained
in detail in various publications and need not be repeated here.[40]
It classified every human being in South Africa according to
race, which determined the extent of the rights and privileges a
person could expect from the state. It designated certain
facilities for whites and others for blacks, sought to direct and
control marriages and sexual relations, designated where people
of different races could live, segregated schools, imposed job
reservation, restricted the free travel and settlement of blacks

---

[38] Thomas Pakenham, *The Boer War* (London: Weidenfeld and Nicolson, 1979),p. 45.
[39] R.F.A. Hoernle, *South African Native Policy and the Liberal Spirit* (Johannesburg: 1945),
p. 55.
[40] See, for example, Muriel Horrell, *Race Classification in South Africa: Its Effects on Human
Beings* (Johannesburg: South African Institute of Race Relations. 1958); *A Survey of
Race Relations*, a series of annual reports issued by the South African Institute of Race
Relations; Arthur Suzman, 'Race Classification and Definition in the Legislation of
the Union of South Africa, 1910–1960', *Acta Juridica*, 1960, pp. 339–67; Jack
Unterhalter, 'Apartheid Legislation and Our Inherited Understanding of the Law',
in *Law, Justice and Society*, Report of the SPROCAS Legal Commission (Johannes-
burg: SPROCAS, 1972); F.P. Rousseau, *Handbook on the Group Areas Act* (Cape Town:
Juta and Co, 1960); John Dugard, *Human Rights and the South African Legal Order*
(Princeton: Princeton University Press, 1978); Francis Wilson and Mamphela
Ramphela *Poverty in South Africa* (Cape Town: David Philip, 1989).

and assigned millions of people to underdeveloped tribal Bantustans. While some of these laws have been modified and others rescinded in recent years, the impact and consequences of the use of parliament and law as an instrument of oppression is likely to haunt South African politics for a long time to come.

The systematic denial of human rights brought about in South Africa through the apartheid system is monumental. The ultimate form of repression is, however, the refusal to allow protest against one's own oppression. In South Africa, since 1948, virtually every form of protest (until the unbanning of the African National Congress and other organisations in February 1990) has been criminalised. And South Africans continue, despite the political concessions associated with February 1990 decisions, to live under some of the harshest security laws in the Western World. Again it is not necessary to discuss this legislation. There are numerous useful books which do precisely this.[41]

As was the case with apartheid legislation, the seeds of the Draconian system of security laws which emerged after 1948, were already sown long before the National Party came to power. Despite these imperfections however, in 1948, 'civil liberties and the rule of law were still vibrant concepts in the political life of the country'.[42] This was a process which the newly elected government vigorously set about destroying. The first important act in this regard was the Suppression of Communism Act of 1950, used as an instrument to ban, restrict and imprison individuals, organisations and trade unions. Then, in the wake of the Defiance Campaign, launched in 1952, came the Criminal Law Amendment Act, the Public Safety Act (allowing the government to declare a state of emergency) and the massive 'show' trial of 156 persons on charges of high treason and related offences – all of whom were ultimately found not guilty! What

---

[41] See, *inter alia* Anthony Mathews, *Law, Order and Liberty in South Africa* (Berkeley: University of California Press, 1972); Anthony Mathews, *Freedom, State Security and the Rule of Law* (Berkeley: University of California. Cape Town: Juta and Co, 1986); John Dugard, *Human Rights and the South African Legal Order* (Princeton: Princeton University Press, 1978); Don Foster (with contributions from Dennis Davis and Diane Sandler), *Detention and Torture in South Africa: Psychological, Legal and Historical Studies* (Cape Town: David Philip. New York: St Martin's Press, 1987). Detainees' Parents Support Committee, *Review* (Bramley, Johannesburg), published annually.

[42] Dennis Davis in Don Foster, *Detention and Torture*, p. 12.

the state could not do through the courts, however, it proceeded to do through parliament.

Within ten days of the shootings at Sharpeville, the government used the Public Safety Act of 1953 to declare a state of emergency, and over 13,000 people were arrested. On 8 April 1960 the African National Congress and the Pan Africanist Congress were banned under the newly enacted Unlawful Organizations Act. From that time on security laws allowing for detention without trial were intensified from provisions for 90 days detention to 180 days detention and ultimately detention for indefinite periods. The freedom of speech was curtailed, organisations and individuals banned and restricted, and virtually every form of protest and resistance criminalised.[43] In the words of Anthony Mathews, the 'security' laws which are 'an integral part of the apartheid system . . . [have] torn the heart out of the Rule of Law and the civilized Roman–Dutch legal system'.[44]

Executive rule

This history of legal repression in South Africa began with the abuse of parliamentary supremacy. It ironically reached its zenith with the restricting of parliamentary power in the implementation of the 1983 constitution. The new constitution provided for a tricameral parliament, giving limited political rights to 'coloureds' and Indians in separate parliamentary chambers, while totally excluding Africans. It further allowed for the election of an executive State President by an electoral college within which a white majority vote was constitutionally entrenched. In the words of J.D. van der Vyver, 'it marks the end of the Westminster system of government in the Republic of South Africa – or, to be more exact, of the South African caricature of Westminster'.[45]

The separation of power between legislative and executive branches of government as exists in the United States of America

---

[43] *Ibid.*, pp. 11–56. Davis provides a summary of these laws.
[44] Mathews, *Law, Order and Liberty*, p. 302.
[45] J.D. van der Vyver, 'Depriving Westminster of Its Moral Constraints: A Survey of Constitutional Development in South Africa', *Harvard Civil Rights–Civil Liberties Law Review*, 20:2, Summer, 1985, p. 291.

has never existed in South Africa. The South African parliament has also functioned outside of the historical tradition of the British parliamentary system. This has resulted in the dominant authority of parliament being used to confer on the executive and ruling party excessive and near absolute powers. Charles I, who the British parliament saw fit to execute in 1649, would have revelled in the South African executive's power to make laws![46]

The 1983 Constitution established this executive and/or party privilege beyond question. Ostensibly designed to incorporate 'coloured' and Indians into the legislative process, it entrenched and intensified the *de facto* power that the ruling party had already grabbed for itself. 'Far from dispersing power, the new constitution would concentrate it even further in the hands of the majority white party', observed Dr F. Van Zyl Slabbert who was at the time leader of the official opposition in parliament. The ruling white party would control not only the white chamber but choose the President. This amounted, he said, to a new form of white 'dictatorial rule'.[47]

Slabbert's assessment of the Constitution is confirmed by the mathematics and provisions contained within it, which provides for whites, 'coloureds' and Indians to be represented in a tricameral parliament on a ratio of 4:2:1. Each separate house is responsible for such matters which are designated 'own affairs', while 'general affairs' are to be approved by all three houses of parliament. Where the three houses are unable to agree on a specific piece of legislation and all attempts at compromise at the level of joint committees fail, the State President is able to refer the legislation to the President's Council – a kind of substitute legislature, whose membership is determined on the same 4:2:1 basis. Its decision on disputed legislation is final.[48] The State

[46] *Ibid.*, p. 312.
[47] *South African House of Assembly Debates*, 16 May 1983, cols 7065–74. Quoted in James Barber, 'White South Africa – into the Political Unknown', *The World Today*, 39:12, December 1983, p. 493.
[48] Of the 60 member Council, 20 members are elected by the majority party in the white House of Assembly and a further 25 are appointees of the State President. While the Constitution requires that ten of the Presidential appointees need to come from opposition parties, the State President can always count on a clear majority in the Council to have the legislature he requires accepted.

President, elected for a five-year period by an electoral college constituted on the set 4:2:1 ratio and therefore invariably a member of the majority white party, is left with unprecedented and almost limitless executive and legislative authority.[49] It entrenches not only unrestrained white power, but single party and ultimately executive rule.[50]

THE BURDEN WEIGHS HEAVILY

As South Africa slowly edges towards the possibility of reconstruction, constitutional debate is again on the political agenda. Ironically it is the ruling party, who have consistently turned away from a Bill of Rights and any form of constraint on parliamentary-executive authority, who are now investigating newly entrenched constitutional clauses and the curtailment of parliamentary supremacy. The most cynical reading on these moves suggests that now that parliamentary supremacy has been exploited as a basis for dispossessing black people of their land and most basic rights, the privileges acquired by whites in the process (such as property ownership and 'other privileges') should be entrenched in a Bill of Rights. Parliamentary supremacy (so this line of argument continues) must now be limited to ensure that a black majority government does not 'indiscriminately' use parliament to undo what whites have so successfully accomplished to their own benefit over the years.

Despite the emotional appeal of this kind of argument, the

---

[49] See, *inter alia, Race Relations Survey*, 1986 (Johannesburg: The South African Institution of Race Relations), Part 1; J.D. van der Vyver, 'Depriving Westminster of its Moral Constraints: A Survey of Constitutional Development in South Africa', *Harvard Civil Rights–Civil Liberties Law Review*, 20:2, Summer, 1985; David Welsh, 'Constitutional Changes in South Africa', *African Affairs*, 83:331, April 1984; Dennis Austin, 'The Trinitarians: the 1983 South Africa Constitutional', *Government and Opposition*, 20:2, Spring 1985; James Barber, 'White South Africa – into the Political Unknown,' *The World Today*, 39:12.

[50] The Constitution contains a series of clauses which are described as 'principles of cardinal importance'. These are entrenched to the extent that the amendment or repeal of these principles requires an absolute majority in each of the three houses of parliament, without the President's Council having the authority to resolve any disagreements that may arise between the houses. One such clause refers to the composition and size of the respective houses. In entrenching the 4:2:1 ratio between the houses and on the President's Council it entrenches white oligarchical rule.

African National Congress' constitutional proposals for a new South Africa include provision for a justiciable Bill of Rights and a Constitutional Court with the power 'to review and set aside legislation and actions which are unconstitutional'.[51] It is designed to extend, rather than restrict, the rights and privileges of *all* South Africans, while claiming the need for 'affirmative action for the advancement of persons who have been socially, economically or educationally disadvantaged by past discriminatory laws and practices'. It requires that special provision be made 'to redress the added discrimination which has been suffered by women and the victims of forced removals'.[52] The working draft of the ANC's Bill of Rights, published in November 1990, in turn, states:

Nothing in the Constitution shall prevent the enactment of legislation, or the adoption by any public or private body of special measures of a positive kind designed to procure the advancement and the opening up of opportunities, including access to education, skills, employment and land, and the general advancement in social, economic and cultural spheres, of men and women who in the past have been disadvantaged by discrimination.

No provision of the Bill of Rights shall be construed as derogating from or limiting in any way the general provisions of this Article.[53]

The interim report of the South African Law Commission, in turn, provides what is in many ways a more restrained (conservative) proposal for a Bill of Rights, focussing on First-Generation rights.[54] It excludes direct constitutional proposals on economic and social rights of the kind found in the ANC proposals, while its limited affirmative action clause fails to make provision for remedial or corrective action to redress the consequences of generations of oppression. This suggests that, while the ANC and the South African government both use the language of international human rights, the gap between their

---

[51] *A Discussion Document: Constitutional Principles and Structures for a Democratic South Africa* (Bellville: Centre for Development Studies, University of the Western Cape, 1991), p. 26.   [52] *Ibid.*, p. 30.

[53] Published in *Monitor*, December 1990, pp. 64–8. See also: African National Congress, *Discussion Document: Constitutional Principles and Structures for a Democratic South Africa* (April 1991).

[54] South African Law Commission, *Interim Report on Group and Human Rights* (Pretoria: SA Law Commission, August 1991).

respective documents is wider than what at first appears to be the case. The constitutional proposals of the ruling National Party underline the extent of the gap.[55] While conceding necessity of one person one vote in a lower house, the proposals prevent the majority party from exercising the kind of power needed to correct the historical imbalances in the country. Although seemingly renouncing all forms of race, the proposals effectively vest power in ethno-chauvinistic formations. In the words of Roger Southall:

We must not be misled into presuming that a viable constitutional consensus will be easily achieved, for what strikes one about the NP (National Party) proposals particularly is their calculated ambiguity; they seek not so much to control a central government as to abolish it, whilst simultaneously rendering what remains of democracy at the centre subject to constraints imposed by an essentially unaccountable 'constitutional state'.[56]

It is around these and related issues that the struggle for a future South Africa is likely to be fought, both before and after a Bill of Rights is adopted. It is an issue that the church can scarcely ignore while facing the issues involved in reconstruction and nation-building.

The different sections of the population in South Africa, divided by generations of colonialism and apartheid, each look to a Bill of Rights for different things. Some look for protection from abuses to which they have been subjected in the past, and for ways of remediating the inequalities of the South African society. Others look for the protection of property and cultural identity. There is, at the same time, a growing consensus between conflicting groups that some form of 'affirmative action' is required at the level of human rights in South Africa if the emerging new structures are to be characterised by justice and human dignity. The details of this process will need to be politically negotiated, making Van der Vyver's counsel regarding a Bill of Rights an important guideline:

A useful means of evaluating any constitutional arrangement is to imagine that one's greatest political opponent, or the person one would

---

[55] National Party, *Constitutional Rule in a Participating Democracy*, September, 1991.
[56] Roger Southall, 'The Constitutional State! The Proposals of the National Party for a New Consitution', *Monitor*, October 1919, p. 90.

least of all want to entrust with the powers of government, were in charge of the affairs of state. Then ask yourself what that party or such person could lawfully do within the confines of the authority sanctioned by the constitution in question.[57]

Such an exercise falls beyond the scope of the present study. Its focus is the articulation of the *theological* principles involved in the process of political reconstruction, as it applies to constitutional, legal and human rights concerns. The contextual focus of the study at the same time demands that this exercise be undertaken retroactively, requiring that a future South African society be structured by learning from past mistakes.[58] Methodologically this requires an inductive, contextual approach which is informed by global human rights developments, while grounded in the resilience and strength of the actual South African struggle for justice. A constitution (or Bill of Rights) capable of bringing justice and peace to society is indeed not made under circumstances chosen by those who happen to draft it, but under circumstances directly encountered, given and transmitted from the past. It is insufficient merely to appropriate the best clauses from the best constitutions of the world. The burdens and struggles of the past need to inform the creation of a new future.

New nations do not spontaneously rise from the ashes of the past on the day of political transition. South Africa is likely to continue to live 'between the times' for several decades beyond its day of liberation. The old will die over many years. The birth of the new will take time. It is the task of those who share in the creation of the new to ensure that great chunks of the past remain dead, and that the spirit of the quest for justice and democracy that has survived the tyranny of the past, is able to shape the new age.

A Bill of Rights in South Africa must ultimately function as a freedom charter designed to maximise the freedom of the individual, within the context of communal exigencies and

[57] J.D. Van der Vyver, 'Constitutional Guidelines of the African National Congress', *South African Journal on Human Rights*, 5, 1985, p. 138.
[58] *Ibid.* Also J.D. Van der Vyver, 'Notes and Comments', *The South African Law Journal*, 106, 1989.

social responsibility. To the extent that theology is, in addition to all else, about the redeeming of human kind from captivity to sin and the worship of false gods and ideologies, the interface between constitutionalism and theology is pertinent for the times within which we live. Given the burden of South African history this involves regulating and promoting, not preventing, socio-economic and other forms of change. It will need to have at least as much to do with 'positive' freedoms, such as the right to education, housing and health-care, as with 'negative' freedoms, such as the protection of the ownership of property. But what if the accumulation of property in the hands of the few prevents the distribution of education, housing and health-care to the many? From a theological perspective a constitution must in such a conflictual situation reveal a bias in favour of those who are without rather than those who have. This is a bias that involves complex legal, economic, theological and ethical issues which are addressed in the chapters that follow.

CHAPTER 3

The rule of law: searching for values

Writing at the time of the French Revolution, the eighteenth century Whig politician and political philosopher Edmund Burke, observed that 'a seasonable extension of rights is the best expedient for the conservation of them'.[1] Two centuries later on the southern tip of another continent it is clear that unless individual human *and* socio-economic rights are extended to all South Africans there are not likely to be too many rights of any kind left to share with anyone. Equal liberties in the absence of a concern for the material well-being of people in South Africa is, at very least, the worst kind of abstraction. The importance of this concern has, of course, vast implications for emerging democracies in Eastern Europe and for established western nations as well, where inequitable distribution in material and social resources fails to match the democratic ideals on which these nations are constructed. The question addressed in what follows is how to integrate both kinds of rights (individual and social). There are not many situations in modern history where this has been accomplished.

The history of the abuse of parliamentary supremacy, as discussed in the previous chapter, shows law-making in South Africa to have been little more than an exercise in providing the white minority with an arsenal of weapons designed to exploit the black majority. The effects of this abusive kind of legal positivism have persuaded an increasing number of participants in the struggle for a new South Africa of the need to establish an

---

[1] *The Works of the Right Honourable Edmund Burke*, x, p. 254. Quoted in Francis Canavan, 'Burke as a Reformer', in Peter J Stanlis (ed.), *The Relevance of Edmund Burke* (New York: P.J. Kenedy and Sons, 1964), p. 91.

alternative system of rule, under the control of a constitution which legally guarantees the rights of all citizens. Human rights declarations which fail to redress past social and economic imbalances, resulting in large sections of the population remaining trapped in poverty and oppression, are similarly being questioned by an ever broadening constituency of people. In a country where 80 per cent of the population has been systematically dispossessed of their material well-being since the beginning of the colonial period, while more and more wealth continues to be located in an ever smaller section of the population, individual (first generation) rights are simply not likely to survive in the absence of a concern for social and economic freedom. The meaning of personal liberty and human dignity simply must be conceived more broadly than is the case in most western liberal democracies.

The conflicting theories of legal positivism and value-based law ('natural law' theory) can in one form or another be traced back to some of the earliest expressions of political formation and social union, although as theories in their own right they have a relatively short history. Each carries within it certain values, pertinent to the issues being faced in South Africa and elsewhere, which cannot be fully understood apart from the context out of which they emerged and on which they invariably continue to draw life. To an identification and explication of these values we now turn.

POLITICS AS THE ART OF LIVING TOGETHER

Contemporary debate on politics and law-making (like all 'modern' debate) has its roots in the Enlightenment rejection of medieval superstition and individual submission to all external or higher forms of authority, whether an omnipotent God, a tyrannical king or unquestioned tradition. It marks the beginning of an age within which humanity has come of age. It is an age within which the individual dares to be autonomous, to think and to exercise 'free' choice. These aspirations are an inherent part of liberalism in the West. To understand the essential values of this tradition we turn to a consideration of the ethical theories of Immanuel Kant and John Stuart Mill. Both theories impose an indelible imprint on contemporary debate.[2]

To empathetically grasp the most basic concerns of Kant and Mill is to understand the liberal values which influence contemporary political and legal debate in the modern world. For Kant the focus is on will-oriented conceptions of autonomy. For Mill the focus is on action-oriented autonomy. Both emphasised the importance of choice – and the 'right to choose', as *the* expression of individual autonomy and human dignity, continues to be the hall-mark of contemporary liberal politics.[3]

Originally the notion of 'autonomy' was used to refer to self-determining political communities, free from foreign rule. 'Kant extended this notion to the self, choosing a legislative, political model of self as his model of the autonomous person.'[4] The result is a system of ethics, built on two central tenets: The self who decides on certain principles as a basis for action is the rational or essential self (the *noumenal* self), not the idiosyncratic empirical self. In other words, this is a self which stands in isolation from all desires or sensual, contextual and manipulative influences.[5] This isolation becomes the basis for Kant being able to argue that the choice of the autonomous person is the choice which *any* strictly rational individual would make, leading him to the second tenet

---

[2] Terry Pinkard's *Democratic Liberalism and Social Union* (Philadelphia: Temple University Press, 1987) focusses on 'two very different conceptions of autonomy', those of Immanuel Kant and John Stuart Mill, as formative of liberal political theory. Other influences in the classical liberal tradition are discussed in Bruce Ackerman's *Reconstructing American Law* (Cambridge, Mass.: Harvard University Press, 1984).

[3] John Rawls, for example, in emphasising two principles as part of his 'theory of justice,' namely the 'principle of greatest equal liberty' and the 'principle of justice' which allows for the distribution of material goods to the benefit of the least privileged members of society, argues that the former principle has *lexical priority* over the second. See *A Theory of Justice* (Cambridge: Harvard University Press, 1971), p. 302. Terry Pinkard, in arguing against the reduction of human dignity to freedom of choice, nevertheless regards the principle of respect for individuals as '*the basic one*' within a democratic liberal society (p. 107). Concerned to emphasise the importance of the individual he offers a broader (communal) notion of self than what is normally associated with liberalism (p. 96f).

[4] Pinkard, *Democratic Liberalism*, p. 5.

[5] In the *Critique of Practical Reason* Kant insists that unless the freedom of the will is presupposed (in isolation from personal and societal passions) it makes no sense to talk of the moral worth of the individual. See also Third Section of *Fundamental Principles of the Metaphysic of Morals. Critique of Practical Reason and Other Works*, translated by Thomas Kingmill Abbott (London: Longmans, Green and Co, 1898).

of his argument: A rational, moral norm is for Kant a norm which can and must be *universally* valid. The two tenets are brought together in his 'supreme principle of ethics': 'Act on a maxim, the ends of which are such as it might be a universal law for everyone to have.'[6]

The obvious question is whether Kant's autonomous person is a *realistic* possibility and, more important for our purposes, whether his radical focus on the individual *noumenal* self is a *helpful* political ethic? His 'sweet dream' of a constitution corresponding to reason alone, is heuristically appealing. Is it practical?[7] The essential problem with Kantian ethics is what has appropriately been dubbed by Pinkard as a 'thin notion of self'. Dissociating the autonomous self from social context and creating an ethic that applies to any rational agent in any context, necessitates a level of abstraction which fails to provide specific ethical content for specific people in specific situations.[8] A Kantian theory of deduction from general principles to more particular norms without allowance for contextual demands is both unyielding and can, some would suggest, be quite immoral. Indeed, Pinkard suggests that Kant's famous example of the absolute immorality of all forms of lying, even if it means surrendering an innocent life to a killer, has probably converted more people to utilitarianism than all the arguments offered by the utilitarians themselves![9]

Marxists would, in turn, argue that any attempt to separate ethical ideals from social context is not only impossible (and that Kant's 'rational self' is simply a reflection of eighteenth-century bourgeois values), but that Kant's sense of a rational ethic militates against a critical discernment of social and contextual values which reside in his supposedly rational, universal ethic.[10] Neil Postman, in turn, reflecting on the impact of mass communications, suggests that corporate and controlled thought have been so imposed on, and internalised by, the contemporary individual that even the *possibility* of a rational,

---

[6] Kant, *Metaphysical Elements of Ethics, ibid.*, p. 306.
[7] Melvin J. Lasky's discussion of Kant's political ethic suggests that Kant himself realised that this was not possible. See, *Utopia and Revolution* (Chicago and London: University of Chicago Press, 1976), p. 593.   [8] *Ibid.*, p. 20.   [9] *Ibid.*, p. 85.
[10] Hugh Collins, *Marxism and Law* (Oxford: Oxford University Press, 1984), p. 63.

thoughtful person is scarcely plausible.[11] Briefly stated, although useful as an heroic ideal, it is difficult to conceive of the possibility of the Kantian autonomous self existing at all.

This and related criticisms of the Kantian ideal have resulted in some within the liberal political tradition looking to other sources for ethical inspiration, where the primacy of the individual is lifted out of pure Kantian isolation, to be rediscovered within a given context. The outcome was the emergence of *utilitarian ethics* (where the 'right' or 'good' is measured by the consequences of an action) – as opposed to Kantian *deontological ethics* (an ethic which argues that something is 'right' or 'wrong' in itself, independent of the consequences of the action).

Important in this regard, whatever one's assessment of utilitarianism, is a *step* towards a theoretical linking of liberal theory on individual rights to democratic decision-making in a pluralistic society.[12] As such it can be seen as an attempt to redress the criticism that liberalism shows a certain indifference to the communal nature of existence. Yet clearly utilitarianism continues to affirm an *individual* ethic, failing to take the differences between individuals seriously. As such it fails seriously to address the political issues at the heart of the act of communal living.

Utilitarian theory has taken many different forms, while adequately summed-up in Jeremy Bentham's axiom, 'the greatest happiness for the greatest number'.[13] The details of the theory were modified by John Stuart Mill and later by others, but, in essence, and more especially at the level of *classical* utilitarianism, it concerns itself (however individually con-

---

[11] Neil Postman, *Amusing Ourselves to Death: Public Discourse in the Age of Show Business* (New York: Penguin Books, 1986).

[12] There are ambiguities and qualifications in John Stuart Mill's commitment to democracy. His infatuation with the middle class as 'the most wise and the most virtuous part of the community', is only one. It allowed him to suggest that in the long run it does not matter who elects the government because the middle class is 'that portion of the community of which, if the basis of representation were ever so far extended, the opinion would ultimately decide'. In R.P. Anschutz, *The Philosophy of J.S. Mill* (Oxford: Clarendon Press, 1953), pp. 33–4.

[13] Jeremy Bentham, *An Introduction to the Principles of Morals and Legislation* (Garden City, New York: Anchor Books, 1973).

ceived) with what can loosely be referred to as the 'common good'.[14] Justice, in other words, is adjudicated by reference to the practical consequences of a particular act or policy, rather than with regard to its Kantian sense of intrinsic worth.

The weakness of the theory, as suggested, is its failure to allow for different perceptions of the common good or the means of realistically resolving the conflict resulting from these differences. It is here that the liberal individualism of the ethic becomes most clear. Despite the different nuances within utilitarian theories, the central objection to all forms of utilitarianism, is derived from the recognition that human well-being or happiness (utility) is not univocal. Whose version of 'well-being' is to be the measure of good in an unequal and heterogeneous society? John Stuart Mill, for example, concludes that the pleasures of the intellect are intrinsically superior to bodily pleasures and pains – an intellectualist understanding of value that not everyone would accept.[15] However pleasure is conceived, at the level of government, utilitarianism must necessarily result in institutional arrangements which require the rights of some to be sacrificed for the sake of others. Ross, for example, asks 'if the only duty is to produce the maximum of good, the question who is to have the good – whether it is myself, or my benefactor, or a person to whom I have made a promise – should make no difference'.[16] As such utilitarianism fails to address the question of distributive justice or whether some within a society have more legitimate claims to certain rights than others, making itself vulnerable to the capricious domination of the weak by the strong. Differently conceived, at worst, it reduces the significance of the individual to a component of what Rousseau called the 'general will', leaving the door open to

[14] The different forms of utilitarianism emerge in relation to the question how to measure the greatest good. Does one take the aggregate of good or the average good? Does each act need to be assessed in its own right (act–utilitarianism), or do certain rules emerge (rule–utilitarianism), which need to be assessed against the utility which they produce? Is justice simply a part of utility? Karen Lebacqz's *six Theories of Justice: Perspectives From Philosophical and Theological Ethics* (Minneapolis: Augsburg Press, 1986), pp. 15–32 provides a useful discussion on the strengths and weaknesses of the different types of utilitarian ethics.

[15] John Stuart Mill, *Utilitarianism* (New York: Bobbs-Merrill, 1957), p. 12.

[16] W.D. Ross *The Right and the Good* (Oxford: Clarendon Press, 1930), p. 22.

individuals being subservient to some greater cause. It is this (however ideologically conceived) that has constituted the curse of most authoritarian regimes which have collapsed in recent times. Within liberal ideology the danger of domination is also present.

TWO NOTIONS OF HUMAN DIGNITY

The challenge that haunts liberal politics, is the challenge that confronts all politics – how to allow the maximisation of individual freedom of choice while at the same time addressing the corporate responsibilities that are part of any social union. If individual liberty is the primary value, then equality may have to be sacrificed. If equality is the primary value, there will be violations of liberty.[17]

The concern of Terry Pinkard's *Democratic Liberalism and Social Union* is to redress this apparent contradiction which resides at the heart of democratic-liberalism, arguing that the affirmation of individual freedom alone constitutes a one-sided view of a fragmented tradition.[18] As such it provides a useful basis on which to address the political issues central to a theology of reconstruction. His concern is to *balance* individual and common values, rather than to propose a compromise within which neither are adequately addressed.[19] The goal is the establishment of a social theory and morality which 'rests on a view of ourselves as co-members of a common world'. It involves a morality within which each individual is necessarily seen as 'one of us', requiring co-existence based on mutual respect and co-operation by a community of individuals who consciously locate themselves within their social context rather than seek (in a Kantian way) to abstract themselves out of it. The quest is for a *thicker* or broader notion of the moral self.[20]

The outcome of the above discussion is two very different

[17] Lebacqz, *Six Theories of Justice*, p. 65.
[18] Pinkard, *Democratic Liberalism*, pp. 51; 101f.
[19] Pinkard views Duncan Kennedy's classification of 'individualism' and 'altruism' as two competing theories and a fragmentation of liberalism. This concern is to transcend rather than choose or reduce the two into compromise. pp. 100f.
[20] Pinkard, *Democratic Liberalism*, p. 15.

notions of self dignity: A classical libertarian understanding which (when pushed) reduces human dignity to individual free choice, and a broader, social (egalitarian) perception of humanity which insists that human dignity involves more than free choice. Precisely what the latter means in any particular society is determined not merely by ideological theory (whether of Kant, John Stuart Mill or Karl Marx) but by values inherent to the historical and social context (with all the political, economic, cultural and religious dimensions) that influence any particular society at a given time. Within this context theories, doctrines and traditions (the theoretical apparatus we bring to a situation) usually need to be reshaped, reconceived and rewritten. As suggested in the introduction, this is an exercise in intellectual and theoretical renewal which is emerging in response to social practice in many areas of conflict around the world today.

The two notions of human dignity – *individualistic and choice oriented* vs. *communal and substance oriented*, reflect two different world views. A nineteenth-century, western, liberal world view formed by important Enlightenment insights in the case of the former. A broader world view in the case of the latter, sometimes expressed in sections of twentieth-century human rights declarations, as well as democratic socialist creeds which give expression to the needs of poor and oppressed people. The affirmation of basic freedoms such as freedom of speech, the freedom of assembly and the freedom to dissent are important and can scarcely be omitted from any inclusive doctrine of human rights. A broad definition of human dignity requiring, however, that attention also be given to such basic needs as housing, health care and education. To affirm the former freedoms without the latter has resulted in the ghettoes and social impoverishment associated with many western democratic liberal societies. The latter in isolation from the former has, in turn, resulted in the oppressive type of societies formerly associated with the eastern bloc countries. The civil rights struggle in the United States of America is enough to emphasise the importance of the basic rights of a black person having the right to sit at a lunch counter like any other American and order a meal. It also exposes the weakness of a tradition of human rights within which certain Americans can order *filet mignon* and the best French wine at a five-star restaurant for lunch as many times a week as they desire, while others can scarcely afford a sandwich.

The challenge facing contemporary societies is how to weld two different but related visions of democracy into a higher and more complete reality. It involves economic and political democracy, giving concrete expression to the highest human rights ideals which affirm the personal and material dignity of people, the right to participation in society and the freedom of choice in every area of life.

The ideological labels attached to this broader kind of democracy are not as important as the outcome. Indeed the socialist/capitalist debate can be set aside for the present, while recognising the importance of economic democracy as an inherent ingredient to the reconstruction process around the world – by which is meant the redressing of the indefensible imbalances between the rich and the poor. Most important in this regard is the discerning of the road to the integration of two different but related notions of human dignity associated with the two economic systems which continue to dominate global structures. This is a goal to be differently fought for and earned within the historical and social context of different societies. All ideological systems and historic traditions must be weighed and shaped in relation to the pursuit of justice and the affirmation of the fullest and widest sense of human worth.

Before turning our attention to the contextual locus of ethical values, it is necessary first to give attention to the two traditions of law-making introduced at the beginning of the chapter, namely *legal positivism* and *value-based law*. These two traditions, much like the ethical theories of Immanuel Kant and John Stuart Mill, stand at the centre of political and legal debate in the West. They are not, however, left unchallenged. To do some justice to contemporary legal debate, attention is given to one of the more prominent challenges to both these systems, namely the radical critique of the Rule of Law associated within the school of critical legal studies (linked essentially to Harvard University).[21]

TWO TRADITIONS OF LAW-MAKING

At the centre of the debate on individual choice and common good is an ineluctable pluralism. Individuals have different and often competing notions of what is good and of maximum utility. Differently stated, there *is* no common good. There is only a plurality of what are likely to be incommensurable goods. Politically, this is a relatively new problem. Differences in western political values reach back, of course, to Aristotle and before, while the radical questioning of *de facto* authority, however, only got seriously underway with the Enlightenment. It became a turning-point in the intellectual quest for the emancipation of political and legal institutions from religious influences. Harold Berman suggests that it was only in the twentieth century that this link was substantially broken.[22]

A major development in the western legal tradition began when the church imposed its political and legal unity on Europe through the Papal Revolution, marked by the publication of Pope Gregory VII's *Dictates of the Pope* in 1075. This early phase of legal reform reached its climax with the laws of another Gregory, Gregory IX in 1234, resulting not only in massive legal enquiry and systematisation of the law within the church, but also the creation and growth of law outside of the church in the form of secular law.[23]

[21] The antagonism between liberal legal theorists and the school of critical legal studies is documented in Andrew Altman, *Critical Legal Studies: A Liberal Critique* (Princeton: Princeton University Press, 1990), pp. 7–9.

[22] Harold Berman, *Law and Revolution: The Formation of the Western Legal Tradition* (Cambridge, Mass: Harvard University Press, 1983). Also 'Religious Foundations of Law in the West: An Historical Perspective', in *Journal of Law and Religion*, 1:1, Summer 1983, p. 3. See also H. Berman, *The Interaction of Law and Religion* (Nashville: Abingdon Press, 1974).

[23] The church needed law to regulate the activities of the clergy (their hitherto independent economic, political and social activities were now brought under the jurisdiction of the pope), the activities of the laity (the church claimed exclusive jurisdiction over such matters as divorces, crimes, moral offences etc.) and its relations with the secular authorities – and *jus canonicum* (canon law) was the outcome.

Gradually two systems of law (civil and canon) developed, reflecting the division of the world into two separate authorities, temporal and spiritual. Cardinal Hostiensis, writing in the thirteenth century, insisted that canon law, built on both civil and theological learning, was superior to both. Just as the mule is better than the ass and the horse, he argued, canon law excels both its theological and civil law parents![24]

Squabbles apart, both ecclesial and secular law were part of a more or less homogeneous world view, which comprised a fundamental belief in God as a God of justice and law, and a shared belief that human law was derived from God's will being manifest in natural law, discernible through reason and conscience.[25] Both ecclesial and secular lawyers regarded it as their duty to articulate God's purpose for society in law.

It took five great revolutions, suggests Berman, to separate the secular law from the religious tradition in the West.[26] The Protestant Reformation in Germany in the sixteenth century, the English Revolutions between 1640 and 1689, the American and French Revolutions of 1776 and 1789 and the Russian Revolution of October 1917. Each progressively separated church and state and further secularised the law.[27]

In essence, the homogeneity of the European world view began to crumble almost at the same time as it emerged as a decisive political and legal factor at the close of the eleventh century. The investiture controversies between emperors and popes, regional struggles and ultimately the national revolutions which followed, all served to magnify the problem of authority that is inherent to pluralism. And then, in the wake of the religious wars in the latter part of the sixteenth century, the primary political question shifted away from what constituted true religion and the absolute 'good' to how people of different religious and ethical persuasions could co-exist. The demand

---

[24] Mulford Q. Sibley, 'Religion and Law: Some Thoughts on Their Intersections', *Journal of Law and Religion*, II:1, 1984, p. 49.
[25] Thomas Aquinas, *Summa Theologica*, Blackfriars Edition (New York: McGraw Hall. London: Eyre and Spottiswoode, 1963), 1a2ae, Question 91, pp. 19–39.
[26] *Ibid.*
[27] A detailed study of these developments is found in Berman's *Law and Revolution*.

was for a *sovereign authority* capable of transcending these differences and holding crumbling nations and communities together. The political shift was essentially away from utopian ideas of what ought to be possible, to a more mundane and pragmatic politics of realism built around compromise and co-existence. The quest for political authority at this point in European history was, in other words, a quest for social stability and nation-building not completely different to the quest within Eastern Europe, South Africa and elsewhere today.

The notion of political authority can be traced back to Aristotle's notion of *legibus solutus* (the sovereign being the one not bound by laws). And certainly Thomas Aquinas thought that in a society with an array of different notions of what is right and good the prince is responsible to God alone. '*Quod principi placuit legis habet vigorem*', (what pleases the prince has the force of law), he wrote.[28] The modern concept of authority is commonly, however, attributed to Jean Bodin's *Six Livres de la République* (1575), written at the height of a series of enduring religious wars in France. While locating the sovereign under the laws of God and nature, and requiring the sovereign to obey the fundamental laws of the constitution, Bodin argued that '*law is nothing else than the command of the sovereign, in the exercise of his sovereign power*'.[29]

Soon the clauses qualifying Bodin's understanding of sovereignty were forgotten, and the way was opened for law to be reduced to no more than such decrees which emanated from an individual ruler or sovereign legislating body. For all its appeal as a problem-resolving device in pluralistic and divided societies, this positivistic understanding of law has always been challenged by a more traditional understanding of law, which requires law to give expression, and conform, to a set of ethical values higher than the law itself. These two different legal traditions: *legal positivism*, which defines law in relation to some form of supreme legal authority, and *value-based law*, which ties

---

[28] Quoted by Stanley J Benn, 'Sovereignty', in *Encyclopedia of Philosophy* (New York: Macmillan Company and the Free Press, 1967), p. 502.
[29] *Ibid.* See also, H.E. Cohen, *Recent Theories of Sovereignty* (Chicago: Chicago University Press, 1937); Pinkard, p. 58.

the legitimacy of law to an anterior set of values, continue to shape legal debate today.[30]

More than an intellectual exercise in legal analysis, the debate reaches to the heart of the legal conflict in newly emerging nation-building situations. To ask whether law is merely what a sovereign legislative authority determines it to be, or whether it is invalidated to the extent that it violates certain values contained in a constitution or common law tradition, is to address the question at the centre of the historical debate on South African law outlined in Chapter 2. Central to this debate are a number of related questions. When is a law a law? What is the essential character of law? By what criteria is a sovereign authority regarded as legitimate? When and by what criteria does a sovereign gain or lose legitimacy? These are historical questions that can best be understood in relation to the ongoing debate between two traditions.

Legal positivism

Jean Bodin (and others, like Thomas Hobbes) explained at the level of political philosophy the need for a sovereign capable of giving commands under the threat of censure. Jeremy Bentham and John Austin took the philosophy a step further. Turning away from any sense of the need to theologically or philosophically 'prove' what a person 'ought' to do, Bentham argued that it could be empirically concluded that most people want happiness.[31] The task of sovereign power, whatever form it might take, was to give expression to the concrete political and economic implications of this desire. The sovereign power was to *command* and the people were to *obey*. Where the people might disagree with the decision of the sovereign power, so the argument went, they were to work within the political system to influence or even change the sovereign power. But law, for Bentham, was law 'as it

---

[30] The encounter in the 1950s between H.L.A. Hart, the Oxford University based legal positivist and Lon L. Fuller, Professor of Jurisprudence at Harvard University, affirming a principle-based understanding of law constitutes an important instance of this debate. See H.L.A. Hart, 'Positivism and the Separation of Law and Morals', *Harvard Law Review*, 71, 1957–8; Lon L. Fuller, 'Positivism and the Fidelity of Law – A Reply to Professor Hart', *Ibid.*   [31] Jeremy Bentham, *An Introduction*, pp. 17–22.

is', not as some might think it ought to be. With this the distinguishing characteristic of legal positivism was established as the stated decree of the sovereign which is legitimate and valid, irrespective of its moral or immoral content.

John Austin took the theory further. His doctrine of state sovereignty, linked as it is to the 'command theory of law', still influences political debate. In brief, a law or legal command (as opposed to other commands or orders) was, for Austin, a command given under censure (or threat) by a *sovereign*.[32] Sovereignty was, in other words, for Austin 'a pre-legal political fact'.[33] It was seen to antecede law. Law was only law to the extent that it was commanded by a *sovereign*. And if it was so commanded (whatever the content of the command) it was to be obeyed.

Most contemporary debate on Austin's command theory of law is related to his understanding of sovereignty. H.L.A. Hart, himself an avowed positivist, emerges as his major critic, essentially because he regards Austin's theory as so important.[34] We consider only his discussion on the 'rule of recognition', because it is here that an important difference emerges between Austin and Hart. And this, in turn, becomes a pivotal point in the debate on authority and the legitimacy of government. For Austin sovereign power is a manifestation of *habitual* obedience given to a person or a body of persons by the majority of the people. For Hart, on the other hand, sovereignty is a result of the *acceptance* of authority by the people. The difference is subtle but important.

There is a sense in which Hart's understanding of sovereignty throws into question the very possibility of there being a sovereign, the implications being that it is better simply to talk of a person or body of people who have 'authority' and 'jurisdiction'.[35] Hart rejects the notion of 'pre-legal' authority by locating ultimate authority and the right to bestow authority

---

32 John Austin, *The Province of Jurisprudence Determined* (New York: Noonday Press, 1954), p. 134.

33 J.W. Harris, *Legal Philosophies* (London: Butterworths, 1980), p. 32.

34 H.L.A. Hart, *The Concept of Law* (New York: Oxford University Press, 1965). Also Hart's 'Introduction' in John Austin, *The Province of Jurisprudence Determined*.

35 Pinkard, *Democratic Liberalism*, p. 58.

and jurisdiction in the electorate, who can threaten, reshape and ultimately withdraw authority and jurisdiction from any person or body of persons as it deems necessary. In so doing Hart seeks an *inside* perspective on sovereignty, law and social value. He seeks to view reality from the standpoint of participation. The outcome is a radically more democratic and participatory understanding of sovereignty, locating legitimate government in what Max Weber calls the 'legal–rational' structures of authority, government based on social contract.[36] This is an important gain which provides the basis for a democratic critique of all *outside* (prescriptive) notions of the common good, whether grounded in legal positivism, natural law or Marxian values. (This is ultimately what Hart has in common with a natural-law theorist like Dworkin, despite the essential differences between legal positivism which he espouses and the value-based approach to law adopted by Dworkin.)

Hans Kelsen writing at more or less the same time as Hart has, in turn, identified 'the principle of efficacy' as the basis of legitimate sovereignty. The basic legal norm (*grundnorm*) which makes law legitimate and obligatory is, for Kelsen, not merely that it is the product of a recognised legislature, but that it is *functional*. The essential question for him is, does it work? Is it politically and juridically effective?[37] The practical importance of this debate is illustrated in the citing of Kelsen's theory of efficacy by judges in revolutionary situations in Pakistan in 1958 and Uganda in 1965, and in response to the Rhodesian Unilateral Declaration of Independence in the same year.[38] In Rhodesia, for example, the Smith regime was found, on the basis of the Kelsenian doctrine of efficaciousness, by the Rhodesian High Court and the Privy Council in Britain, to be *de iure* legitimate because it was *de facto* able to maintain control of the

---

[36] Max Weber identifies three sociological models of authority: Traditional–sacral, legal–rational and charismatic–revolutionary. See *From Max Weber: Essays in Sociology*, translated and edited by H. Gerth and C. Wright Mills (London: Routledge and Kegan Paul, 1948), pp. 294–300. Also *Economy and Society*, I, edited by G. Roth and C. Wittich (Berkeley: University of California Press, 1978), pp. 212–45.

[37] Hans Kelsen, *General Theory of Law and State*, translated by Hans Wedberg (Cambridge: Harvard University Press, 1945), p. 118.

[38] Harris, *Legal Philosophies*, p. 71.

country.[39] Only when the bush war had intensified to the extent that *de facto* chaos prevailed were Britain and the West ready to conclude that the Smith regime was illegitimate and worthy of being removed from power.[40]

There is a certain harshness about legal positivism. To adopt a Kelsenian position, law is that which can be effectively imposed. There is also a simple political appeal to Hart's understanding of law and law-making. For him law is simply what has passed through recognised and accepted law-making precedures.[41] Hart, for example, soundly rejected the Nazi death-camp laws, but insisted that there was nothing to be gained by arguing on the basis of some ideal theory of law that they could simply be dismissed as unworthy of being called law.[42] He went further. 'If laws have reached a certain degree in iniquity', he suggested, 'there would be a plain moral obligation to resist them and to withhold obedience.'[43] Hart is certainly not indifferent to ethical values, arguing that *if* there is a moral right it is the right to be free.[44] But in a strict doctrine of sovereignty even such rights are seen as a limitation on sovereign power.

It is this that has persuaded people, especially those whose lives are daily exposed to tyrannous rule, to turn away from legal positivism. The problem with legal positivism, suggests Lon Fuller (in his celebrated debate with Hart) is that on the one hand we (can) have an amoral datum called law, which has the peculiar quality of creating a moral duty to obey it. On the other hand, we have a moral duty to do what we think is right and decent. When we are confronted by a statute we believe to be

---

[39] Donald B Molteno, 'The Rhodesian Crisis and the Courts', in *The Comparative and International Law Journal of Southern Africa*, 2:2, July 1969, pp. 425f.

[40] The employment of Kelsens' principle of efficacy by the Rhodesian High Court and the Privy Council in Britain to provide judicial recognition to Ian Smith's regime is discussed in my 'Theology, Law and State Legitimacy', in *Journal of Law and Religion*, V:2, 1987. The argument is also included in Charles Villa-Vicencio, *Civil Disobedience and Beyond: Law, Religion and Politics in South Africa* (Cape Town: David Philip. Grand Rapids: Eerdmans, 1990), pp. 114–15.

[41] Hart, 'Positivism and the Separation of Law and Morals', p. 603.

[42] *Ibid.*, pp. 615–21. After the defeat of Germany he argued that the correct way for these laws to be dealt with was to pass retroactive legislation which effectively annulled them.   [43] Hart, 'Positivism', p. 617.

[44] H.L.A. Hart, 'Are There Any Natural Rights?', *Philosophical Review*, 64, 1955, pp. 175–91.

thoroughly evil, we have to choose between the two duties.[45] The importance of legal positivism on the other hand, as Hart and other legal positivists see it, is that it affirms the importance of the law-making procedure and encourages democratic participation within these structures; arguing that it is here that the struggle for individual rights is to be fought and won. This dimension to legal positivism appeals to people on both sides of the political divide, even those who affirm a separate Bill of Rights which limits sovereign power.

Robert H. Bork, a conservative American legal scholar, has argued that the tying of the legitimacy of law to morality has the effect of lifting ethical debate out of the electoral and legislative process and leaving it to a panel of judges. The measure of law, for him, is the will and mores of the people expressed in the constitution and through the legislative process. The task of judges is to impose *that* morality, and not to become involved in the legislative process by allowing their own moral views to influence their judgments.[46] Albie Sachs, who does not share Bork's conservative political values, nevertheless shows indications of a similar procedural concern to that of Bork. While supporting a Bill of Rights for a democratic South Africa, he argues that such a Bill should be left to emerge over a period of time, in order to ensure the maximum involvement of the broad population in the creation of new post-apartheid values and ideals. His fear is that a 'mountain-top' judiciary, operating under too many antecendently imposed ethical restraints could act against the fullest participation of the people in the reshaping of South Africa.[47] The values that should eventually shape a new South Africa, Sachs argues, are yet to be formed. At least in the transitionary phase, he suggests, these values should emerge out of a largely unrestrained democratic legislative process. The question facing Sachs is what it is that ultimately constrains the law-making process, preventing the kind of abuse of power which characterised the tyranny of the past.

The appeal and the possible success of legal positivism presupposes an open democratic process. It also suggests that

---

[45] Fuller, 'Positivism and the Fidelity of Law', p. 656.
[46] Richard Neuhaus (ed.), *Law and the Ordering of Our Life Together* (Grand Rapids: Eerdmans, 1989), p. 127.   [47] Sachs, 'Towards a Bill of Rights.' p. 308.

parliamentary supremacy in an open democratic society will be morally and responsibly used. The framers of the American Constitution were not prepared to make this assumption. There are sufficient twentieth-century and Third World experiments in post revolutionary government which, in turn, show that even while new values are yet in the making there are certain minimum values needed to guide this process. These situations seem to suggest, without providing any guarantees, that such values are most effective when explicitly stated by the legislature and watched over by a body separated from the legislature. The moral vision behind this insistence has kept alive an alternative value-based theory of law, even when legal positivism was accepted as the dominant form of law in most countries around the world.

Hart's notion of *acceptance* over against Austin's *habitual* understanding of political authority is probably not sufficient to prevent the abuse of government power. Nicolas Wolterstorff suggests that, although questions concerning the legitimacy of government action or of our rulers repeatedly emerge in our political lives, most of us obey even such laws and rulers which we question 'not because we believe that we ought to do so. We do so from habit, habitually.' 'Obeying one's state', he continues, 'is . . . as non-problematic as any of the other things we do habitually.'[48] The story of submissive obedience to tyrannous dictators through history is enough to make the point. The popularisation and celebration of explicit values in a Bill of Rights which affirms the essential values that characterise the identity of a people and their struggle could contribute to the breaking down of the kind of political acquiescence which people ranging widely from Hart to Bork, Sachs and Wolters-dorff are seeking to overcome.

Value-based law

The doctrine of legal positivism, despite the concern for morality which Hart and others have sought to promote, has contributed to what Berman identifies as a nervous breakdown located at the

[48] Nicholas Wolterstorff, 'Theology, Law and Legitimate Government.' Occasional paper No. 2, published by Theology in Global Context Association, New York, n.d.

heart of modernity in the West, related to the loss of moral integrity.[49] Symptomatic of this is a loss of confidence in, *inter alia*, law and religion which, suggests John Witte, is attributable to a positivist concept of law and a privatist understanding of religion.[50]

Conflicting interests have at times given rise to a sterile, adjudicating, balancing, non-promotional notion of legal positivism. Eager to offend no one, the sovereign has sought simply to balance conflicting interests without affirming any one set of values in preference to another. Without a clear sense of direction legal positivism has often left people in panic, suggests Berman, without direction in life. In situations like South Africa legal positivism has conversely been used to disregard all sense of balance and moral responsibility, in reducing law to the command of 'the guys with the biggest guns'. In the former situation, law is in danger of leaving people without a sense of purpose or moral value, in the latter it drives people with blind fury in a direction shaped and manipulated by a narrow ideological sense of value. Both situations suggest that a doctrine of law is required which shows more moral aggression, resulting in the re-establishment of the organic link between value and law.[51]

This has resulted in the rediscovery, despite the many philosophical attacks against it, of the natural-law tradition. From the time of the early Greek philosophers, scholars have grappled with the problem inherent to the question concerning the status of unjust or tyrannical laws, recognising the need to discern a 'higher law' against which to measure all laws. 'One does not have to believe in the devil', writes Albie Sachs, 'to accept that evil is multifariously seductive.'[52] The varied

---

[49] Harold Berman, *The Interaction of Law and Religion* (Nashville: Abingdon Press, 1974), p. 21. Also *Law and Revolution*, pp. 33–41.

[50] John Witte, 'The Study of Law and Religion: An Apologia and Agenda', in *Ministry and Mission*, 14:4, Fall 1988.

[51] This has resulted in a new found concern for human rights within the legal process. It has also resulted in renewed interest in the relationship between religion and law. See Howard J. Vogel, 'A Survey and Commentary on the New Literature in Law and Religion', *Journal of Religion and Law*, 1:1, 1983, pp. 79f.

[52] Albie Sachs, *Protecting Human Rights in a New South Africa* (Cape Town: Oxford University Press, 1990), p. 7.

manifestations of the quest for a common understanding of justice, as a standard by which to test the particular laws of any society, need not be addressed here. It is enough to recognise what Lourens Ackermann has called the 'common ancestry' of the various attempts in history, both secular and theological, to affirm a kind of universal 'common law' or sense of 'common good' as a norm which reminds us who and what we ought to be.[53]

This quest is, of course, haunted by David Hume's insistence that there is no rational procedure by which we can objectively know what is morally right or wrong.[54] For him 'ought' simply cannot be derived from 'is'. In some circles this, together with certain Protestant reactions against natural law, put paid to serious philosophical debate on natural law for several generations. This situation is changing. In restating Thomas Aquinas' approach to natural law in the light of Hume's noncognitivism, J.M. Finnis has made a significant contribution to re-opening this debate. At the centre of his argument is an insistence that true classical doctrine never purported to derive 'ought' from 'is'.[55] He sees it rather as a first reflective grasp of what is self-evidently good. Allowing that people may reasonably differ on details, and that justice may require different ways of reaching a specific goal, Finnis argues that there are nevertheless certain basic goods and forms of behaviour which, based on a realistic understanding of human nature, together constitute the universal and unchanging principles of natural law. Ernest Baker defines this 'new' approach to the natural law debate as producing a 'conceptual natural law' which constitutes a certain 'way of looking at things, a spirit of "humane interpretation" . . . which may and does affect the law which is actually enforced, but does so *without being law itself*'.[56] Leaving

---

[53] Lourens Ackermann, 'Introduction' to *Human Rights for South Africans*, edited by Mike Robertson (Cape Town: Oxford University Press, 1919), p. 6.

[54] David Hume, *A Treatise of Human Nature*, edited by L.A. Selby-Bigge (Oxford: Clarendon Press, 1964) p. 469.

[55] J.M. Finnis, *Natural Law and Natural Rights* (New York: Oxford University Press, 1980).

[56] Ernest Baker, '*Translator's Introduction*', in Otto Gierke (ed.) *Natural Law* (Boston: Beacon Press, 1957), p. xxxvii. Italics added.

aside the details of contemporary debate on natural-law theory and the content of the 'admonitions' contained within it, value-based law is an attempt to articulate a minimum set of values which apply to the rights of individuals within a social union. If law is not legitimated by the acceptance/efficacy of sovereign command, as legal positivists suggest, then what is it that provides this legitimacy? Value-oriented theories of law are an attempt to answer this question.

Lon Fuller suggests it is the presence of a moral foundation which provides the minimum criteria whereby a decree is worthy of being a law. He uses the poignant hypothetical example of 'a country just emerging from a period of violence and disorder in which any thread of legal continuity with previous governments has broken', to make his point.[57] Within a society where all dominant values, customs, traditions, culture and moral appeal have collapsed, law *can* only be legitimated by the acceptability of its moral content to all concerned. John Rawls' projection of moral social principles from behind what he calls a 'veil of ignorance', from which vantage point no one knows who will play what role in society shaped by these principles, constitutes a detailed and courageous attempt to forge such a set of moral values. These values or principles are discussed in a later chapter. For the present the content of the values being asked for can be bracketed out. It is enough to note Fuller's observation: 'The provisions of the constitution should . . . be kept simple and understandable, not only in language, but also in purpose.'[58] It has to do with what Anthony Mathews refers to as an 'elusive but real quality of law' against which to assess all particular laws, and in terms of which the power of government is to be limited.[59]

Arguing that judges are to rule without discretion where the law is explicit and clear, Ronald Dworkin recognises that in 'hard cases', where there are no clear rules, the judge is obliged to show discretion. In so doing the judge cannot, he argues,

[57] Fuller, 'Positivism and the Fidelity of the Law', pp. 642–3.
[58] Fuller, *Ibid.*, p. 643.
[59] Anthony Mathews, *Law, Order and Liberty in South Africa* (Berkeley: University of California Press, 1972), p. 11.

operate with the freedom of a legislator. The judge's discretion is undertaken in relation to principles of morality *embedded in the broader value-system of the community*, already formed by legislators in response to the demands of the community. They include, he suggests, specific community goals and general principles of moral value which form part of society's ethical milieu.[60] These rules (implicit in the constitution and laws of the land) constitute the basis of all court-based judgments.

The burning question concerning Dworkin's principles (embedded in the value-system of the community) in a period of radical political reconstruction as envisaged in South Africa (which includes some of the traits envisaged in Fuller's example of a country emerging out of a period of discontinuity), concerns the specific nature of these principles. The social conflict and plurality of values in any society, and especially in post-revolutionary situations, poses the question concerning the nature and content of the principles. *Whose* values and priorities are to be relied on beyond the letter of the law? The dominant values implicit to a particular society and an established legal system are invariably the values of the dominant classes. It is this which suggests Dworkin's theory of law is more positivistic than what it appears to be at first reading. It also points again to an appeal inherent to the argument in favour of parliamentary supremacy in a fully democratic society. History shows, however, that even in the most 'democratic' of parliaments the concerns of the poor are not necessarily promoted.

The burden of former generations weighs perhaps most heavily, on newly emerging societies, at the level of internalised values. It takes time for the character of the new society to emerge. Legal systems like cathedrals, suggests Berman, take centuries to construct![61] Revolutions are, however, also fragile entities which sometimes die in the very process of being born. They require an early life-support system. Leo Strauss has poignantly observed that sometimes when a nation is defeated on the battlefield and annihilated as a political entity it still has the capacity to 'deprive its conquerors of the most sublime fruit

---

[60] Ronald Dworkin, *Taking Rights Seriously* (Cambridge: Harvard University Press, 1977), p. 22.   [61] Berman, 'Religious Foundations of Law in the West', p. 12.

of victory by imposing on them the yoke of its own thought'.[62]
The ghost of past dictatorships is likely to threaten newly
emerging societies in many parts of the world for some time to
come – not least South Africa. This is why it is important that the
essential values of the new society, which has emerged through
the long years of struggle, be entrenched in a constitution as a
basis against which a minimum moral foundation of law can be
measured. Without this the chances of something new emerging,
which radically transcends all past tyranny, are made that much
more difficult.

CRITIQUE OF THE RULE OF LAW

The most serious criticism against the suggestion that the
solution to the acute problem against which Strauss warns is to
be found in the affirmation of a Bill of Rights within the liberal
tradition of the rule of law, comes from adherents to the school of
critical legal studies. With varying degrees of conviction they
argue that inherent to the very idea of the rule of law is the
perpetuation of a system of law which favours a particular group
within society. No attempt is made here to outline the different
trends within this school of thought.[63] The more radical
dimensions of critical legal scholarship, which amount to a total
rejection of the virtue of the rule of law, are left aside. Attention is
given solely to the more moderate manifestations of legal
deconstructionalism, and only with a view to identifying certain
latent presuppositions and contradictions associated with liberal
legal theory which often militate against its own highest ideals.
For our purposes the critique of liberal legal theory, emanating
from the critical legal studies movement, can be reduced to three
points.

1. The familiar problem of pluralism, characterised by a range
   of fundamentally different and incompatible moral and

---

[62] Leo Strauss, *Natural Right and History* (Chicago: Chicago University Press, 1953), p. 2.
[63] The debate is introduced in, *inter alia*, Mark Kelman, *A Guide to Critical Legal Studies*
    (Cambridge: Harvard University Press, 1987). A liberal response to this debate is
    found in Andrew Altman, *Critical Legal Studies: A Liberal Critique* (Princeton: Princeton
    University Press, 1990.)

political viewpoints, is identified by critical legal studies scholars as the all-pervasive ingredient of social existence. They insist that judicial values and legal procedure are an inherent part of this reality. The liberal suggestion, that judicial values and legal procedure can be lifted above politics and moral conflict into a 'neutral' legal sphere, is rejected as obscurantist. Duncan Kennedy states the position bluntly:

Teachers teach nonsense when they persuade students that legal reasoning is distinct, *as a method for reaching correct results*, from ethical or political discourse in general . . . There is never a 'correct legal solution' that is other than the correct ethical or political solution to that legal problem.[64]

The commitment of adherents of critical legal studies is to take away the mystique in which the judiciary is draped. Their concern is for liberal–legal values and judicial process to be seen for what they are – not a neutral set of rules which treat all contestants equally, but the manifestation of a political struggle within which one group asserts its values over those of others.

2. All human values and ideals are a reflection of a particular context out of which they emerge. They 'rely tacitly if not explicitly upon some picture of the forms of human association that are right and realistic in the areas of social life with which they deal'.[65] This means that normative arguments produce norms which are internal to a particular world view within a particular context. Liberal values contained, for example, in the Bill of Rights attached to the American Constitution are a reflection of a prior commitment to individualism and a free market economy. To accept the values promoted under the rule of law within this tradition is therefore to accept the legitimacy of this particular political–economic decision, whereas it is precisely this commitment which critical legal studies scholarship is insisting needs to be

[64] Duncan Kennedy, 'Legal Education as Training for Hierarchy', quoted in Altman, *Critical Legal Studies*, p. 14.
[65] Roberto Unger, *The Critical Legal Studies Movement* (Cambridge: Harvard University Press, 1986), p. 8.

questioned. Contemporary political and economic problems made explicit in the exploitation of marginalised people in democratic–liberal societies require critical scholars to challenge certain western political and economic presuppositions rather than merely to assume them.

3. All political programmes (whether liberal or socialist) need to be investigated at the inter-face between social ideals and actual practice. In democratic–liberal societies, political and economic institutions, formations and practices which have emerged out of a radical commitment to individual rights and democracy need to be investigated with a view to determining whether in practice they are not a contradiction of these fundamental values. This, suggests Unger, requires a level of internal critique, rearrangement and destabilising of existing structures to ensure the maximum protection of individual rights and promotion of political and economic democracy.[66]

In brief the moderate strand of critical legal studies, of which Roberto Unger is among the most consistent and systematic exponents, is committed to an exploration of what he calls the 'subversive implications' of the above critique of liberal scholarship.[67] His concern is to offer a 'total criticism' (which does not, for him, equal 'total rejection') of the liberal tradition.[68] It is designed to 'open-up the petrified relations between abstract ideals and categories, such as freedom of contract or political equality, and the legally regulated social practices that are supposed to exemplify them'. He 'takes the preconceptions of liberal legal and political theory seriously and pushes them to their conclusions'.[69] His critique of value-based law is that it fails to take its own values and principles seriously enough.

In contemporary society a (perhaps *the*) primary human right is the *right to participation* by individuals in the creation of their

---

[66] *Ibid.*, pp. 52–6.
[67] *Ibid.*, p. 6. For comment on Unger as a moderate critic, see Altman, p. 19.
[68] Roberto Unger, *Knowledge and Politics* (New York: Free Press, 1975), pp. 1–3, 10, 15, 17–18. See discussion in Altman, *Critical Legal Studies*, p. 17.
[69] Unger, *Critical Legal Studies*, pp. 16, 24.

own future.[70] Unger uses the concept of 'formative contexts' to make his point. Functioning for him much as 'modes of production' operate for Marx, he argues that society's formative contexts are most evident in society when 'defeated or exhausted people stop fighting'.[71] It is then that the fixed routines, set attitudes, firm practices and circles of existence associated with these formative contexts (which are a product of the dominant culture and players of society) control society. Unger argues that Marx was correct in rejecting all such modes of existence which manipulate and control the individual, but *wrong* to the extent that he failed to press the repudiation hard enough.[72] For Unger social changes short of total rejection are not necessarily mere conservative tinkering. They can be the prologue to more radical things to come. Milner Ball's review of Unger's critique of Marx is helpful. 'Freedom does not lie in an endless flight from one context to another but in revising the context in which we find ourselves, thereby making them more fully human.'[73] Different situations demand different tactics, and the roles of conflict, violence and revolution in social change are central categories in Unger's understanding of politics. Vitally important for him is, however, the right of individuals to take charge of and shape social structures in which they find themselves. His commitment, in other words, is to radical and uncompromising democracy in all its social, political and economic dimensions. Sachs' fear is well founded when he suggests that 'authoritarianism is even more deeply ingrained in what is called the "South African way of life" than is racism'.[74] To the extent that authoritarianism is an ingredient of any society, including both Eastern Europe and the Western World, radical democracy is only learned with difficulty.

A critique of the liberal understanding of the rule of law,

---

[70] Roberto Unger, *Social Theory: Its Situation and Its Task* (Cambridge: Cambridge University Press, 1987), pp. 169–90; *False Necessity: Anti Necessitarian Social Theory in the Service of Radical Democracy* (Cambridge: Cambridge University Press, 1987), pp. 475; 524–39. [71] *Social Theory*, p. 151.
[72] See Milner Ball, 'The City of Unger', *Northwestern University Law Review*, 81:4, Summer 1987, pp. 628. [73] *Ibid.*, p. 629.
[74] Sachs, *Protecting Human Rights.* p. 32.

which itself demands the affirmation of the fullest implications of individual rights and democratic participation, must be an important part of the quest for human rights and political formation in situations of political reconstruction, in much the same way that it is identified as being crucial to debate within Unger's own Brazilian context. It also provides the basis for theological dialogue in the chapter that follows, dealing with human rights.

WHEN IS A MINIMUM TOO MUCH?

There are wide differences in international debate concerning the moral basis for a viable doctrine of individual rights, democracy and social justice. There is, however, a hard won consensus emerging in situations of crisis concerning the need for what James Harrington, as early as 1656, called the 'empire of laws and not of men'. Two centuries later this same notion came to be a moral and political basis for the American republic, seen in the words of Chief Justice John Marshall, as a 'government of laws and not of men'.[75] In the late twentieth century the contextual demands (both historical and contemporary) in South Africa and many other situations require that the fundamental rights presupposed in any notion of the rule of law be investigated, scrutinised and applied with all radical consistency as demanded by Unger and others.

Debate has long ranged concerning precisely what the 'rule of law' as opposed to (what Aristotle called) the 'passion of individuals' means politically. The objective in what follows is a limited and contained one. It is to show that there is within recent legal and political scholarship, representative of a wide range of ideological positions and schools of thought, a body of literature which represents the emerging of common ground in favour of the concept of the rule of law as a common basis in terms of which society can best be managed and directed. In essence, it is argued, that concern for the rule of law has to do with the affirmation of *a moral and procedural minimum* which

[75] E.S. Corwin, *Liberty Against Government: The Rise, Flowering and Decline of a Famous Judicial Concept* (Baton Rouge: Louisiana State University Press, 1948), pp. 13f.

protects the governed from the possible abuse of those who govern, while allowing maximum flexibility and freedom to any government to deal with the changing needs of society.

The concept of the rule of law first gained recognition with the publication of A.V. Dicey's *Introduction to the Study of the Law of the Constitution* in 1885. The extensive debate that followed is summarised by Anthony Mathews, in which he identifies four different interpretations of the rule of law:[76] The *law enforcement approach* which legitimises even the most totalitarian decrees. The *procedural justice approach* which recognises that all members of society, private citizens and government officials alike, should have equal access to the law and be equally responsible before the law. The *material justice approach* which makes the rule of law synonymous with the attainment of full social and political justice. The *protection of basic rights approach* which goes beyond the administration of law as included in the procedural justice approach (which can result, suggests Mathews, in the possibility of a tyranny of laws which makes it potentially an instrument of government power rather than a restraint on it). For Mathews the protection includes 'the freedom of the person, freedom of expression, freedom of movement and the right to hold meetings'.[77] Dugard shows that in South Africa liberal lawyers have largely confined themselves to what Mathews identified as the second understanding of the rule of law. And yet, in so doing they have also sought to uphold the freedoms of the individual identified in Mathews' fourth model.[78]

Current debate of the rule of law is essentially between the third and fourth models of rights as outlined by Mathews. The central question is whether a viable minimum moral foundation to the rule of law is adequately covered by Mathews' fourth example of basic rights (the protection of basic rights approach),

---

[76] Anthony Mathews, *Freedom, State Security and the Rule of Law: Dilemmas of the Apartheid Society* (Cape Town: Juta and Co, 1986). See also Anthony Mathews, *Law, Order and Liberty in South Africa*: John Dugard, *Human Rights and the South African Legal Order* (Princeton: Princeton University Press, 1978). Richard A Cosgrave, *The Rule of Law: Albert Venn Dicey, Victorian Jurist* (Chapel Hill: University of North Carolina Press, 1980) traces the concept 'rule of law' to W.E. Hearn in 1876.

[77] Mathews, *Freedom, State Security and the Rule of Law*, pp. 1–22.

[78] Dugard, *Human Rights*, p. 39.

or is more required. Ivor Jennings argues that Dicey's formulation of basic rights, being a product of nineteenth-century Whig *laissez-faire* philosophy, is essentially meaningless in a complex modern society, precisely because it fails to protect the individual against the violation of individual rights by the all-powerful structures of state and society.[79] In an age where people are, in turn, politically, socially and economically deprived as a result of the social, economic, educational and cultural structures of society, Dicey's formula is simply *too narrow*. For Mathews, on the other hand, the commitment of the Universal Declaration of Human Rights and the European Convention on Human Rights is *too broad*. He is particularly concerned about the report of the International Commission of Jurists that emerged from its Delhi conference held in January 1959, which has consciously broadened the rule of law into an instrument of political, social and economic change:

Broadly speaking, in the historical development of free societies the main emphasis has been laid on the right of the individual to assert his freedom from state interference in his spiritual and political activities, a freedom which finds expression in such classic rights as freedom of worship, speech and assembly. The recognition that rights of this kind without a certain standard of education and economic security may for large sections of the population be more formal than real has led to greater emphasis being put on a second kind of individual rights. These latter are concerned with the claim of every individual in the State to have access to the minimum material means whereby he may at least be in a position to take advantage of his spiritual and political freedom.[80]

Mathews' concern is that by broadening the rule of law to the point where it becomes 'a vehicle for an entire social and political philosophy, its juridical significance [is diminished] to vanishing point by submerging the legality principle in which the source of that significance lies'.[81] In other words Mathews

[79] Ivor Jennings, *The Law and the Constitution* (London: University of London Press, 1956), pp. 54f. See also the discussion of this critique in Dugard, *Human Rights*, pp. 45–49.
[80] Mathews, *Law, Order and Liberty*, pp. 27–8. The full text of the declaration is found in *The Rule of Law in a Free Society* (Geneva: International Commission of Jurists, 1959).
[81] Mathews, *Law, Order and Liberty*, p. 29.

suggests that, in seeking to include in the notion of the rule of law an entire socio-economic and political programme, the quest for a minimum anterior legitimating principle against which to test all political programmes is lost. The testing principle is equated with a particular political programme and this, *inter alia*, contains 'the danger of social policies being frozen through law'.[82] At the level of constitutional law, the danger is that particular law is elevated to foundational norms.

The fundamental question is: When is an entrenched minimum moral foundation to law too much? Mathews' concern is to be carefully noted. Not all the values and requirements of any particular society need to be entrenched to the point of restricting the freedom of future societies. Sachs realises this in pleading for time to allow the values of the new society to emerge. Leo Strauss, in turn, identifies the danger of allowing the 'yoke of [present] thought' from being imposed on future generations. But it is here that any agreement that may exist between those who adhere to the narrow and broad definitions of human dignity already identified come to an end.

There is agreement between those holding to these different perceptions of human dignity on the values contained within the First Generation of rights which emerged from the anti-colonial, bourgeois revolutions of the eighteenth century. There is less agreement concerning the Second Generation of rights which affirm the social, economic and cultural values contained in the *International Covenant on Social, Economic and Cultural Rights*, eventually ratified only in 1976 in response to the *Universal Declaration of Human Rights* adopted (but not intended as a legally binding document) by the United Nations in 1948. An emerging Third Generation of rights which affirms development, peace, social identity and ecological issues evokes even less legal support among most nations.[83]

The Magna Carta, the seventeenth-century English Bill of Rights, the United States Bill of Rights, the French Declaration of the Rights of Man were all formulated and adopted by the middle and upper classes with a view to redressing the violation

---

[82] Mathews, *Freedom, State Security and the Rule of Law*, p. 21.
[83] Sachs, 'Towards a Bill of Rights', p. 295.

of their rights by arbitrary rulers. The Second Generation of human rights were written under the impact of the East–West conflict, making the question of socio-economic rights as central to human rights debate as the question of individual First Generation rights. The Third Generation of human rights, in turn, addresses the needs of under-developed and developing nations. In situations of contemporary reconstruction the particularity of the historical context of the oppressed people must be taken into account in defining the minimum moral value as it relates to both legitimate laws and the fullness of humanity.

Sociologists of law argue that in reality this is precisely what does happen in the normal process of values. They emerge from within the rough and tumble of politics within which different theories, doctrines and ideologies are brought into conflict with one another. In a careful sociological study, Eugen Ehrlich, for example, describes how what he calls 'living law' (the untroubled acceptance of essential values and social transactions, whether or not these are found in particular laws) emerges as a result of the dialectical interplay between social forces and existing value-systems.[84] This sociological understanding of the way in which fundamental societal values emerge finds (ironically for some) common ground with many contemporary understandings of natural law which, in addition to all other cultural and mythical accretions, is a rational attempt to articulate certain fundamental principles of human existence in the light of historical and lived experience.[85] And some Marxian theorists, given an historical materialist commitment to scientific observation of data, find themselves drawn, with some qualifications, to a position where they too are ready to acknowledge the gains associated with the rule of law tradition.

There is little support in contemporary critical Marxian scholarship for a literal interpretation of the withering away of

[84] Eugen Ehrlich, *Fundamental Principles of the Society of Law* (New York: Arno Press, 1975).
[85] See discussion in Richard John Neuhaus (ed.), *Law and the Ordering of Our Life Together* (Grand Rapids: Eerdmans, 1989), p. 121.

the law.[86] Most scholars affirming this tradition have turned away from a crude materialistic understanding of law as the simple reflection of the economic base, or the unqualified weapon of the ruling class, which needs to be rejected by oppressed people at every opportunity.[87] The increasing common ground between Marxian and other sociologists of law is that all societies are made up of conflicting groups (disagreement remains whether these groups can be reduced to social classes), and that law is mixed up in the business of preserving social order and giving some sense of political direction to society.[88] E.P. Thompson has done as much as any to expand this common ground, paving the way for a political space in relation to phrases like 'law and order' and the 'rule of law' that had hitherto been almost the exclusive terrain of liberal and right-wing theorists.[89] In so doing his concern is similar to those already identified as belonging to the critical legal studies movement.

Locating himself in the Althusserian tradition, Thompson recognises law to be 'by definition a part of a "superstructure" adapting itself to the necessities of an infrastructure'. It is therefore 'clearly an instrument of the *de facto* ruling class'. It reinforces, legitimates, masks and mystifies social relations and class rule.[90] Like any Marxian, he further regards law to be an inherent part of the fabric of society. It cannot, as supposed by some within the liberal tradition, be separated off into a sphere apart from social conflict, supposedly providing neutral rules which constrain conflicting classes and interest groups. It serves

---

[86] E.B. Pashukanis's work contributed significantly to contemporary debate on this ideal. See E.B. Pashukanis, *Selected Writings on Marxism and the Law*, Piers Beirne and Robert Sharlet (eds.) (New York: Academic Press, 1980). See also R. Sharlet, 'Pashukanis and the Withering Away of Law in the USSR', in S. Fitzpatrick (ed.), *Cultural Revolution in Russia 1928–1931*. (Bloomington: Indiana University Press, 1978).

[87] Hugh Collins, *Marxism and Law*, pp. 23–34.   [88] *Ibid.*, p. 45.

[89] Steve Redhead, 'Marxist Theory, the Rule of Law and Socialism', in Piers Beirne and Richard Quinney (eds.), *Marxism and Law* (New York: John Wiley and Sons, 1982), pp. 328–42.

[90] E.P. Thompson, 'The Rule of Law', in Beirne and Quinney (eds.), *Marxism and Law*, p. 130.

[91] E.P. Thompson, 'The Poverty of Theory', in *The Poverty of Theory and Other Essays* (London: Merlin Press, 1978), p. 288.

the dominating role of the ruling class, it functions 'at every bloody level' he tells us, influencing and shaping everything from the relations of production to philosophy, religion and the quest for personal self-identity.[91] Yet, in a consideration of the struggle of the English people in the sixteenth and seventeenth centuries against royal absolutism, Thompson allows that law cannot simply be reduced to class power. Law, he says, has become 'less an instrument of class power than a central arena of conflict'.[92]

The pertinent question is 'how can law be both of a class and yet *not* of a class?'[93] Thompson's answer is that, despite the domination of the ruling class, certain hard fought victories have been won by the working-class movement in the sphere of law-making and judicial procedure.[94] In an Ungerian sense workers have insisted on the right to participation in the process of political formation. Thompson views the victories which have resulted from this participation as constituting a contradiction of the dominant status of the dominant classes. 'This', says Thompson, 'is to me a cultural achievement of universal significance.'[95] He continues:

I am insisting only upon the obvious point, which some modern Marxists have overlooked, that there is a difference between arbitrary power and the rule of law. We ought to expose the shams and inequalities which may be concealed beneath this law. But the rule of law itself, the imposing of effective inhibitions upon power and the defence of the citizen from power's all-intrusive claims, seems to me to be an unqualified human good.[96]

The problems which Thompson's critics have concerning his perceptions of the rule of law can be left aside. What is clear is

---

[92] E.P. Thompson, 'The Rule of Law', p. 133.
[93] Redhead, 'Marxist Theory', pp. 331.
[94] Thompson specifically identifies the importance of trial before jury in eighteenth-century English law as one such procedural advantage against the power of the state. N. Blake in 'Juries and Civil Liberties: A Political History', *Bulletin of the Haldane Society of Socialist Lawyers*, No. 11, Autumn 1979, shows that a jury in the twentieth century does not necessarily perform the same function.
[95] Thompson, 'Rule of Law', p. 135.
[96] *Ibid*. Redhead speaks for many of Thompson's critics in identifying his 'Rule of Law' comment as the 'infamous last ten pages' of *Whigs and Hunters* (from which it is extracted) to 'rest rather uneasily on top of the preceding 250 or so [pages]'. In Beirne and Quinney (eds.), *Marxism and Law*, pp. 329, 330.

that some within the historical materialist tradition (Thompson, Unger and others) have moved away from a preoccupation with Marxian ideology about law giving attention to the material base (political context) out of which specific laws emerge.[97] In so doing they have returned to Marx's own primary concern not with ideas, but with the material source of these ideas. The task of an historian and materialist, argues Thompson, is always to be specific. Debate of 'the rule of law, in this sense, must *always* be historically, culturally and, in general, nationally specific'.[98] Thompson's critique of the liberal notions of the rule of law at the same time allows for the important gains made within the rule of law tradition. The point has already been made. Thompson's concern, like that of some within the critical legal studies movement, is to push the liberal tradition to take its own rights seriously. Not least of all, his concern is to ensure the active participation by all ranks and classes of people in the creation of their own future.

AUTHORITY AS EVENT

Central to the argument of this chapter is the presence of an apparent contradiction within society between a commitment to personal freedom, radical independence and self-reliance on the one hand, and democracy, social dependance and corporate responsibility on the other. The affirmation of the one set of values to the exclusion of the other denies the quest for a social union at peace with itself. Can the apparent contradiction be overcome? How can an individual enjoy both the personal autonomy associated with the libertarian tradition, while at the same time allowing the most fundamental socio-economic provisions identified in Second and Third Generation human rights instruments to flourish? Can we do no more than choose one side or the other and then fight for our values at the cost of other values? Can no more be hoped for than a grim compromise

---

[97] The shift is away from a peculiar kind of Marxian idealism, back to Marx's own concern with the material base. See also Collins' chapter in 'Class Struggle and the Rule of Law', in *Marxism and the Law*, pp. 124–146.

[98] E.P. Thompson, 'Trial by Jury', *New Society*, 29, November 1979. Italics are added.

which violates both individual and social values? Alternatively, is there a possibility of rising above the conflict in the creation of an alternative order which does not violate anyone's rights, while affirming the essential values incorporated in the two traditions to which reference has already been made? The quest must be for what Pinkard calls a balancing or harmonising of values, 'a workable consensus about what values are constitutive of the good life, in which individuals find a point to living, and in which individuals find their fulfilment as communal beings of a sort'.[99] Differently stated, this is a relationship within which individuals find their individual fulfilment in community with others. No ready-made set of values is in existence, waiting to be drawn on to satisfy this need. Jerome Frank makes the point in insisting that we abandon,

> the fairy tale of a pot of golden law which is already in existence and which the good lawyer can find, if only he is sufficiently diligent; the phantasy of an aesthetically satisfactory system and harmony, consistent and uniform, which will spring up when we find the magic word of rationalizing principle. We must stop telling stork-fibs about how law is born and cease even hinting that perhaps there is still some truth in the Peter Pan legends of the juristic hunting-ground in a land of absolutes.[100]

The question posed in this penultimate section of the present chapter is: If law be more than what the strict positivists suggest and at the same time there is no pot of golden laws waiting to be tapped – what is the source of values which shape the quest for a better society? These values are not found in what Dworkin refers to as 'celestial secret books'.[101] Values emerge rather as the insights of former generations, and existing theories are tested and reshaped to meet the needs of the present with its commitment to a new future. In the words of Paul Lehmann, the values of each new age emerge as 'one generation tells another how the future shapes the present out of the past'.[102]

[99] Pinkard, *Democratic Liberalism*, p. 99.
[100] Jerome N. Frank, *Law and the Modern Mind* (New York: Brentano Books, 1930), p. 244.
[101] Ronald Dworkin, 'Seven Critics', *Georgia Law Review*, 11, 1977, pp. 1201, 1249.
[102] Paul Lehmann, *The Transfiguration of Politics* (New York: Harper and Row, 1975), p. 7.

Milner Ball illustrates this point in his discussion on the values enshrined in the American constitution.[103] Leaving aside debate on the actual merit and formation of these values, it is important to recognise that their authority is not ultimately vested in the constitution *per se* nor in the power of the state, but in a people who, at a certain time in history, committed themselves to a process of government under the rule of law and according to a certain set of principles. He draws on Hannah Arendt to show that it is the *constituting act* which gives the constitution its enduring authority.[104] The founding event within which the framers of the constitution were able to forge sufficient agreement to create the American *politeia* as a 'fundamental political fact' is the source of authority.[105] For Ball the *politeia* is more than a formula for government. 'It is a great spirit. It is a high and noble assertion . . . a vindication of the morality of government.'[106] The pity for Ball lies in violations it has suffered in excluding and/or marginalising blacks, native-Americans and women in society, despite two centuries of celebrating this 'great spirit'! For Unger it is evidence of a failure by the nation to take its own values seriously enough. Arendt shows that the Greek word *arche*, and its Latin equivalent *principium*, mean both 'beginning' and 'principle'. As long as the founding principle within which the nation had its beginning is truly affirmed as the guiding principle of the nation, she argues, the nation as constituted will endure.[107] To the extent to which it is violated by the exploitation of marginalised Americans, it is under threat.

Few nations affirm constitutionalism with the same relish as do Americans. The point made by Arendt is important. The quest for fundamental values emerges in the event of history within which a nation is founded. For a nation to survive other

---

[103] Milner Ball, *The Promise of American Law: A Theological Humanistic View of Legal Process* (Athens: The University of Georgia Press, 1981), pp. 7–15.

[104] H. Arendt, *On Revolution* (New York: Viking Press, 1965), p. 193.

[105] *Ibid.*, p. 9. The Greek word *politeia* is sometimes translated to mean 'constitution' of, for example, the human body. John Adams, she suggests, on this basis likened a political constitution to the constitution of the human body. *Ibid.*, p. 140, n. 10.

[106] Milner Ball, *Lying Down Together: Law, Metaphor and Theology* (Madison: The University of Wisconsin Press, 1985), p. 17.

[107] Arendt, *On Revolution*, p. 214, n. 9. Ball, *The Promise of American Law*, p. 10.

than by force, agreement must be reached on certain principles to guide the ensuing life of the nation. The event has a beginning when the people (often in the wake of conflict) agree to seek consensus on fundamental values. The event is also process. Changing circumstances result in the founding principles acquiring new meaning, and sometimes the founding principles themselves need to be changed. Those adhering to constitutionalism argue, however, that the process by which such changes may occur (such as a two-thirds majority vote in the legislature or a referendum) ought to reflect the same tough process of struggle which gave rise to the initial constitutional principles. Ideally the amendments should unite a coalition or constituency of people which extends beyond any one social or economic group in society, uniting people of different persuasions, values and social beliefs.

Constitutionalism is, in a sense, primarily a contemporary and democratic manifestation of Bodin's doctrine of sovereign power. Its concern is the articulation of values and procedure which allow people with conflicting values to co-exist and create a society within which good is maximised for as many people as possible, while the fundamental rights of everyone are protected. Arendt's understanding of the *constituting act* within which this commitment occurs is related to what has earlier been identified as a workable consensus in law-making. It is a consensus which emerges among autonomous individuals who have earned one another's trust and learned to show loyalty to one another, sometimes as a result of conflict and mutual suffering. All this is part of the event of nation-building.[108]

The struggle against tyranny in Eastern Europe has in many instances already given rise to nation-building events. South Africa is, in turn, closer today to culminating in such an event than at any time in history. Certain lessons have been learned in these struggles and values have emerged that constitute the embryonic values of the new societies. They are values which must be nurtured, in order to be developed and carried into the future.

Except in the most rigid forms of legal positivism there is a

[108] Pinkard, *Democratic Liberalism*, p. 108.

broad perception of the need to create a moral base for law, law-making and judicial procedure which maximises individual and social rights; against which all government action and specific laws need to be tested. These values are not 'given' or found 'waiting' to be discovered, they are earned in hard fought battle. The rule of law, in this sense, has to do with the creation of a social system of values and practices which make it possible for people with different principles to live together. More than that; what Unger, Thompson and others teach is that there is a continuing need for these values to be tried, tested and shaped by the ongoing active participation of the ruled in the process of ruling.

A THEOLOGICAL OBSERVATION

The identification of legal values as a basis for law-making within, and in response to, a specific historical event has, of course, for theologians a familiar ring about it. Biblically the 'Law of Moses' emerges in response to the liberating event of the Exodus. It is not ascribed to Moses as the leader of the liberated slaves but to the God of the event which gives the people their life together. At the heart of the Hebrew community that grew up in response to the liberating activity of God was the concept of the covenant, binding the former slaves to one another and to the life-giving spirit of God. In their 'Foreword' to Walter Harrelson's important study, *The Ten Commandments and Human Rights*, Walter Brueggemann and John Donahue view the Commandments in their own context as a kind of 'charter for free persons'.[109] It gave form and content to the spirit and promise of the Exodus event.

Clearly the law as we know it today was unknown in ancient Israel. Israel was not a secular state. The Torah, in turn, contains more than 'law'. It includes the teaching of the prophets, wisdom writings, poetry, mysticism and spirituality. Culturally this tradition has nevertheless informed secular legal debate in a way that legitimates metaphorical hermeneutical

[109] Walter Harrelson, *The Ten Commandments and Human Rights* (Philadelphia: Fortress Press, 1980), p. xiii.

links being made between biblical reflection of law and the contemporary quest for social and legal renewal.

For Norman Gottwald the Decalogue 'gives an unmistakable skeletal structure to the religion of Yahweh as the religion of a particular egalitarian social system. To worship Yahweh, to be an Israelite, meant above all else to practice a specific way of life.'[110] Gottwald's monumental study on the tribes of Israel prior to the establishment of the united monarchy shows (*inter alia*) how this essential idea energised the Israelite social system of laws and practise over against other social systems. In the words of Abraham Heschel, the Torah (which is more than law but never devoid of it), given in response to the Exodus event, is 'the indispensable and loving instrument holding the community of God and Israel together'.[111] Julius Wellhausen, writing in an earlier period, in turn saw prophecy develop in response to the changing needs of the community of Israel. 'The prophets do not speak out of the law, but out of the spirit . . . Their 'torah' is worth just as much as that of Moses and it issues from the same perennial source.'[112] And in the New Testament, despite the criticism levelled against Jesus by the protectors of temple religion, he was seen by others to stand within the tradition of the law and the prophets (Matt. 5:17), as the faithful interpreter of the law for his situation.[113]

There are numerous different methodological approaches to the study of law in the Bible.[114] What they have in common is a recognition of the appropriation by biblical writers of laws and customs of neighbouring peoples and traditions. It is this that has prompted Anthony Phillips to argue that the study of biblical law is best left to lawyers, who have the necessary skills to analyse and discern the presence of these different traditions in

[110] Norman K. Gottwald, *The Tribes of Yahweh* (Maryknoll: Orbis Books, 1985), p. 59.

[111] Abraham Heschel, *The Prophets* (New York: Harper and Row, 1962), p. 230.

[112] Julius Wellhausen, *Sketch of the History of Israel and Judah* (London: A. and C. Black, 1891), p. 88.

[113] Gerard S. Sloyan, *In Christ the End of the Law* (Philadelphia: Westminster Press, 1978), pp. 49, 69.

[114] Bernard Jackson in his article 'The Ceremonial and the Judicial Biblical Law as Sign and Symbol', *Journal for the Study of the Old Testament*, 30, 1984, p. 40, identifies six different methodological approaches.

biblical law.[115] For our purposes, the process whereby biblical laws emerged is more interesting than the sources of these laws. This is a process which shows a willingness by the early Hebrews and Christians alike to appropriate existing laws from other cultures and environments in which they found themselves. Harrelson, for example, shows the influence of the laws and customs of other Near Eastern societies on the Decalogue.[116] Sometimes laws and customs were simply taken over. Often they were modified, and in other situations rewritten. The single theological concern was the same. It was to use the resources available in any given situation and in each changing situation to give expression to the central liberating message of the Exodus – the specific way of life associated with the worship of Yahweh. The laws and customs of different societies were, in other words, used to give expression to what Milner Ball, in a different time and place, refers to as the 'great spirit' which emerges out of a constituting or life-giving event. Law, narrative, poetry and teaching in the two biblical testaments are essentially a repetition and elaboration of the liberating events of God in the Exodus and life of Jesus.

The task of law-making in the Bible has always been a creative act of putting together the necessary ingredients in fulfilment of the covenant promise of God to God's people. Each generation of prophets and apostles realised that there was no blueprint to be found in the past simply to be applied to the present. In the Introduction to this study reference has been made to the radical break which occurred with the return of the Hebrews from exile. The challenge facing those who entered the new age was to discern a new message and a new set of values for a new time in history. It is this challenge that faces South Africans, Eastern Europeans and others at this point of their history – with important lessons for other societies within which the socio-political and economic contradictions have not yet manifest themselves in revolution. An important question is whether the church has the will to share in the creation of these values.

[115] Anthony Phillips, *Ancient Israel's Criminal Law* (Oxford: Blackwell, 1970).
[116] Harrelson, *The Ten Commandments*, p. 23f.

Theologically it has something important to say. The theology of the people of the Book (Muslims, Christians and Jews) speaks of the individual dignity of each person created in the image of God, insisting that individuals realise their full potential as persons within the community of others, and that it is the calling of each person to share in the creation of the reign of God on earth. These affirmations speak to the political and legal concerns outlined in this chapter, including the right to active participation in the formation of their own future.

In a radically pluralistic society the church can (and should) have no monopoly over this process. It needs to learn with Bonhoeffer what it means to speak of its most fundamental values in a religionless or secular way. This is perhaps the only way in which it will be heard. For this to be achieved the church is obliged to address human rights. Without this basic commitment it is likely to find itself marginalised from the political quest for reconstruction. It may have no other tangible social contribution to make to the creation of a new age.

CHAPTER 4

Human rights and theology

Political definitions and formulae often give rise to different theories. Jean Bodin's understanding of 'political authority' in his *Les Six Livres De La Republique* (1577), was this kind of study. As already shown, he defined a sovereign as someone capable of rising above the conflicting interests of society, and law as 'nothing else than the command of the sovereign'.[1] The later definition gave rise to the tradition of legal positivism. The debate which followed in the wake of this tradition, in turn, resulted in the quest for a set of fundamental values; a moral understanding of the rule of law, able to protect the general welfare of all people, without capitulating to the partisan demands of any one group and worthy of being a basis for effectual rule. The outcome was two different perceptions of law as discussed in Chapter 3. In what follows attention is given to the values which have come to shape the moral understanding of law, and more especially the human rights debate as a basis for law-making.

Human rights, as we understand the concept today, emerged as part of a slowly evolving process, part of an idea whose time had come. *Magna Carta* had already been signed in England in 1215. The *Petition of Rights* followed four centuries later in 1628, and after the Glorious Revolution came the *Bill of Rights* in 1689. Almost a hundred years later, in 1791, came the *Bill of Rights* of the United States Constitution, making America the first state to

---

[1] Jean Bodin, *Les Six Livres De La Republique* (Paris: Chez I du Puis, 1583). See discussion in Terry Pinkard, *Democratic Liberalism and Social Union* (Philadelphia: Temple University Press, 1987), p. 58. Also Stanley J. Benn, 'Sovereignty', in *Encyclopedia of Philosophy* (New York: MacMillan Co. and Free Press, 1967).

be ruled in submission to a constitution which defines human rights 'as the basis and foundation of government'. It was preceded in 1789 by the French *Declaration of the Rights of Man and Citizen.*

Written within the epoch of the social establishment of the bourgeoisie, the major concern of the American and French constitution (which made liberal rights theory a part of established modern politics) was the defence of the interests of citizens as free individuals, free producers and free proprietors.[2] This resulted, almost from the time when they were written, in the twin concerns of these documents – socio-economic freedom and political equality on the one hand, and individual rights, due process of law and the right to own private property on the other – being interpreted with a bias in favour of individual rights. Subsequent centuries saw the emphasis on free choice and the protection of the individual from interference by the state and other people become the unquestioned dominant concern of liberal western political theory and praxis.

The 1918 Russian Revolution sought to correct this imbalance in a constitution which committed the Russian Socialist Federated Congress of Republics 'in struggle to destroy every exploitation of man by man, every class division of society, unmercifully to crush the exploiters . . .', severing itself from the tradition of middle-class human rights which had become a part of the political pursuits of the West.[3] A *different* set of human rights was affirmed – not the rights of the merchant class revolting against the divine right of kings, but the rights of workers against those who owned the industries and exploited the poor.

[2]   C.B. Macpherson, 'Natural Rights and Justice in Hobbes and Locke', and John W. Chapman, 'Natural Rights and Justice in Liberalism', in D.D. Raphael, (ed.) *Political Theory and the Rights of Man* (Bloomington: Indiana University Press, 1967), pp. 1–15; 27–42. Also Zechariah Chafee, Jr., *How Human Rights Got into the Constitution* (Boston: University Press, 1952) and Ernest Barker, 'Natural Law and the American Revolution', in *Tradition of Civility* (Cambridge: Cambridge University Press, 1948), pp. 263–355.

[3]   This development is outlined in the World Alliance of Reformed Churches' study on the theological basis of human rights. See Jurgen Moltmann, 'The Original Paper: A Theological Basis of Human Rights and of the Liberation of Human Beings', in Allen O. Miller (ed.), *A Christian Declaration on Human Rights* (Grand Rapids: Eerdmans, 1977), pp. 26–29.

Then came the Nazi and Fascist terror of the 1930s, and again the need became obvious to protect the rights of individuals. On 24 October 1945 the United Nations Charter was established, with a Preamble giving expression to the determination of the new body to 'save succeeding generations from the scourge of war, which twice in our lifetime has brought untold sorrow to mankind', to 'reaffirm faith in fundamental human rights, in the dignity and worth of the human person, in the equal rights of men and women', and 'to promote social progress and better standards of life in larger freedom'. One of four main goals of the United Nations, as stated in Article 1. 1, is to foster international cooperation in 'promoting and encouraging respect for human rights and for fundamental freedoms for all without distinction of race, sex, language or religion'. Three years later, on 10 December 1948, the *Universal Declaration of Human Rights* was adopted by the General Assembly of the United Nations. Forty-eight of the 56 member states of the United Nations voted in favour of the adoption of the Declaration, while 8 states abstained from voting. Subsequently 6 of the abstaining states have adopted the Declaration as well as over 100 of the states which became members of the United Nations after 1948. Only South Africa and Saudi Arabia, of the original members, have failed to do so. It took until 1966 before the *International Covenant on Economic, Social and Cultural Rights* and the *International Covenant on Civil and Political Rights* were adopted, and they were not ratified until 1976. They then became legally binding on the states that voted for ratification.[4]

Despite the tardiness in making the Declaration a viable and binding means of protecting international human rights, Lourens Ackermann (the first occupant of a chair in human rights in South Africa) argues that 'if anything, it (the Declaration) has achieved greater status because of the delays . . .' In the process people came to 'feel a deep need for a universal human rights instrument to whose terms they can hold governments and societies to account'. 'The Declaration', he continues, 'has become a standard by which to test state

---

[4] Lourens Ackermann, 'Introduction', to *Human Rights for South Africans*, edited by Mike Robertson (Cape Town: Oxford University Press, 1991), p. 1.

constitutions, a weapon in international diplomacy, and a set of principles to which the UN organs refer when confronted by human rights issues.' As such, he argues, the Declaration has become a source of 'customary international law, very much like the customary domestic law, or "common law" of a country'.[5]

A number of additional international and regional covenants and treaties have, of course, followed in the wake of the *Universal Declaration of Human Rights* and the two International Covenents.[6] Each of these, like the *Universal Declaration of Human Rights* itself, have, to varying degrees stressed the importance of both individual and political rights on the one hand, and socio-economic rights on the other; recognising that the two different categories or generations of rights need to be protected in different ways. This has given rise to a growing international recognition of the need for the two generations (and more recently a third generation of developmental and ecological rights) to form a comprehensive whole.

The need for harmony between individual and political freedoms (the freedom of speech, religion, assembly and dissent) and socio-economic well-being (the right to work, housing, health-care and education) at the same time continues to tear at the heart of the human rights struggle. In Eastern Europe, for example, it could be argued that one set of human rights have recently been traded for another. People have demanded the individual rights denied to them by undemocratic socialist dictatorships, while at the same time being thrust into social and economic anxiety as the cost of living spirals and unemployment escalates. Poland, for example, is 'caught in the vice of the International Monetary Fund and World Bank, which is creating unemployment, an inflation rate of 1,000 per cent and a foreign debt that has surpassed 45 billion US dollars'.[7]

---

[5] *Ibid.*, pp. 3:5.

[6] Some of the other major international human rights treaties are: the *Convention on the Elimination of All Forms of Discrimination Against Women*, the *Convention Against Torture and Other Cruel Inhuman or Degrading Treatment or Punishment*. The regional declarations include: *The European Convention of Human Rights. The American Convention of Human Rights, The African Charter of People's and Human Rights.*

[7] A speech by Erich Weingartner, former executive secretary of the World Council of Churches' Commission of the Churches for International Affairs. Published as an occasional paper by the Institute for Christian Ethics, Waterloo Lutheran Seminary, Waterloo, Ontario, Canada. 1990.

The need for an inclusive understanding of human rights is further accentuated by the bitter class distinctions and conflicts which characterise western society. This is a quest which remains unfulfilled despite the euphoria promoted in some quarters of capitalism concerning the 'failure of socialism' in Eastern Europe. The question posed in what follows is *whether theology has a contribution to make toward transcending the historic contradiction between individual and socio-economic rights*. Does it provide a theoretical framework within which to move beyond the impasse of secular debate as outlined in the last chapter?

WHY THEOLOGY?

Bodin's understanding of political sovereignty came in the wake of a succession of religious wars in sixteenth-century France. He saw the need to locate law-making above religious controversy. Liberal political thought, following Locke and others, has since turned this insight into the secular political tradition which characterises the western debate on politics and human rights. This important gain, earned in the wake of centuries of religious-motivated human suffering, has persuaded Leo Strauss, as a political philosopher, to argue that the quest for human rights 'should be kept independent of theology and its controversies'.[8] 'A pluralistic society that tries to make its unifying political and moral principles religious in any nontrivial sense is in for trouble,' argues Frederick Olafson in similar fashion.[9] Some Christians have, in turn, rejected talk of the theology of human rights for very different reasons. Seeing it as a humanistic development, bordering on personal arrogance and pride, they argue that the image of God has been destroyed within humanity, leaving humankind irremediably sinful, deserving of no recognition and worthy of no intrinsic rights.

This is a theological argument that has on occasions been used politically to defend the most flagrant violations of human rights. J.M. Potgieter, professor of private law at the University

[8] Leo Strauss, *Natural Rights and History* (Chicago: University of Chicago Press, 1953), p. 164.
[9] Frederick A. Olafson, 'Two Views of Pluralism: Liberal and Catholic', *Yale Review*, 51, 1962, p. 531.

of South Africa, employs the argument as a basis for rejecting all proposals for a Bill of Rights in South Africa intended to defend and promote the rights of all its citizens.[10] Insisting that the image of God can only be restored through conversion to Christ, he regards the masses as having no essential rights. Linked to an ideology of white (Afrikaner) Christian nationalism in South Africa, this of course, has the most serious moral and political implications. Similar arguments were used during the crusades to justify the slaughter of human beings seen as 'infidels', less than fully human and worthy of extermination because they refused to submit themselves to the ideology of the medieval church. Potgieter's argument is but a small step from the reactionary kind of apartheid ideology which has traditionally located rights and privileges exclusively in the hands of whites as the carriers of the gospel and 'civilised values', extendable by derivation only to those blacks who conform to white ('Christian') understandings of civilisation and government. The argument further lends itself to amoral and uncompromising notions of 'law and order'. Right-wing Christians have, for example, taken this argument to the point of absurdity in citing Potgieter's argument as a basis for attacking church leaders and theologians who have supported the call for a Bill of Rights in South Africa. Within the context of indiscriminate violations of the most basic human rights by the South African state, a right-wing Christian group has argued: 'An honest person needs no special "rights" in order to associate, disassociate, assemble, read, speak, perform or travel'. 'The rights [demanded by human rights activists] . . . for the arrested, accused and convicted', the statement continued, 'seem to be aimed primarily at limiting the power of the police.'[11]

So why theology? Would it not be better for theologians to learn the bitter lessons of history and leave politics to the politicians and human rights to those secular, 'value-free' disciplines which best equip society to rise above what are too often the sectarian interests of religious and secular ideologues? To the extent that

[10] J.M. Potgieter, 'Gedagtes oor die nie-Christelike Aard van Menseregte', *Tydskrif Vir Hedendaagse Romeins Hollandse Reg*, 52:3, August, 1989, pp. 386–408.
[11] *The Gospel Defence League Newsletter*, June 1989.

theology is ideologically captive to one or another political agenda, the answer is an unqualified 'yes'. To the extent that it provides a basis for ideological critique, while contributing to a better understanding of humanity, as a basis for the promotion of such rights that sustain human dignity, a theological silence in the face of human rights violations can only be construed as morally repugnant and socially irresponsible.

The primary task of theology is not, however, to 'reinvent the wheel', in reworking the list of human rights already defined and defended by countless human rights agencies around the world. There is consensus within the major Christian traditions that the rights identified in most human rights declarations are worthy of theological support, while emphasising the need for support to be given to socio-economic (Second Generation) as well as developmental and ecological (Third Generation) human rights alongside more generally accepted First Generation rights. As such the consensus reflects a broad global perspective on human rights, incorporating the liberal values of western bloc countries and social values of eastern bloc countries as well as First and Third World perspectives. This is best seen in the 'Common Ground on Human Rights' which emerged as part of the World Council of Churches' study on human rights at the St Polten, Austria, conference in October 1974.[12] With participation in the study project by representatives of socialist and Third World countries, the findings of the study reflect a priority concern for those whose rights were at the time seen to be most under threat in the world as a whole. The proposed list of human rights begins with the right to life. Then comes the right to cultural identity, followed by democracy, the right to dissent, personal dignity and freedom of religion:[13]

a. There is a basic human right to life – inclusive of the entire question of survival, of the threats and violations resulting from unjust economic, social and political systems, and the equality of life.

b. There is a right to enjoy and to maintain cultural identity –

---

[12] *Human Rights and Christian Responsibility*, vols. 1–3 (Geneva: WCC-CCIA, 1975).

[13] See Jurgen Moltmann, *On Human Dignity: Political Theology and Ethics* (Philadelphia: Fortress Press, 1984), p. 8.

which includes issues such as national self-determination, the rights of minorities etc.

c. There is a right to participate in the decision-making process within the community – which comprises the entire issue of effective democracy.

d. There is a right to dissent – which prevents a community or a system from hardening into authoritarian immobility.

e. There is a right to personal dignity – which implies, for example, the condemnation of all torture and of prolonged confinement without trial.

f. There is a right freely to choose a faith and a religion – which encompasses the freedom, either alone or in community with others, in public or in private, to proclaim one's faith or one's religion by the means of teaching, practice, worship and ritual.[14]

The listing of rights by the Roman Catholic *Magisterium* provides a similar, although slightly varied emphasis, stating:

a. That all men are equal in nobility, dignity and nature, without any distinction of race, sex or religion.

b. That everyone therefore has the same fundamental rights and duties.

c. That the rights of the human person are inviolable, inalienable and universal.

d. That everyone has a right to existence, to bodily integrity and well being, to everything necessary to maintain a decent standard of living, such as food, clothing and shelter, means of subsistence and any other services indispensable to social security.

e. That everyone has a right to a good reputation and respect, to protection of privacy and to an honest representation.

f. That everyone has a right to act in accordance with the right norms of his own conscience and to investigate the truth freely following the ways and means proper to man. This may in certain circumstances involve the right of dissent for reasons of conscience from some rules of society.

[14] Quoted in Jan Milic Lochman, 'Human Rights from a Christian Perspective', in Allen O. Miller (ed.), *A Christian Declaration on Human Rights: Theological Studies of World Alliance of Reformed Churches* (Grand Rapids: Eerdmans, 1977), p. 17.

g. That everyone has the right to express his ideas and opinions freely and to be correctly informed about public events.

h. That everyone has the right to worship God according to the right norm of his conscience, to practise his religion both in private and public, and to enjoy religious liberty.

i. That the person's fundamental right is to have all his rights safeguarded by law; namely, to a protection that is impartial, inspired by the true norm of justice, and at the same time effective. This means that all are equal before the law and any judicial procedure should give the accused the right to know his accusers and also the right to a proper defence.

j. Finally, the *Magisterium* asserts that fundamental human rights are inseparably interconnected in the very person who is their subject with just as many respective duties; and that rights as well as duties find their source, their sustenance and their inviolability in the Natural Law which grants or enjoins them.[15]

There is general consensus among Christian churches on the rights affirmed in the WCC and the Roman Catholic declarations, although debate on the prioritising of rights necessarily continues. Some might even argue an ecumenical study on human rights in the 1990s would require both the St Polten and the Vatican priorities to be reshuffled. It would probably also be necessary to include an affirmative action clause concerning the participation of black people and/or women in most, if not all, nations on earth. The continuing debate that has not changed is the theological consensus on an *inclusive* perception of rights. The essential theological task is, however, at a deeper level. Jan Milic Lochman makes this point in arguing that, if the church is to make a serious contribution to the human rights struggle, it involves more than fine-tuning, or even over-hauling, the existing secular human rights debate. The church, he argues, is obliged rather to engage in 'a deepened theological reflection in order to work out the specifically Christian contribution to the further development of the human rights issue'.[16] Heinz-Eduard

---

[15] Pontifical Commission (Justitia et Pax', *The Church and Human Rights* (Vatican City, 1975), p. 22.

[16] Lochman, 'Human Rights from a Christian Perspective', in Miller, (ed.), *A Christian Declaration*, p. 17.

Todt goes further in arguing that while the St Polten conference produced a 'new classification' of rights, more useful than the 'bewildering mass of codified human rights conventions' in existence, 'what was offered here was *not* a theological basis'.[17] The plural character of contemporary society suggests that the primary task of the church is perhaps not so much to promote the 'specifically Christian' (Lochman) contribution to human rights as much as to share with others in establishing a popular cultural, spiritual and theoretical basis which defines and promotes human rights. Briefly stated, from a theological perspective, human rights have to do with the realisation that all people are created in the image of God, enjoying equal human worth. In order to realise and fulfil their destiny as the bearers of God's image, the fundamental rights of all people are to be fully claimed and concretely appropriated, recognising that without certain basic rights (as outlined by the WCC and the Vatican) people are not able to realise their full God-given potential. To deny these rights to people is to oppose the work and purpose of God in the world. As such it is a sinful act requiring repentance and reparation. Popular ecclesial culture does not view the violation of human rights in this serious manner. The issue does not enjoy the kind of prominence nor the urgency that many other issues enjoy in the liturgy, teaching and witness of the Christian church.

The church's primary task is clearly to facilitate *Christians* to promote and appropriate the values of a human rights culture. It is understandable (and correct) therefore that it is essentially the identifying of a Christian theological basis for human rights that has become the focus of most ecumenical and denominational human rights studies.[18] Because of the wide acceptance of the St Polten and Vatican cataloguing of human rights, the primary

---

[17] Heinz-Eduard Todt, 'Theological Reflections on the Foundations of Human Rights', *Lutheran World*, 24:1, 1977, p. 45.

[18] See, inter alia, WARC study in Miller (ed.), *A Christian Declaration of Human Rights*; the Lutheran World Federation of Churches' study in Jorgen Lissner (ed.), *Theological Perspectives on Human Rights* (Geneva: Lutheran World Federation, 1978); The Pontifical Commission 'Justitia et Pax', *The Church and Human Rights* (Vatican City, 1975); John Paul II, *On Social Concern (Sollicitudo rei socialis)* (Washington DC: US Catholic Conference, 1988); Theological Studies Department of the Federation of Protestant Churches in the German Democratic Republic, 'Theological Aspects of Human Rights', *WCC Exchange*, 6 (December, 1977); United Church of Christ in the

aim of the various ecclesial studies which have emerged in their wake has not been a listing of rights as much as the articulation of a political ethic grounded in a theological understanding of what it means to be human. In the words of Winston Ndungane:

The doctrine of human rights is man's attempt at exercising his responsibility as God's steward on earth in that it seeks to challenge all the injustices that distort the image of God in man. It is an attempt to establish a social condition where there are harmonious and peaceful relations among the people of the world, and where people are able to realise their full potential as God created them. There is some kind of relation that exists between the notion of human rights and the Christian doctrine of man . . .[19]

The obligation of the church at the same time reaches beyond the confines of its own membership – it is to share in the promotion of a wider culture within which there is sensitivity to, and support for, human rights. It must be shown that these human rights claims are not merely theoretical 'political options' or a set of moral values to which certain religious and/or moral people adhere. Indeed, until such time as it is acceptable that the pursuit and realisation of these rights are inherent to what it means to be human, the human rights agenda will never occupy its rightful place in political struggle. Addressing St Andrews University in 1934, the Rector of that university observed:

Freedom is the most ineradicable craving of human nature. Without it peace, contentment and happiness, even manhood itself, are not possible. The declaration of Pericles in his great funeral oration holds for all time:

'Happiness is Freedom, and Freedom is Courage.'

That is the fundamental equation of all politics and all human government, and any system which ignores it is built on sand.[20]

United States of America, 'A Pronouncement on Human Rights', in Alfred Hennelly, S.J. and John Langan, S.J. (eds.), *Human Rights in the Americas: The Struggle for Consensus* (Washington DC: Georgetown University Press, 1982,), pp. 150–8.

[19] Winston Njongo Ndungane, *Human Rights and the Christian Doctrine of Man*. A dissertation towards the degree of Master of Theology submitted to the Faculty of Theology, King's College, University of London. September 1979.

[20] Quoted in M.M. Corbett, 'Human Rights: The Road Ahead', *Human Rights: The Cape Town Conference*, C.F. Forsyth and J.E. Schiller (eds.) (Cape Town: Juta and Company, 1979), p.2.

The Rector was General J.C. Smuts. Unable to inject this dynamic into his political vision for South Africa, he unwittingly predicted the inevitable outcome of the policy of apartheid.

Until such time as the human rights agenda is seen to be the ineradicable centre of human coexistence, it is likely to continue to function as no more than a rhetorical appendage to the more important political agenda of hegemony, national security and trade. It will continue to be picked up and dropped at the will and pleasure of rulers whose own 'rights' (privileges) are too often realised at the cost of the fundamental rights of others. *The task of theology is help locate the human rights struggle at the centre of the debate on what it means to be human and therefore also at the centre of social and political pursuit.* It is to help invest the existing human rights agenda with a dynamic to fulfil its ultimate goals, by sharing (with other disciplines) in defining the nature and ultimate purpose of humanity.

Differently stated, unless human rights values are grounded in the cultural and political ethos of a nation and become a part of the motor that drives society, they tend to be little more than of decorative value, often used to conceal the harsh reality of human abuse and exploitation. Jeremy Bentham once referred to *such* moral ideals as 'nonsense – nonsense on stilts'. His words are sobering: 'A reason for wishing that a certain right were established, is not that right – want is not supply – hunger is not bread'.[21] At the risk of repetition, *the question is whether it can be shown that the pursuit of rights is inherent to what it means to be human.* If this is the case, the failure to have these rights fulfilled will necessarily result in social and political conflict. This, in turn, means that the pursuit of human rights could become the most essential and viable cultural and spiritual lever available to social reformers and ethicists in the mobilising of people for the pursuit of a more just world order.

Jurgen Moltmann poses a pertinent theological question in enquiring in what manner theology can serve this end. Its primary concern is not, he suggests, in some idealistic or abstract way simply to promote more sensitivity and awareness of human rights. It is rather a *revolutionary* task. It has to do with unleashing

---

[21] Jeremy Bentham, 'Anarchical Fallacies', in Fredrick A. Olafson (ed.) *Society, Law and Morality* (Engelwood Cliffs: Prentice Hall, 1961), p. 347.

'the dangerous power of liberation', which is inherent to a theological understanding of what it means to be human, into the socio-political and economic structure of society.[22] In other words, it is in the struggle for human rights that theology has its best chance to be materially grounded in the political and socio-economic struggle for a world that conforms more closely to the demands of the gospel.

A theology of human rights is an inherent part of theological anthropology. It gives expression to an understanding of humanity which transcends both the individualistic bias of the dominant forms of western liberalism and the unqualified collectivism of rigid Marxist notions of humanity. Neither have provided a satisfactory sense of what it means to be a person with inherent personal dignity realisable in relationship and community with other people. In the words of Max Stackhouse, the secular alternatives 'leave us relying only on the *fluxus quo*' – with people torn between individual desire and social responsibility.[23]

The *inclusive* notion of human rights, inherent to a theological understanding of humanity, constitutes an important theological contribution to the human rights debate. Theology is at the same time obliged to take the criticism, coming from Iredell Jenkins and others, seriously. His concern is essentially that attempts to expand human rights to cover ever greater areas of social and economic needs ultimately undercut the legitimacy of a more limited list of political or First Generation rights which can and need to be immediately fulfilled. The critique, of course, echoes the concern of Anthony Mathews (discussed in Chapter 3), that the broadening of the notion of the rule of law to include all social and political concerns ultimately transforms it into less than a minimum anterior principle against which to test all political ideologies, allowing it to become synonymous with a particular political agenda.[24] Jenkins writes:

---

[22] Moltmann, 'The Original Study Paper: A Theological Basis of Human Rights and of the Liberation of Human Beings', in Miller, *The First Liberty: Religion and the American Republic*, (New York: Paragon House Publishers, 1988), p. 32.

[23] Max Stackhouse, 'A Protestant Perspective on the Woodstock Human Rights Project', in Hennelly and Langan, *Human Rights in the Americas*, p. 146.

[24] Anthony Mathews, *Law, Order and Liberty in South Africa* (Berkeley: University of California Press, 1972), p. 29.

There is so much unnecessary suffering and wanton abuse and neglect of men in need that a doctrine that cries out against these conditions and demands their correction merits both our thanks and our attention ... But there is also much in this doctrine [of human rights] that seems unsound and imbalanced, arousing doubts and reservations in the minds of many ... The doctrine seems altogether devoid of internal restraints and controls. It is a dangerous doctrine because it advances no criteria, whether theoretical, empirical or practical, for determining its reach. It grounds rights in humanity, and then leaves the notion undefined, so that the content of rights is indefinite and indeterminate.[25]

The theology of human rights, which grounds rights in an understanding of what it means to be human, is essentially about contributing to the kind of theoretical control for which Jenkins asks. Correctly interpreted it circumvents ideological captivity, by providing an understanding of humanity which functions as a standard against which to measure all ideological systems. At the same time it lifts human rights claims above the level of mere rhetoric by focussing on praxis.[26] Theology is about ultimate meanings and the significance of these ultimates for daily living. As applied to human rights this has to do with a theological understanding of what constitutes the dignity and meaning of life, what it means to be truly human, and what essential rights are needed to protect this humanity.

Clearly theological answers to these questions will be 'ideologically' or 'contextually' coloured in the same way as answers that emerge from any other discipline. Theological and secular human rights declarations which have emerged from western liberal democracies are clearly different to those that have come out of socialist situations, and First World human rights priorities usually differ from those that come out of Third World situations. There is at the same time remarkable consensus regarding the very foundation of human rights, which can be reduced to the freedom and well being of people. It is this that ultimately places the human rights agenda above the desires of

---

[25] Iredell Jenkins, 'From Natural to Legal to Human Rights', in Erwin H. Pollack (ed.), *Human Rights* (Buffalo: Jay Stewart, 1971), p. 213.

[26] See also David Hollenbach, S.J. *Claims in Conflict: Retrieving and Renewing the Catholic Human Rights Tradition* (New York: Paul, p. 33.

some to justify particular ideologies and/or legitimate the practices of their own nations.

As a way of developing the theoretical basis asked for, and the communally based understanding of humanity sought after in the last chapter, attention is given to some of the important contemporary theological studies on human rights in the Roman Catholic and Protestant traditions.

Roman Catholic rights theory

Post Vatican II Roman Catholic doctrine on rights is best characterised in a statement made by John XXIII in 1961. He describes the modern tradition of the church as 'dominated by one basic theme – an unshakable affirmation and vigorous defense of the dignity and rights of the human person'.[27]

This emphasis is developed in *The Pastoral Constitution on the Church in the Modern World* (*Gaudium et Spes*) published during the last session of Vatican I in 1965, and *Message Concerning Human Rights and Reconciliation* published by the Roman Synod of Bishops in 1974. It is further elaborated in a paper prepared by the Papal Commission, *Justitia et Pax*, entitled *The Church and Human Rights*, published in 1975.

The traditional Thomistic understanding of nature and grace is seen throughout these documents. The *Justitia et Pax* paper observes: 'The teaching of the *Magisterium* on fundamental human rights is based in the first place or is suggested by the inherent requirements of human nature ... within the sphere of Natural Law.' What this means is that the affirmation of the *Magisterium* 'that all men are equal in nobility, dignity and nature, without distinction of race, sex or religion', together with a series of related rights ranging from food, clothing and shelter to judicial procedure and the rights of women included in the *Justitia et Pax* document are seen to be part of the order of

---

[27] Quoted in Hollenbach, *Claims in Conflict*, p. 42.

creation made known in natural law and discernible through reason.[28] These are rights which the *Magisterium* regards, in the language of liberal natural rights theory, to be self-evident – there to be seen by any fair minded person as made known and verified in common experience.

The document then goes further. It affirms what has always been part of the Thomistic and Catholic tradition, but often neglected prior to Vatican II. This is the insistence that it is ultimately through the revelation of Christ that the basic rights of humankind are made known in a fuller and more decisive manner. Echoing *Gaudium et Spes*, we read in *The Church and Human Rights*: 'The truth is that only in the mystery of the Incarnate Word does the mystery of man take on light . . . Christ, by the revelation of the mystery of the Father and His love, fully reveals man to man himself'.[29] John Paul II's words to the Pueblo Conference in 1979 underscore this emphasis, giving the kind of Christological focus to Roman Catholic doctrine which has made post Vatican II Catholic–Protestant dialogue so much easier:

The truth that we owe to human beings is, first and foremost, a truth about themselves . . . Thanks to the Gospel, the Church possesses the truth about the human being. It is found in an anthropology that the Church never ceases to explore more deeply and to share.[30]

Hollenbach's important survey of the development of Roman Catholic rights theory shows why particular claims or human rights (which include such basic needs as food and shelter) have come to be regarded by the *Magisterium* as indispensable for the protection of the true identity of humankind.

Human dignity is not an abstract or ethereal reality but is realized in concrete conditions of personal, social, economic and political life. The history of the papal teaching has been a process of discovering and identifying these conditions of human dignity. These conditions are called human rights.[31]

---

[28] *The Church and Human Rights*, pp. 21–8.   [29] *Ibid.*, p. 28.
[30] John Paul II, 'Opening Address at Pueblo', in John Eagleson and Philip Scharper (eds.), *Pueblo and Beyond* (Maryknoll: Orbis Books, 1979), p. 63.
[31] Hollenbach, *Claims in Conflict*, p. 68.

Locating John Paul II's social teaching within this broader framework, John Langan explains why he finds himself both attracted and disconcerted by a Pope whose moral and religious teachings tend to find little support among many people whose concern it is to promote social justice. Focussing mainly on *Sollicitudo Rei Socialis* (*On Social Concern*) (1988) at a recent major papal social encyclical, Langan identifies the theological significance of the way in which the document approaches the fundamental structures of society which shape and determine the quality of human life.[32] Rejecting both liberal capitalism and Marxist collectivism as 'imperfect and in need of radical correction', the encyclical regards both as 'subject to the structures of sin'.[33] John Paul II had already spoken of the structures of sin in the 1984 Apostolic Exhortation, *Reconciliatio et Paenitentis* (*Reconciliation and Penance*).[34] He importantly refuses 'to draw a comforting line between a sinful social realm of powerful institutions and a private realm of passive innocents whose lives are occasionally marred by personal vices'. Responsibility for socially significant sin is located not merely before 'a relatively small number of "movers and shakers" who initiate harmful practices or who derive substantial benefits from them . . . Almost all who count as citizens or (social) agents' have a responsibility to do something about it.[35]

Personal sin remains a fundamental category for John Paul II, but in *On Social Concern* the power of the structures is seen to be such that they extend 'far beyond the actions and the brief lifespan of an individual'. They interfere 'in the process of the development of peoples' and 'work against a true awareness of the universal common good'. 'The sum total of these negative forces', he argues, constitutes 'an obstacle which is difficult to overcome'.[36] The Pope's sense of social and corporate sin, which strikes at the very identity of what it means to be human, has profound human rights implications. To say the least it requires

---

[32] John Langan, 'Personal Responsibility and Common Good in John Paul II'. A paper delivered at Claremont Graduate School, Claremont, California, 2–3 February 1990.
[33] *On Social Concern*, pars. 21, 36, 41.
[34] John Paul II, *Reconciliation and Penance* (*Reconciliatio et Paenitentis*) (Washington DC: US Catholic Conference, 1984). [35] Langan, 'Personal Responsibility', p. 6.
[36] *On Social Concern*, par. 36.

the human rights agenda to reach into the socio-economic and political sphere precisely because these structures inescapably shape the very fabric of what it means to be human.

The full implications of the Pope's insights concerning the power of the structures of sin cannot be fully developed here. There are sentences in his encyclical which suggest that social structures can become so powerful that they become a demonic presence not only shaping the character of our lives, but also determining our perceptions of the common good, and therefore our understanding of good and evil. The tone and moral concern of the encyclical concerning the potentially destructive force imposed by social structures on people as moral agents is tantalising. It can provide the basis for a link with the work of writers like Trent Shroyer, Franz Hinkelammert and others who would take the insights of the encyclical a step further. For Shroyer cybernetics has become the dominant instrument shaping contemporary society, limiting the power of the individual as a moral agent and restricting social change.[37] Hinkelammert defines the interlocking synthesis of political, economic, military, scientific and technological as modernity's 'ideological weapon of death'. It virtually excludes the possibility of moral agency or debate.[38]

Against this background the Pope's suggested solution could, of course, be dismissed as simply inadequate. He calls for conversion and the emergence of new spiritual attitudes as a basis for transforming action. He at the same time strikes at the heart of what he regards as the controlling ideologies behind the structures of sin – 'the all consuming desire for profit' and 'the thirst for power'. Without specifically identifying profit with the West and the ideology of state power with earlier manifestations of eastern bloc socialism, he sees these two forces as the controlling mechanisms of the modern world. More than that, 'in today's world', he suggests, the two are 'indissolubly united, with one or the other predominating'. This sometimes results in human life being shaped by decisions that are inspired only by

---

[37] Trent Shroyer, *The Critique of Domination: The Origins and Development of Critical Theory* (New York: Brazilier, 1973).
[38] Franz J. Hinkelammert, *The Ideological Weapons of Death* (Maryknoll: Orbis Books, 1986).

economics or politics. All this, he continues, results in 'idolatry: of money, ideology, class and technology'.[39] Here, of course, John Paul II's social teaching (ironically) finds common cause with *The Road to Damascus*, a document signed by oppressed Christians engaged in liberation struggles in South Africa, Namibia, South Korea, Philippines, El Salvador, Nicaragua and Guatemala, which argues that 'the sin of idolatry lies at the heart of the imperialism of money' which motivates the exploitation and oppression of Third World countries by western imperial nations.[40] The Pope moves even further in the direction of liberation theology in calling for the empowerment of the poor and for solidarity with those who suffer as a consequence of the sinful structures which exemplify this idolatry. And solidarity, he insists, 'is not a feeling of vague compassion or shallow distress at the misfortunes of so many people . . . It is a firm and persevering determination to commit oneself to the common good.'[41] The empowerment of the poor, for the Pope, involves an ethic of non-violent self-assertion for the poor and an ethic of generous self-giving for the rich.[42]

The essential concern that Langan understandably has with *On Social Concern* is what he defines as 'a profound tension between the affirmation of the possibilities for conversion and the recognition of the ways in which people are involved with or enmeshed in structures of sin'.[43] Differently asked, is conversion and the generation of new spiritual attitudes (asked for by the pope) possible in the kind of world defined by Shroyer and Hinkelammert? Unless this fundamental tension is resolved, suggests Langan, the danger exists that the Pope's call to conversion will be 'little more than the moralistic exhortations designed to convict all of us of sin and likely to produce in many a reaction of defensive or even derisive dismissal'.[44] The failure of the encyclical to address all that is involved in this tension is what ultimately separates the social teaching of the Pope from liberation theology and the *Road to Damascus* document.

Having identified this tension, Langan shows the direction in

---

[39] *On Social Concern*, par. 37.
[40] *The Road to Damascus: Kairos and Conversion* (Johannesburg: Skotaville, 1989), p. 10.
[41] *On Social Concern*, par. 38.   [42] *Ibid.*
[43] Langan, 'Personal Responsibility', p. 21.   [44] *Ibid.*

which the church would be obliged to move for the implications of the Pope's demanding articulation of social living to be realised:[45]

1 The denial of the essential goods necessary for survival and for functioning as free and equal citizens would need to be seen as an act of sinfulness, requiring the church to commit itself to a process of redistribution and reallocation of goods.

2 Rights (including, for example, the right to shelter, food and health care) that are necessary for survival with decency and for full participation in society as free and equal citizens would need to be regarded as primary. This means that the rights to private property and the rights to goods and services not included in the primary requirements would probably need to be restricted and/or renunciated in order to fulfil the primary rights.

3 A range of psychological, social and spiritual considerations facilitating the redistribution process would need to be devised.

The implication of John Paul II's teaching is to locate the struggle for human rights within the context of questions of political economy. It recognises that in a world controlled and manipulated by dominant life-shaping social and economic structures, questions concerning full participation in life on the basis of freedom and equality involve more than the right to the freedom of expression and choice or even the right to food and shelter. They necessarily involve questions concerning which ideologies and structures allow for the possibility of these ideals being realised. The importance of *On Social Concern* for the human rights debate concerns its theological understanding of the inescapable social character of life and human behaviour. It contributes to a theoretical understanding that links liberal individual rights to a social agenda which includes socio-economic and political concerns. The Roman Catholic doctrine of rights further necessarily locates the human rights debate fully within the theological and pastoral ministry of the church. *On Social Concern* shows that the struggle against human rights

[45] *Ibid.*, pp. 14–19.

violations on both the personal and the social level is synonymous with the fight against sin. To share in the quest for human
rights as the essential concrete requirements for decent human
living is, in turn, an inherent part of the evangelical task of the
church to proclaim personal and social conversion.

This comment on Roman Catholic rights theory, brief as it is,
necessarily requires mention of John Paul's latest encyclical,
Centesimus Annus, in which a similar argument is developed to
that contained in *On Social Concern*. In responding to the collapse
of socialism in the Soviet Union and Eastern Europe, the need is
again stressed to transcend the limitations of both free-market
capitalism and eastern bloc socialism. Without taking the
debate significantly beyond what is already outlined, *Centesimus
Annus* reiterates the essential challenge facing contemporary
Roman Catholic social ethics as being the need to move beyond
the existing social structures of both East and West. In so doing it
unequivocally recognises the struggle for economic justice to be
an inherent part of the church's evangelical calling. It also views
democracy as a quest that stands central to the gospel.[46]

Protestant teaching on human rights

There is, of course, no one Protestant doctrine on human rights –
or anything else. There are a variety of different Protestant
approaches. These differences can largely be traced back to the
origins of Protestantism in the sixteenth century. In what follows
attention is given primarily to two major emphases within
Protestantism: Lutheran and Reformed or Calvinist theology,
representative of two different theological ways of approaching
social ethical questions.

The sixteenth century was, of course, a century within which
the resourcefulness and responsibility of humanity had already
been re-established in the events of the Renaissance. The
Protestant Reformation was a different kind of celebration of the
worth of humankind.[47] Turning away from any suggestion of a

[46] John Paul II, *Centesimus Annus* (Vatican City, 1991). The encyclical appeared after the
manuscript of this book was already with the publisher.
[47] For a discussion of these developments as they pertain to the human rights debate see
Stackhouse, *Creeds, Society and Human Rights*, pp. 54–65.

humanistic understanding of inherent human worth or basic rights, Protestantism was a celebration of salvation as a free and undeserved gift of God. It was soon realised, however, that a person liberated from the medieval preoccupation with earning his or her salvation through ecclesial restraints and obligations was a person spiritually emancipated to participate in society in a free and uninhibited manner. It had to do with learning 'to live in Christ through faith and [one's] neighbour through love'.[48] Leaving aside the complicating question of some being chosen as recipients of God's grace and others not, those who understood themselves to be saved from forces of degradation and sin participated in life and made demands on society with a zeal that had not been witnessed in Europe for generations past.[49]

The Lutheran tradition

Martin Luther's primary concern was, of course, to reform the church, particularly regarding its audacious claims that the destiny of the human soul after death could be determined by the purchase of indulgences, with the wealth generated by this system being used for the benefit of the ecclesial and political elite. His objective was the rediscovery of a simple spirituality which linked the individual soul directly to God through faith, devotion and honest living. The far-reaching political implications of this gospel soon, however, became obvious to everyone concerned. The church in Rome realised that it was striking at its established theological and political hegemony. The German princes saw it as an opportunity to wrench further power from Rome, relocating the spiritual centre of the German people within the context of German nationalism. The poor in Germany and elsewhere, in turn, saw spiritual freedom to carry within it a host of different socio-economic and political rights, to which they laid claim through a series of peasants' revolts.

The outcome was that, within a decade of Luther having proclaimed his message of justification by faith alone, he found

---

[48] Martin Luther, 'The Freedom of a Christian', *Works of Martin Luther* (Philadelphia: Muhlenberg Press, 1959), vol. III p. 341.

[49] Stackhouse suggests Protestantism was part of the same world of thought as Conciliar Catholicism which the Council of Constance tried to crush in 1415. *Creeds, Society and Human Rights* (Grand Rapids: Eerdmans, 1984), pp. 44–9.

himself drawn essentially onto the side of the princes. Like Augustine before him, Luther regarded history as, at best, a place of tentative peace to be endured while awaiting the dawn of God's kingdom. He believed there was a natural hierarchy in society, and that the German princes were the legitimate rulers equipped 'to patch and darn as best we can while we live, punish the abuses and lay bandages and poultices over the sores'.[50] Required to rely more and more on the supportive and benign Frederick the Wise and his immediate successors in Saxony, he was content to leave the direct political ordering of society to them. He theologically opposed the peasants and plebeian priests who promoted the cause of rebellion in the name of a God-given freedom, and in similar fashion he opposed those within the Anabaptist movement who renounced involvement in the political realm. The task of the Christian, Luther taught, was to live in obedience to his or her conscience as informed by the Word of God, giving obedience to those who rule, except where their commands contradicted the Word of God. In brief, Luther's two kingdom doctrine stood at the heart of all that he had to say on human relations and social ethics. The task of the church, in the words of the *Augsburg Confession* (written by Melanchthon in consultation with Luther), 'was to preach the Gospel and administer the sacraments', while 'temporal authority is concerned with matters altogether different from the Gospel'.[51]

This doctrine has been interpreted in different ways by separate Lutheran theologians, as it tended to be employed in different ways by Luther himself.[52] A balanced reading of the doctrine suggests that the 'spiritual kingdom' (which is the concern of the church) and the 'temporal kingdom' (which is the concern of civil authorities) are both manifestations of the 'kingdom of Christ' over against the 'kingdom of the devil'. It is

---

[50] See 'Treatise on Good Works', *Works*, vol. 44, p. 95; 'To the Christian Nobility', *Works*, vol. XLIV, pp. 212–15; 'To the Nobles of Germany', *Works*, vol. XLV, pp. 355–78.

[51] Article 28, The Augsburg Confession, in T.R. Tappert (ed.) *The Book of Concord* (Philadelphia: Fortress Press, 1959).

[52] See the discussion in Jurgen Moltmann, *On Human Dignity: Political Theology and Ethics* (Philadelphia: Fortress Press, 1984), p. 63.

the understanding of the two kingdom doctrine which explains Luther's willingness to be politically involved, at least to the extent of counselling and criticising the princes, while persuading his followers to become involved in politics. For him there was no blueprint in scripture or special insight among Christians which provided a specifically 'Christian' answer to the complexities of political reality. The Christian, renewed by the spirit of God, he believed, was nevertheless better equipped to deal with these problems than the person unexposed to the redeeming power of God. He never, however, tired of proclaiming: *simul justus et peccator* – those who are justified are at the same time still sinners. This, he thought, was what made politics such a messy business! Moltmann's summary statement on the two kingdom doctrine is worthy of special attention:

Luther's two kingdoms doctrine is in truth a critical–polemical separation between God and Caesar. It permits neither a Caesaro-papalism nor a clerical theocracy. It intended to teach that the world and politics may not be deified, nor may they be religiously administered. One should give to Caesar what belongs to Caesar – no more and no less – and give to God that which is God's. One should turn the self-deified world into the world, and let God be God. One should deal rationally with the world, with the law and with force. The world is not and it never will become the kingdom of God; rather it is a good earthly order against evil chaos. One should deal spiritually – which means with faith – with God and his gospel. The gospel does not create a new world but saves people through faith.[53]

All this means, of course, that from a Lutheran perspective the human rights debate is a part of the temporal or secular agenda. A few examples are enough to make the point. Martin Honecker affirms a strong Lutheran distinction between theology (dogmatics) which he regards as deriving knowledge from revelation, and ethics which is an exercise of universal reason in response to the revealed tenets of faith. To try to base human rights (as an exercise in ethics) on the special postulates of faith involves for him the danger of absolutising human endeavour while undercutting its universality.[54] Trutz Rendtorff takes a

---

[53] *Ibid.*, pp. 70–1.
[54] Discussed in Todt, 'Theological Reflections', in *Lutheran World*, p. 52.

slightly different approach to the same end. He identifies a parallel between the concept of human rights and the Christian doctrine of justification by faith. In the same way that the doctrine of justification by faith affirms God's unconditional acceptance of the sinner, human rights must be conferred on all people unconditionally. The actual task of defining these rights, however, remains a secular phenomenon.[55] In brief, in Lutheran theology human rights must be taken seriously as a basis for creating the very best world possible. At the same time it needs to be recognised that it is not *the* ultimate solution to life's problems. This emphasis within Lutheran theology is jealously guarded as the exclusive realm of the gospel. Only as people are transformed by the power of the gospel are they truly able to love one another and live in harmony and community.

The Lutheran World Federation's (LWF) study, *Theological Perspectives on Human Rights*, published in 1977 is a thorough and insightful study which illustrates Lutheran social ethics at its best.[56] Having identified *freedom, equality* and *participation* as 'the three inviolable basic elements of worldly rights', the document is careful to insist that there is, however, no simple identity between these rights and the gospel. Concepts such as 'structural parallels' and 'analogy' are used to describe the link and yet the difference between 'the justice which applies in the kingdom of God and that in worldly law'. In so doing the essential task of the gospel is underlined.[57] It is *constructively* and *critically* to challenge all human rights proposals from the perspective of faith and love, which should enable Christians to engage in the struggle for human rights with a level of hope and courage that surpasses what the law alone can generate within us. In so doing, we are at the same time to be conscious of boundaries of the gospel 'and not seek to achieve by force of law things which can only emanate from spontaneity and love'.[58] This, in turn, requires us to 'promote in an unconstrained way' the best human rights proposals which appear at any given time.[59] That is, without

[55] *Ibid.*
[56] Lutheran World Federation, *Theological Perspectives on Human Rights*, (Geneva: Lutheran World Federation, 1977). Also Jorgen Lissner and Aren Sovik (eds.), *A Lutheran Reader on Human Rights* (Geneva: Lutheran World Federation, 1978).
[57] LWF, *Ibid.*, p. 15.   [58] *Ibid.*   [59] *Ibid.*, p. 16.

reducing the social ideals of the gospel to any specific set of human rights claims, the gospel requires us to commit ourselves without constraint to the goals of the current human rights endeavours.

In a study on human rights published at the same time as the LWF study, Heinz Eduard Todt and Wolfgang Huber focus attention on the same theological imperative. They perceive within human rights debate 'elements of transcendence' which point to the content of the gospel.[60] Elsewhere Todt speaks of the human rights struggle as 'a parable of the kingdom of God'.[61] In so doing Todt and Huber address the immediate concern of Lutherans while at the same time, as will be shown shortly, giving expression to a concern that is central to the Evangelical Reformed tradition. As such (reflecting perhaps the encounter between Reformed and Lutheran theologies in the Heidelberg ecclesial context), they give expression to the heart of the ecumenical focus on human rights. This is a focus which gives clear moral support to the human rights agenda, while seeking constantly to subject this agenda to the renewing power of the gospel.

The similarities between the theological basis of Catholic rights theory and the Lutheran approach to human rights are extensive. Not least among these is the way within which transcendence is viewed in relation to human rights. Commenting on the approach of *Gaudium et Spes* to ethical commitment, Hollenbach identifies what he regards as a tension inherent to human existence – a tension between the drive of the human spirit toward a value worthy of absolute commitment and an awareness of the shifting and limited nature of all historical values. Two equally wrong consequences can follow:

The quest for transcendence could be focussed on an historically limited value in a way that absolutises this value. The result would be idolatry and enslavement. On the other hand, a complete or premature withdrawal from historical engagement in the name of pure transcendence is also a temptation.[62]

---

[60] Wolfgang Huber and Heinz Eduard Todt, *Menschenrechte. Perspektiven einer menschlichen Welt* (Stuttgart: Kreuz Verlag, 1977). Quoted in Moltmann, *On Human Dignity*, p. 12.
[61] Tödt, 'Theological Reflections', p. 57.   [62] Hollenbach, *Claims in Conflict*, p. 72.

This tension stands central to all theological debate. All human efforts to define or create the ethical ideal need to be assessed and critiqued from the perspective of the divine absolute which always demands more than human endeavour can deliver. The affirmation of the transcendent absolute can, however, never become an excuse not to commit oneself to the best human alternative available.

The Lutheran ethic can be (and has been) incorrectly read in support of both errors, by a distorted and one-sided interpretation of its content. By requiring the church to focus on the postulates of the faith, while recognising that human endeavour can never be more than sinful, the urgency of the human rights struggle has been seriously undermined. In its most extreme forms this approach has led to the church confining itself to the saving of souls, content to leave politics to the politicians. The other reading of Lutheran ethics (which is at the centre of the contemporary Lutheran human rights studies) requires *serious commitment to the best human rights proposals possible, while affirming that it is through the gospel alone that ultimate human harmony is achieved.* This ethic, Lutherans argue, ultimately injects the human rights debate with precisely the kind of critical urgency that is needed. In so doing it also provides an important incentive against allowing the human rights debate (and the theological question concerning the nature and identity of true humanity) from becoming captive to any particular ideological agenda.

The Reformed tradition

The Reformed or Calvinist side of Protestantism was obliged to address a side of the theological tension (or dialectic) with an urgency that never imposed itself on Luther. Geneva was an independent city of refugees and social reform was a priority if it was to survive at all. John Calvin had been expelled from the city eighteen months after his arrival, and when he returned it was with a sense of reluctance. He did not enjoy the full confidence of the rulers, and he never fully trusted them. In this context his sense of covenant, with an obligation to fulfil God's will in every area of human existence in the face of a host of conflicting loyalties, ultimately gave his theology a dynamic and a sense of social urgency which Luther, operating essentially with the same theological principles, was not required to realise. Calvin insisted that the civil authorities were under divine mandate to deliver 'legitimate and just government' providing for the essential needs of God's people.[63]

If for Luther politics was the *affairs of people* hammered out in debate and compromise, for Calvin politics was the *affairs of God* to be discerned within Scripture and rationally tested within the community of faith. If Lutheran theology can be criticised for containing the capacity to distract from the 'religious' zeal required to save the world from human rights violations, Calvinism carries within it the capacity to assimilate religion and politics into an uncompromising theocracy.

Calvin's Geneva, consisting largely of exiles, was clearly a centre of social reform by the time Calvin's ministry drew to a close.[64] It also evidenced the first signs of popular participation in government.[65] At the same time it experienced its 'moments of pronounced imperialism'. This was, of course, equally true of Puritan Massachusetts in colonial America, and is still true of 'hard-line heretical Calvinism in South Africa'.[66] 'Imperial Calvinism' soon hardened into a dogmatic fundamentalism, which replaced the freedom inherent to the sovereignty of the biblical God with a God of undeviating order, whose unquestioned authority was given to an equally intractable chosen elect. Calvinist theology also spawned two very different kinds of Reformed thought: 'Evangelical Calvinism' and 'Free-Church Calvinism' or Puritanism.[67] Affirming the absolute freedom of God in the building of human community and the re-establishing of the Kingdom of God on earth, Evangelical Calvinism has in recent times come to be associated with the theology of Karl Barth and its radical critique of all existing

[63] John Calvin, *Commentaries on the Epistle of Paul the Apostle to the Romans* (Grand Rapids: Eerdmans, 1948), p. 469.

[64] Andre Bieler, *La pensée économique et sociale de Calvin* (Geneva: Librairie de l'universite, 1959). Also Andre Bieler, *The Social Humanism of Calvin* (Richmond: John Knox Press, 1964).

[65] Paul Lehmann, *The Transfiguration of Politics* (New York: Harper and Row, 1975), p. 41. See John Calvin, *Institutes of the Christian Religion*, IV, XX, 31a; a passage Ernest Barker calls 'the seedbed of modern democracy'.

[66] Stackhouse, *Creeds, Society and Human Rights*, p. 56.   [67] *Ibid.*, pp. 55–7.

social structures, as an incentive for what Paul Lehmann has referred to as Barth's theology of 'permanent revolution'.[68] Free-Church Calvinism was, on the other hand, influenced by Protestant developments in Switzerland, Holland, France and elsewhere, but essentially emerged as a distinctive ecclesial type in England and later in America. Concerned essentially with the right ordering of the community of faith rather than society as a whole, this family of churches within the Reformed tradition unleashed a theological dynamic that eventually reached beyond ecclesial boundaries into secular politics. Its impact would come to be felt not only through the Congregational churches, the Baptists, Society of Friends (Quakers) and various 'separatist' groups, but also indirectly through the Anglican Church and later the Methodists, as well as the English and American libertarian political traditions.

The unifying theme within the Reformed tradition is freedom through the grace of God to share in building a society that reflects the values and ideals of the gospel. Responding to the freedom of the gospel as understood by Luther, Calvinists developed the claim of God on their lives within an organised, disciplined and political ethic that has made Reformed theology a significant ingredient in the struggle for human rights within the western political tradition. Within the contexts of Geneva and Puritan Anglo-America, both of which demanded participation in the process of nation- and community-building, the appropriation of biblical symbols (the Exodus, the covenant, a calling to be saints and an obligation to share in building the Kingdom of God on earth) seemed a natural and obvious development. Max Weber's formative study, *The Protestant Ethic and the Spirit of Capitalism*, describes the political and economic sense of vocation central to this experience.[69]

The outcome was an ethic closely related to the secular liberal debate on natural rights, democracy and social contract. What distinguished Puritan ideas from those of Locke, John Stuart Mill, Rousseau and others was essentially a twofold emphasis:[70]

---

[68] This theme is discussed in Chapter 1.
[69] Max Weber, *The Protestant Ethic and the Spirit of Capitalism* (New York: Harper and Row, 1958). [70] Stackhouse, *Creeds, Society and Human Rights*, p. 62.

A theology of reconstruction

One, the ethical ideal shaping the covenantal community is not merely socially *constructed* and *discerned* within the revealed will of God. Puritan spirituality taught that to the extent that individuals respond to and live in accordance with the 'given' or revealed realities of life they experience fulfilment as persons. It brought a spiritual incentive to liberal politics, and, as Weber showed, those who committed themselves to the Puritan ideals came to understand their social and economic prosperity as a sign of God's favour and assurance of their election as the chosen people of God. This ultimately gave rise to a momentum which carried its adherents well beyond religion into a secular life style that held onto only the most distant rudiments of its historic origins. Two, the biblical symbols out of which Puritanism shaped its ethic carried within them communal values. Despite the strong sense of individualism which emerged within Puritanism as it reached toward ever more secular and material goals, the communal values grounded in its origins theoretically distinguished Puritan theology from liberal individualism. The Puritans and liberals shared the view that society should be governed according to 'self-evident' truths.[71] For the Puritans this meant the laws of God (tested by reason within the community of saints) such as the freedom of religion and the right to assembly. For liberals this meant ideas and values (seen to be self-evident within the experience of any hard-working individual) such as the right to own property.

In reality the encounter between Puritans and liberals was, of course, more complicated than this. Liberals shared many of the values affirmed by the Puritans, and the Puritans were able to find theological reasons for legitimating those values cherished by liberal individualists. Despite the 'privatisation' of Puritanism and its eventual absorption into liberalism, the theological roots of Calvinism continue to challenge the individualism of the West. In contemporary debate it continues to operate as a potential 'dangerous memory' ready to activate the communal and democratic ideals so desperately needed to bridge the chasm between liberal individualism and socialist collectivism. It symbolises a form of communalism being sought for on the

[71] *Ibid.*, p. 70.

social–democratic side of liberalism. It, in turn, finds common ground with people in Third World situations, both theologically and in human rights declarations such as the *African Charter on Human and Peoples' Rights*, affirming communalism as the basis of human rights.

The 'coming together' of traditions was seen in the meeting in Nairobi in 1970 of the World Alliance of Reformed Churches (WARC) which initiated a study programme on human rights as a 'first step towards an ecumenical "Christian Declaration on Human Rights".' The conscious response by the WARC to Third World demands and the early history of the Reformed tradition is explicit in the theme of the study, entitled a 'Theological Basis of Human Rights and Liberation'.[72] Like the WCC's St Polten report and the documentation of the Vatican, the WARC report reflects a consciousness of Third World demands in placing the right to life, to nourishment and to work at the beginning of the list of human rights. It locates the human rights struggle within the context of people breaking out of colonial dependence, cultural alienation and political oppression.

Within this context the theological point of departure for the WARC study is located in the liberating message of the Bible, as seen in an 'original study paper' prepared for the study project by Jurgen Moltmann.

In the Old Testament, theological thought begins with Yahweh's liberation-history with Israel in the Exodus and only afterward, and on this basis, comes to the confession that this God of liberation is the Creator of all things and the Redeemer of all people. In the New Testament, too, theological thought begins with the confession of Christ as the liberator and only then, and on this basis, comes to the doctrine of creation and eschatology.[73]

From this focus the parameters of the WARC study follow:[74]

---

[72] The documentation of the study which culminated in a meeting of the Theological Department of the WARC in London in 1976 is published in Allen O. Miller (ed.), *Christian Declaration on Human Rights* (Grand Rapids: Eerdmans, 1977).

[73] Jürgen Moltmann, 'The Original Study Paper: A Theological Basis of Human Rights and of the Liberation of Human Beings', in Allen O. Miller (ed.), *A Christian Declaration*, p. 31.

[74] *Ibid.*, pp. 32–4. These directives are given here in summarised form.

1 *Christian theology is a theology of liberation.* 'The sick, the possessed, the leprous, the humiliated and the godless experienced Jesus as a concrete liberator from their concrete misery and they believed in this liberation.'

2 *The theology of liberation is a theology of people.* Theologically speaking, the human rights debate is located within the doctrine of anthropology. Theologically people are to be understood and defined 'in similitude [as a counterpart] to God'. Created and redeemed by God, human beings have God-given rights. They also have certain ethical claims made on them.

3 *The theology of liberation is a theology of the future.* 'How can there develop out of the ideal of human rights a concrete utopia which relates the intended human future of man to the specific political, social and racial injustice of the present in order to overcome opposition and resistance?' 'Does the struggle for the realization of human rights not presuppose an inner break in the national egoism and the class intellect or the racial mind-set? If Christians find their identity in the crucified Christ, then what relevance can national, cultural and economic identity still have for them?'

The study, located within the context of the quest for liberation, gives rise to certain fundamental theological insights concerning human rights: The struggle for liberation is not only inherent to what it is to be human, but the call to liberation is the call of God. This essential call teaches us what it means to be truly and fully human. Human beings, created in God's image have rights and responsibilities not only for the world within which they live but for future generations. The final document or 'definitive study paper' presented at the conclusion of the WARC study develops this aspect under the rubric 'God's Claim on Human Beings'. The quest for basic rights is here directly related to an obligation to live a life that is befitting of one bearing the image of God, redeemed by Christ and empowered by the Holy Spirit to accomplish the will of God on earth. *This means that the pursuit of human rights comes to be seen as an inherent part of what it means to be human.* In the words of the

'Resolution on Human Rights' adopted by the General Synod of the United Church of Christ in the USA, 'human rights are the gift and demand of God'. 'The fundamental human right is the right to be responsible to God . . . to fulfil the fundamental task of becoming human persons . . . '[75] The implications of this theology for political systems and social practices within which women are marginalised and not permitted (let alone facilitated) to participate fully in society are significant. It similarly challenges many global situations where people are denied the fullest human participation in life on the basis of religion, class and race. Without explicitly addressing such particular concerns, the WARC report provides theological space within which contextual concerns can be addressed.

The Reformed emphasis on human rights is located in the vision of humanity made known in the scriptural doctrine of the covenant. It 'involves the bonding of persons to others under God's law, for God's Kingdom, empowered by God's love'. In an ecumenical sense it gives expression to what John Paul II defined as the 'truth about the human being'. In the WARC study this focus is developed in relation to both the implications of God's creation and the promise of the eschaton as a basis for engagement in the struggle for human rights.

What this means is that the WARC study locates the human rights doctrine decisively within the context of the evangelical task of the church. This ultimately is its strength. Tödt asks a question, however, which all theology is obliged to address if its contribution to human rights is to go beyond the level of motivating people to commit themselves to a set of unrealistic ideals. 'What', he asks, 'is the relationship between the WARC "Theological Basis of Human Rights" and the conventions which have recently become part of international law?' Todt's concern is to make a clear (Lutheran) distinction between 'the universal postulates on human rights' which emerge from theological discussion and the 'codified human rights agreements of the United Nations'.[76] The challenge is twofold: Theology, he argues, has a responsibility to identify the

---

[75] Published in Hennelly and Langan, *Human Rights*, pp. 150–8.
[76] Tödt, 'Theological Reflections', in *Lutheran World*, pp. 45–6.

difference between the rights and duties of the people of God inspired by faith in the ideals of the gospel and love of one's neighbour on the one hand and the values which form part of the various human rights declarations on the other. A theology which fails to do this carries within it not only the danger of reducing the demands of the gospel to the liberal and/or socialist ideals of the different human rights conventions, but in so doing it undermines the particular contribution of theology to the human rights debate, which includes a vision of a reality that transcends the present debate. This is a distinction which evangelical Calvinism readily understands. It has to do with what Barth called God's 'No' to human endeavour in order that God may say 'yes' through the gospel.[77] The second concern implied in Todt's question concerns the theological status of codified human rights agreements and international law. Representing a consensus of enlightened commitment to human rights, they deserve, in the words of the LWF study the support in 'an unconstrained way' as 'structural parallels' which anticipate the kind of society which the gospel requires us to strive for.[78] Differently stated, a concern to promote the ideals of the gospel should never cause us to deviate from promoting existing human rights declarations, as a step towards a more perfect social order.

TOWARDS THEOLOGICAL CONSENSUS ON HUMAN RIGHTS

The debate between Lutheran and Reformed theology ultimately serves to stimulate and refine rather than undermine the respective approach of these two traditions. A consideration of other denominational studies on human rights also shows that the essential emphases of these traditions constitute the poles between which all Protestant human rights theologies are located.

Together with the Roman Catholic studies on human rights, they provide a basis for theological discussion which incorpor-

---

[77] Karl Barth, *Epistle to the Romans* (London: Oxford University Press, 1960), pp. 475–502. See the discussion on this Barthian distinction in Chapter 1.
[78] LWF, pp. 15–16.

ates most doctrinal approaches to human rights. The Anglican and Methodist churches, for example, while showing theological tendencies which reflect the various strands of their respective histories, tend more toward the Catholic and/or Lutheran approaches. Affirming the *Universal Declaration of Human Rights*, the 1948 Lambeth Conference of the Anglican communion, for example, states:

The Conference declares that all men, irrespective of race or colour, are equally the objects of God's love and are called to love and serve Him. All men are made in His image: for all Christ died; and to all there is made the offer of eternal life. Every individual is therefore bound by duties towards God and towards other men, and has certain rights without the enjoyment of which he cannot freely perform those duties. These rights should be declared by the Church, recognised by the State and safeguarded by international law.[79]

The most recent 1988 Lambeth Conference again endorsed the *Universal Declaration of Human Rights*, stressing the importance of 'highlighting human interdependence and the need to eliminate exploitation', in a way (which accords with the ecumenical consensus) that allows for Second and Third Generation rights to take a more central location within the human rights struggle.[80]

In its recent publication on human rights, the United Methodist Church in the United States also affirms its support for the *Universal Declaration of Human Rights*, adopting a similar position to that of the Anglican church, in affirming the God-given worth and dignity of all people, while stressing that as a covenant people 'we are called to responsibility rather than privilege'. The statement continues: 'As a people "committed to Christ" and "called to change" we are responsible for securing the integrity of our covenant in the midst of new imposing human rights developments.' Special attention is drawn to the need to critically analyse trends and developments which may impinge on human rights in the modern world. These include

---

[79] *The Resolutions of the Lambeth Conferences, 1867–1978*, compiled by the Rt. Revd Philip Russell and the Revd Arthur Gosling. Published by the Secretary General of the Anglican Consultative Council for the Lambeth Conference, 1988.

[80] *The Truth Shall Make You Free: Lambeth Conference 1988, the Reports, Resolutions and Pastoral Letters from the Bishops* (London: Church House Publishing, 1988) pp. 223–4.

the impact of capital intensive technology, the use of data banks to provide pervasive information, the growing phenomenon of an underclass of persons domestically and internationally excluded from full participation in society owing to educational, cultural, economic and political conditions, the technological and social displacement of these people, the escalation of militarism, the growth of racist movements, the rising expectations of developing countries and the disproportionate sharing of global resources.[81] Again the focus is on Second and Third Generation rights without denying basic First Generation rights. In stressing the covenant relationship and responsibility within which the church finds itself, the Methodist declaration carries within it tones of a Reformed emphasis, while the concern for the captivity of humankind within the structures of the modern world reflects an analytical concern for structural sin as expressed in post Vatican II social concerns. In brief, a variety of ecumenical influences are seen within the Methodist position on human rights (in much the same way that ecumenical factors shape most theological positions in most churches today) – as is the theological eclecticism which has traditionally shaped the Methodist heritage.

Other churches, notably those in the Anabaptist tradition and, to some extent, some under the influence of Evangelical Calvinism have given attention to the 'community of believers' emphasis, over against the liberal emphases which eventually emerged in many churches within the Puritan tradition. Differences aside, the Roman Catholic doctrine of rights finds a point of departure in a Thomistic understanding of nature and grace, while the Lutheran–Calvinist tradition within Protestant teaching on human rights is located within a tradition of sin and grace. The former begins with a definition of humanity as given in creation and revealed in Christ. The latter begins with humanity as it is, bound in captivity, crying out for liberation, emphasising that it is only in redemption that the insights inherent to the doctrine of creation and eschatology can be fully appreciated. The point has, however, already been made. The

---

[81] *Faithful Witness on Today's Issues: Human Rights* (Washington DC: The General Board of Church and Society, n. d), pp. 3–5.

effects of ecumenism have imposed what would once have been regarded as a Roman Catholic position on many Protestant churches while, as already noted, post Vatican II Catholic social teaching has come to include emphases readily acceptable to the churches in the Protestant tradition. The above analyses of the different theological approaches suggest sufficient common ground to project an ecumenical consensual statement on human rights. To this we turn in the next chapter as a basis to presenting a vision of humanity which takes the existing secular debate on human rights a step further.

CHAPTER 5

Transcending individualism and collectivism: a theological contribution

Human rights are what Ronald Dworkin calls 'political trumps'.[1] They constitute the basic minimum respect and dignity which is the right due to any person by virtue of being human. These are rights which can be claimed in spite of the particular laws which may appear on the statute books in South Africa, Palestine, El Salvador, Iraq, Romania, the Baltic republics, the United Kingdom, the United States or anywhere else on earth. It is not the task of theology 'to deduce [these rights] theologically from specifically Christian premises'.[2] They are rights for all people, whether they choose to live under the gospel or not. Human rights are simply 'there' to be claimed and appropriated by all of humankind. The *Swakopmund Declaration*, written in the midst of the Namibian struggle for independence in 1975, captures this emphasis in affirming that 'the dignity of human personality is a gift of God, which cannot be conferred, and must not be infringed by any human political authority'.[3]

Theology, at the same time, sensitises and makes Christians aware of the nature of these rights, providing them with an incentive to live in accordance with their demands. 'The Word of God sharpens our insight into reality', states the LWF study.[4] The statement by John Paul II in his address to the Pueblo Conference (cited earlier) views human rights in the same way: 'Thanks to the Gospel, the Church possesses the truth about the

[1] Ronald Dworkin, *Taking Rights Seriously* (Cambridge, Mass: Harvard University Press, 1977), p. xi.   [2] LWF, p. 13.
[3] Jørgen Lissner and Arne Sovik, *A Lutheran Reader on Human Rights* (Geneva: Lutheran World Federation, 1978), p. 50.   [4] LWF, p. 17.

human being.' It is at the same time a truth for all to see and claim for themselves.[5] The World Alliance of Reformed Churches, in turn, locates the theological basis of human rights in 'Yahweh's liberation-history with Israel in the Exodus', and 'the confession of Christ as liberator'.[6] The call of the gospel is for people to live lives transformed by the power of God, to love one another and to grow in social and spiritual holiness. In addition to all else (and there is more to Christian holiness) it involves treating one another in the very best possible way. This requires Christians to affirm human rights. To fail here is for Christians to fail in the most rudimentary dimensions of the Christian faith. Above all it is to fail as a decent human being.

Building thus on different aspects of the same theological affirmation of God-given rights, the various theological–ethical studies on human rights offer an understanding of humanity and the rights of people which address the most important questions asked in the current human rights debate. They address the need for what Pinkard has called a 'broad' understanding of humanity, within which individual and communal values are 'balanced' and fulfilled in each other, rather than compromised to the detriment of both. In so doing the theological contribution does not introduce anything qualitatively new to the existing (secular) human rights debate. It does, however, (like some within critical legal studies) challenge the most progressive constituency within the liberal–democratic camp to take its own deepest values seriously. Theologians do so as a step towards fulfilling the higher social ideals of the gospel.

Theology grounds the human rights debate within a personal–communal sense of existence which transcends the divide between western individualism and collectivist notions of human rights, characteristic of much within the secular debate on human rights. Hendrikus Berkhof, for example, insists that in theological discussion we are obliged deliberately to use the word 'person[al]' rather than 'individual'. The individual

---

[5] John Paul II, 'Opening Address at Pueblo', in Eagleson and Scharper, (eds.), *Pueblo and Beyond*, p. 63.
[6] Moltmann, 'The Original Study Paper', in A. Miller (ed.), *A Christian Declaration*, p. 31.

(literally, what cannot be divided any further; Gk. *atomos*) is a person in abstraction from the world. 'A human being is not an individual . . . but a person, a being existing in relation to an entire world and especially to other persons, in an unremitting process of receiving and giving.'[7] Theologically understood, a person can only be a person within the context of the real world which includes other people, the natural order and an awareness of divine transcendance. To withdraw from life or to live in conflict with this order of relations is to live in social, psychological, environmental and spiritual alienation. Theologically it is to be less than human.

In locating the human rights struggle at the centre of the quest for an understanding of what it means to be human, theology brings to the human rights struggle a dynamic and a sense of urgency which makes human rights an issue that, correctly understood, no person can afford to ignore without denying his or her full potential. As such it shows the human rights struggle to be a concern central to the churches task of proclaiming the gospel, as a means of the fullness of life.

Beginning with the theological presuppositions which inform this understanding of human rights, attention is next given to a transformed vision of humanity which goes beyond the impasse which requires a choice between individual and communal values. Finally the process of implementing human rights is addressed as part of a pastoral plan.

A THEOLOGICAL UNDERSTANDING OF HUMAN RIGHTS

We return to the *theological* focus as it emerged in the wake of the WCC and Vatican declarations on human rights. With general agreement among the churches that the rights articulated within these and other declarations of human rights (notably the *Universal Declaration of Human Rights*) demand the support of the churches, the agreed theological task is to ground the struggle for human rights within a fundamental theological understanding of what it means to be human.

---

[7] Hendrikus Berkhof, *Introduction to the Study of Dogmatics* (Grand Rapids: Eerdmans, 1985), p. 23.

What is a human right?

'A human right is a right that a human person has simply by virtue of being a human person, irrespective of his or her social status, cultural accomplishments, moral merits, religious beliefs, class memberships, or cultural relationships.'[8] Human rights are inalienable or fundamental rights which people can claim independently of and prior to their acknowledgement by any society, doctrine or ethic. Says Henkin:

> Human rights are *rights*; they are not merely aspirations, or assertions of the good. To call them rights is not to assert, merely, that the benefits indicated are desirable or necessary; or, merely, that it is 'right' that the individual shall enjoy these goods; or even, merely, that it is the duty of society to respect the immunity or provide the benefits. To call them 'rights' implies that they are claims, 'as of right', not by appeal to grace, or charity, or brotherhood, or love; they need not be earned or deserved. The idea of rights implies entitlement on the part of the holder in some order under some applicable norm; the idea of human rights implies entitlement in a moral order under a moral law, to be translated into and confirmed as legal entitlement in the legal order of a political society. When a society recognizes that the person has a right, it affirms, legitimates, and justifies that entitlement, and incorporates and establishes it in the society's system of values, giving it important weight in competition with other societal values.[9]

Theologically understood, they are God-given rights, intended to enable human beings to become fully human. In the words of a statement on human rights, which emerged from the Evangelical Lutheran Church in the German Democratic Republic in 1975, 'Christians can look upon the debate concerning the further extension of human rights as *a concrete field of action* in which they themselves must bear witness to God's liberating acceptance of the world.'[10] The human rights struggle was, in other words, seen by the church in Eastern Europe prior to the 1989/90 collapse of communist domination, to be a part of

---

[8] John Langan, 'Defining Human Rights: A Revision of the Liberal Tradition', in Alfred Hennelly and John Langan, *Human Rights in the Americas*, p. 70.

[9] Louis Henkin, *The Age of Rights* (New York: Columbia University Press, 1990), p. 3.

[10] Committee on Church and Society and the Secretariat of the United Evangelical Lutheran Church, 'The Theological Relevance of Human Rights', in Lissner and Sovik, *A Lutheran Reader*, p. 30. Italics are added.

its obligation to proclaim the gospel. The challenge facing the church under the new dispensation is to ensure that this commitment remains a part of its agenda now that it is exposed to that set of pressures and temptations which constitute western political reality. Simply because these pressures are more subtle and the temptations more seductive, the challenge facing the church in a united Germany and in Eastern Europe generally is that much greater. The struggle for human rights in a legally segregated society similarly forces people to be either 'for' or 'against' apartheid. As racial laws are scrapped, however, the choices confronting people will become far more complex and the moral choices increasingly ambiguous.

The point has already been made. The primary task of theology is not, however, to legitimate the human rights debate. It is not to confer rights. These are given by virtue of birth and (theologically speaking) God's redeeming love for the entire world in Jesus Christ. It is rather, in dialogue with all other disciplines whose task it is to study the nature of humanity and human relations, *to explore the ways in which human dignity can inform the political order*. To do so Christians turn to their own doctrinal and traditional teaching on what it means to be human, and discern within the biblical story of creation and redemption a spiritual and theological model for living in harmony with God, other people and the whole of creation. In the words of the WARC statement:

Human beings in the fullness of their life and in all life's relationships – economic, social, political and personal – are destined to live 'before the face of God', to respond to the Word of God, and responsibly to carry out their task in the world implied in their being created in the image of God. They are persons before God and as such capable of acting on God's behalf and responsible to him. As a consequence of this, a person's rights and duties as a human being are inalienable and indivisible.[11]

This means that people have certain rights and duties (a God-given calling) to share in the struggle for the implementation of concrete human rights designed to enable humanity to live in

---

[11] Moltmann, 'The Original Study Paper', in A. Miller (ed.), *A Christian Declaration*, p. 132.

harmony and compliance with God's purpose for creation. 'Nowhere', suggests Bernard Lategan, 'is [this] stated so clearly as in Gal. 5:1: Christ set us free to be free – so exercise this freedom!'[12]

Within the Catholic tradition these rights are a part of the natural law, given new visibility in the gospel. Reformed Christians discern the essence of these rights within Scripture, understood and articulated within the Christian community. Lutheran human rights theory, in turn, emphasises the importance of defining these as 'political' or 'secular' rights, always under the critique of the gospel. They carry within them, however, what Huber and Todt define as 'elements of transcendence'.

Each tradition has its own way of making the quest for human rights a central ingredient of the gospel, while recognising that the specificity of human rights agendas is shaped by the context within which they are proclaimed. The findings of the St Polten conference, for example, reflect the priorities of the poor and the demands of newly independent nations by prioritising the 'right to life – inclusive of the entire question of survival'. This is an essential right which the established middle classes in developed nations tend to take for granted. Without reading too much into the sequence within which rights are listed in the various human rights declarations, it is interesting to note that in accordance with the priority concern for the needs of the poor expressed in the WCC St Polten declaration, individual (First Generation) rights are listed after the affirmation of socio-economic (Second Generation rights). More significant is the fact that the right to own property is not listed at all as part of the 'common ground on human rights' in this statement.[13] The *Universal Declaration of Human Rights*, celebrated at the time (and subsequently) by the Roman Catholic Church, the World Council of Churches and its member churches was, on the other hand, written from the perspective of developed nations in the

---

[12] Bernard Lategan, 'Anthropological Perspectives in a Time of Reconstruction.' A paper read at the University of South Africa, January 1991.

[13] Quoted in Jan Milic Lochman, 'Human Rights from a Christian Perspective', in A. Miller (ed.), *A Christian Declaration*, p. 17.

wake of World War II. The primary concern at the time with the violation of individual rights by Nazi and Fascist regimes helps to explain why the right to work appears in the Declaration as late as in Article 23, and the right to adequate food, clothing and housing only in Article 25.

The difficult question concerning human rights priorities is returned to later. Suffice it to say, while bound to develop its teaching within the context of these complexities, a Christian theology of rights, grounded in the history of the Old Testament and the incarnational teaching of the New Testament, cannot easily turn away from a comprehensive understanding of rights, and *ultimately it is obliged to favour the poor and marginalised members of society in defining and prioritising human rights.*

This necessitates concern for such basic rights which enable the poor and marginalised people of society to take their legitimate place in society, responding to the claim of God on their lives to be full, productive and creative members of society. For this to happen all people have a right to food, housing, health care and education. These are an inherent part of the God-given right to life. The right to the freedom of speech, the freedom of religion and the right to vote are vitally important. If they are not, however, linked to socio-economic rights they are rights of limited value. In other words, any intrinsic separation of First and Second Generation rights is theologically quite unacceptable, although from an enforcement point of view it is useful to distinguish between negative and positive right.

Precisely how both generations of rights are to be actually realised in society is a political issue involving complicated economics, careful planning and realistic development within which all people have the fullest right and obligation to participate to the maximum of their ability. In other words, a biblical perspective on human rights must necessarily include responsibilities.

This involves the right to freedom, equality and participation in all the responsibilities and privileges of society.[14] This means more than the right to participate in regular elections. Theologically understood, democracy necessitates the fullest participa-

[14] Moltmann, 'The Original Study Paper', p. 133; LWF, p. 12.

tion of all people in the creative process of making the world a better place. This, in turn, requires a careful assessment of all socio-political and economic structures and institutions with a view to determining the extent to which they promote the well-being and participation in society by all people. Given this priority, the churches are obliged to support the right of people to organise themselves in political parties, trade unions and other groups as a basis for collective bargaining and participation in forming the dominant structures of society which shape and govern the lives of millions of people. It also requires careful analysis to determine to what extent the institutions and structures of society have become what John Paul II has called 'structures of sin' which interfere 'in the process of the development of peoples' and 'work against a true awareness of the common good'.[15]

Whether approached from a biblical covenantal perspective, in pursuit of a 'common good', or as a basis for loving one's neighbour, a theological affirmation of the dignity and rights of people encourages the fullest possible participation by people in the political and economic ordering of society. For this to happen it is important that theology be exposed to the challenge to liberal notions of the rule of law presented by critical legal studies scholars (as discussed in Chapter 3). In so doing theology is obliged to empower those deprived of their most essential democratic and human rights, as well as to challenge those whose claims on the social resources of society often prevent others from acquiring the most essential needs that constitute the right to life. The message of the Bible for the latter group is, ironically, that in being prepared to act against one's own self-interest one acquires not only personal fulfilment, but also the satisfaction of one's most essential material and social needs. This is a message containing the most profound political insights for those who have an excess of resources and privileges as the scramble for resources and rights takes on new dimensions in situations of reconstruction in South Africa and elsewhere. A failure to redistribute resources in a rational manner in societies emerging from generations of oppression and conflict, could well

[15] John Paul II, *On Social Concern*, pars. 21, 36, 41.

lead to more radical options for redistribution, if not a cataclysmic collapse of all political and economic structures. There could then be no resources or rights realistically available for anyone.

Personal and social renewal

The ethic being appealed for requires an outlook on life significantly different to that contained within the creeds of liberal individualism. At the same time it affirms the democratic right and the ability of all people to share in the shaping of society; something often denied ordinary citizens within centrally controlled collectivist societies, ruled by a political elite. It is an ethic which is grounded in a vision of humanity within which each will no longer be responsible solely for him or herself. For this to happen the will and identity of people will need radically to be transformed. It is this that ultimately links a theological–ethical understanding of human rights to a theology of redemption and renewal.

Human rights are seen theologically to be a specific and concrete response to the gospel message which offers life in the midst of suffering and death. 'Sin' is a descriptive word used in the Bible to identify a perversion of people's relationships with God, with one another and with the natural world of which they are an inherent part. It involves living a life of enmity, of violation and inhumanity. It is the incapacity to be truly human.[16] The gospel message of redemption, restoration and renewal, in turn, affirms the essential values which constitute true humanity. Addressing essentially a Reformed audience *The Option for Inclusive Democracy: A Theological–Ethical Study of Appropriate Social Values for South Africa* insists that a programme of human rights is necessary *because of sin*. Sin destroys our perception of who we are, resulting in 'theories and attitudes of superiority, arrogance and elitism'.[17] Reconciliation with God

---

[16] Moltmann, 'The Original Study Paper', in A. Miller (ed.), *A Christian Declaration* p. 139.

[17] Bernard Lategan, Johann Kinghorn, Lourens du Plessis, Etienne de Villers, *The Option for Inclusive Democracy: A Theological–Ethical Study of Appropriate Social Values for South Africa* (Stellenbosch: Centre for Hermeneutics, Stellenbosch University, 1987), pp. 4, 15, 19.

involves accepting the claim of God on one's life. But this can be little more than homiletical appeal if it is not translated into cultural, legal and structural controls and incentives designed to order our lives. At best, under the continuing challenge of the gospel, these structures can become part of the process of renewing, transforming and redirecting personal and social goals.

Commitment and critique

At the centre of theological social ethics is what has earlier been defined as a tension between the drive of the human spirit toward a goal that is worthy of absolute commitment, and an awareness that what in one context is regarded as worthy of such commitment can in another be seen as a reactionary ideology. The affirmation of individual bourgeois rights in the wake of the American and French Revolutions was a progressive step forward (which many within the churches refused to support, hankering after the ecclesial-aristocracy of the past). To affirm these rights in an *exclusive* manner in the present global context, to the neglect of the social and economic demands of the poor would, however, be a part of a reactionary political agenda, which Christians living in obedience to the gospel can scarcely afford to support.

The challenge central to the theological debate on human rights is how to inject a sense of religious zeal into the attainment of human rights capable of being met in a particular context, without suggesting that these rights are necessarily absolute ends in themselves, worthy of uncritical and universal support in all situations for all times. To emphasise the absolute ideals of the gospel over against the limited and relative nature of the human rights debate can distract from the need for immediate commitment to the needs of people which are being met by such relative rights. Unquestioned theological support for a particular political programme can, on the other hand, result in a form of legitimisation for these particular rights which restricts a growing sensitivity towards the changing needs of people within the context of ever-changing socio-economic and political structures. The basis of effective theological–ethical social commitment is to be worked out within the tension between an immediate (near absolute) commitment to what is humanly the best programme possible in a given situation – what John Bennett called 'the next step that our generation needs to take' and an enduring commitment to renewal and transformation.[18] This is a tension that requires all human rights proposals to be theologically dealt with *constructively* and *critically* to ensure the very best immediate affirmation of human dignity, regardless of whether the particular proposal orginates from theological or secular sources.[19]

The gospel is good news in a concrete situation. This requires theology to focus human endeavour on the specific needs of a particular society. Its task does not, however, end here. It is relentlessly to discern within the context of the struggle for human rights what the gospel of love means beyond these rights. It is this that makes the gospel an ally of any regime which promotes the interests of the poor, while at the same time being the harbinger of critique that keeps alive the highest ideals of the revolution of the poor.

A NEW VISION OF HUMANITY

A theological–ethical study of human rights is ultimately about a vision of what society can become. By holding up a vision of a transformed society it constantly challenges the existing order to become more than it is at any given time. The church does so by proclaiming the stories which form part of its heritage in relation to the ever-changing demands of society.

A communal vision

This is a heritage which proclaims a message about human nature which provides an alternative to both western notions of individualism and ideological Marxist perceptions of collecti-

---

[18] John Bennett, *Christian Ethics and Social Policy* (New York: Charles Scribners' Sons, 1946), pp. 76–7. See also the discussion in the Introduction to this volume.
[19] LWF, p. 13.

vism. It at the same time affirms such truths which stand central to these traditions which are too frequently overlooked. From a western human rights perspective the idea of individual freedom is far from isolationist. The right to freedom of assembly, association, franchise, language, culture and religion are all 'associational individual rights'. The Marxist concern for socio-economic rights, such as the right to food, shelter and housing, is at the same time a concern for the right of all individuals to participate in society in solidarity with others.

Despite the failure of communist constitutions in the Soviet Union and elsewhere to limit the power of the state over the individual, these constitutions do, in principle, allow for certain individual rights. A reading of the constitutions of the Soviet Union and the People's Republic of China are enough to make the point.[20] There are at the same time, suggests Henkin, certain significant differences between these constitutions and those of western democracies. The former take the form of a manifesto (rather than law) which presupposes individual rights being subject to the political will of the state as perceived by the political elite, whereas western constitutional law is a higher form of law which protects the individual against the state.[21] This important difference aside, both traditions (in principle) allow for individual and communal or associational rights, suggesting a measure of common ground that is often overlooked in comparative constitutional studies.

The message contained in the biblical vision of society is a message concerning the individual worth and dignity of all people, *realised in community with others*. More specifically, it is a heritage grounded in the story of people who are the focus of God's special care, despite their lowly and despised status in the world – whether they be slaves in Egypt, the poor of Israel, widows, orphans, the sick or the oppressed of society.

Jesus' parable of the lost sheep is often interpreted in western society within the context of extreme individualism to stress the concern of the shepherd for the individual sheep, seemingly at the cost of neglecting the other ninety-nine (Luke 15:3-7). In middle eastern (and other communal) contexts the parable is

[20] Henkin, *The Rights of Man*, pp. 61–78.   [21] *Ibid.*, p. 70.

viewed differently. It focuses as much on the incompleteness of the flock of ninety-nine as it does on the return of the one lost sheep.

The people of God must be aware of the solidarity of the true community; if one organ suffers, they all suffer together. If one flourishes, they all flourish together (I Cor 12:26). It is in the sense of such a community that all people of God must realize their oneness with humankind and must mobilize all their energies, so that all people and every stratum of human society may regain and keep their human dignity.[22]

There can, within this ethic, be no healing or sense of completion in the individual without the restoration of health, purpose and security of the entire community. At the same time the individual cannot experience the restoration of health, purpose, security or fulfilment outside of the community. Biblical teaching on creation similarly shows that it is only in fellowship with other people that the image of God is fully realised (Gen. 1:28). Affirming a similar communal ethic of existence, an African understanding of humanity is summed up in the axiom: 'I am because we are, and because we are therefore I am.'[23]

The dominant western, libertarian, individualistic understanding of humanity (seen in the American *Bill of Rights*, the *Rights of Man* included in the French constitution and, to a lesser extent, in sections of the *Universal Declaration of Human Rights* read in isolation from the entire text) stands in contradiction to this emphasis. In these declarations the rights of individuals all too often in reality means the rights of *some* individuals at the cost of other individuals. In socialist countries, while recognising that the rights to work, to minimum levels of nutrition and housing cannot be enforced against the state, the social culture has at the same time been such that it is has been recognised that individual choice and related individual rights are an abstraction (and evasion of moral responsibility) if not grounded in economic and social security. Despite the failures of Soviet and

---

[22] The Lutheran Church in Hungary, *In Christ – A New Community* (1977), included in Lissner and Sovik (eds.), *A Lutheran Reader*, p. 31.

[23] John S. Mbiti, *African Religions and Philosophy* (New York: Doubleday, 1970), p. 141.

Eastern European socialism, this cultural gain is something that should not be easily turned away from in a theological understanding of human rights. A similar distinction characterises the debate between the North and South. The northern debate takes place within a prior commitment to political and economic freedom of choice. The southern debate is often the other way around. Here freedom of choice is regarded as realistically obtainable for the majority of the population only if and when the basic requirements of nutrition, housing, health care and basic education are provided.

Declarations and study documents on human rights, which emerge from ecclesial situations where the various global constituencies are adequately represented (reflecting the concerns of East and West as well as North and South) often include both liberal individualistic and socialist, collectivist ideals. This prompts debate on the need to decide which of the apparently contradictory rights (the freedom of choice or the right to food) are the most important. By simply 'adding' rights to the growing list of declared rights, the appeal from Iredell Jenkins and others (as discussed in Chapter 3) for an integrated theory of rights continues to be left without attention.

John XXIII's challenge in *Pacem in Terris*, issued at the time of Vatican II begins to address this need. Turning away from the earlier Catholic model of society grounded in western values and defended on the basis that it supposedly corresponds to the demands of natural law, he emphasised a social ethic within all social systems, and indeed the international order itself, is held accountable to the demands of the gospel.[24] Paul VI, taking this a step further, explicitly stated that the basis of Christian engagement in the political economy 'is above and sometimes opposed to the ideologies' and is 'beyond every system' whether capitalism, socialism, liberalism or Marxism.[25] And in *On Social Concern* (as already shown), John Paul II stresses the need for theological critique of the ideologies of both West and East.

---

[24] John XXIII, *Pacem in Terris*, Nos 9–27 in Joseph Gremillion (ed.), *The Gospel of Peace and Justice: Catholic Social Teaching Since Pope John* (Maryknoll: Orbis Books, 1976). See also Hollenbach, *Claims in Conflict*, pp. 62–9, 89–100.

[25] Pope Paul VI, *Octogesima Adveniens*, Nos. 27, 36, in Gremillion (ed.), *The Gospel*, pp. 498, 501.

Lutheran theology, while recognising that politics and economics are necessarily an exercise in compromise, similarly recognises that this is an exercise to be engaged in in the light of the gospel – which impinges on all 'temporal' solutions in both grace and judgment. Evangelical Reformed theology similarly affirms a gospel critique of all socio-economic and political proposals as a continuing incentive to renewal. In effect what is being called for is a constructive theory of rights designed to integrate the seemingly contradictory demands of East, West, North and South.

The WARC study comes close to doing this in locating the human rights debate in a biblical anthropology grounded in the Genesis myth. The *African Charter on Human and Peoples' Rights*, in turn, provides a useful example of a non-western focus on a communal understanding of human rights.[26] It is a useful catalyst for considering an alternative approach to human rights, despite the criticism levelled against it from both western and African perspectives. Olusola Ojo and Amadu Sesay, for example, in assessing Africa's record on human rights, conclude that the Charter is ultimately too state-centric, leaving the Commission on Human and Peoples' Rights (proposed in the Charter) without enforcement power and 'peoples' rights' sufficiently undefined to legitimate the violation of individual rights.[27] Others have, in turn, asked to what extent the western biases of contemporary international human rights instruments address the social and cultural needs of peoples from non-western cultures.[28] In relating western and African notions of humanity in a cross-cultural study Josiah Cobbah, on the other hand, discerns important African communal insights within the Charter that function as an important corrective to western

---

[26] Adopted by the Organisation of African Unity in Nairobi, Kenya, 27 June 1981. It is reprinted in *International Legal Material*, 21:58, 1982.

[27] Olusola Ojo and Amadu Sesay, 'The OAU and Human Rights: Prospects for the 1980s and Beyond', *Human Rights Quarterly*, 8:1, 1986.

[28] Dunstan M. Wai, 'Human Rights in Sub-Saharan Africa', in Adamantia Pollis and Peter Schwab (eds.), *Human Rights: Cultural and Ideological Perspectives* (New York: Praeger, 1979); Jack Donnelly, 'Human Rights and Human Dignity: An Analytic Critique of Non-Western Conceptions of Human Rights', *American Political Science Review*, 76, June 1982.

individualism.[29] The growing concern on the social democratic side of liberal scholarship to broaden the liberal tradition to include communal concerns, can only be enriched by both biblical and African insights.

Liberal individualism, emerging largely in reaction to medieval feudalism, resulted in the western understanding of persons able to draw a sharp distinction between 'natural duties not to harm others and minimally altruistic acts' on the one hand, and 'so called supererogatory acts of benevolence and mercy, of heroism and self-sacrifice' on the other.[30] This is a tradition within which people in need are dealt with at the level of charity, with the person exercising charity being insulated from direct communal responsibility for the person in need. It lacks an incarnational emphasis which requires solidarity and acceptance of communal responsibility and accountability. Biblical, African and other communal cultures are different – all people (both the strong who can contribute and the weak in need) are part of a community which carries within it an obligation to regard individual successes and failures as inescapably the successes and failures of the entire community, to be shared in, and responded to, by the community.

A further consequence of the emergence of liberal ideals in the wake of the collapse of feudalism under the weight of industrial capitalism and urbanisation in the seventeenth and eighteenth centuries was the disappearance of, or increasingly limited role played in society by, intermediary agencies such as medieval towns, guilds, community structures and religious groups. This has often resulted in what James Luther Adams has referred to as the 'atomistic individual' seeking to confront the all-encompassing power of the state, leaving limited institutional space for realistic dissent, the development of democratic skills or a social basis for participatory democracy.[31] A retroactive approach to

---

[29] Josiah A.M. Cobbah, 'African Values and the Human Rights Debate: An African Perspective', *Human Rights Quarterly*, 9:3, 1987. I am indebted to Cobbah in the argument that follows.

[30] Edward Allen Kent, 'Taking Human Rights Seriously', in Martin Tammy and K.D. Irani (eds.), *Rationality in Thought and Action*. (New York: Greenwood Press, 1986), p. 38.

[31] James Luther Adams, *Voluntary Associations (Socio-Cultural Analyses and Theological Interpretation* (Chicago: Exploration Press, 1986).

human rights, one which learns from the lessons of history, is obliged to weigh the effects of this development. The arm of the state has reached deep into South African life, as it has done in many other oppressive societies. The suppression of academic freedom and control of educational institutions, interference in religious autonomy, the control of trade unions, the restricting of civic and community organisations and the manipulation of local government has virtually destroyed all sense of accessible intermediary structures through which individuals can organise themselves and give expression to their goals and needs. The structures of civil society, between government and people, were virtually eliminated.

Emerging democracies need to be constitutionally protected from the haunting possibility of this kind of all-powerful state ever again emerging in the future.[32] The protection of First Generation type individual rights are probably not sufficient to limit government to its proper sphere of interest. The right to local, community, workplace and other forms of organising is an essential part of democracy. It is a key ingredient to the 'balancing' of individual and communal rights. Significantly, the influential study on the church's role in nation-building in India, published a little more than decade after independence in that country, stressed the need for limiting state power in the economic, social, educational and cultural fields. Accepting the difficulty involved in identifying the exact time and place for such limits, the study declares:

While State planning is essential for rapid social development, there are grave dangers to responsible citizenship when State initiative oversteps the proper limits.[33]

The isolated individual is simply unable to stand up against the power of economic barons and bosses in the private sector or the all-powerful state at the political level. Frug, in an article on the declining influence of the city in modern politics, traces the way in which this process reduced modern notions of community

---

[32] See Van der Vyver, 'Constitutional Guidelines of the African National Congress', *South African Journal of Human Rights*, 5, p. 141.

[33] M.M. Thomas, *Christian Participation in Nation-Building*, p. 8.

to the 'sum of its individual members', giving rise to an abstract 'fictional person', required to live directly subject to the state.[34] To the extent that no individual is capable of effectively resisting state power without organised communal support, the destruction of an intermediary community marks the beginning of the loss of effective democracy and a consequent loss of influence by ordinary people over their own affairs. It is a social and psychological malady of significance, subtly affecting increasingly larger sections of modern society.

Hegel's earlier corrective to the abstraction of humanity has, for a variety of reasons, either gone unnoticed or simply not been taken with sufficient seriousness in liberal philosophy and politics.[35] Lewis Hinchmann shows how liberal philosophers came to imagine that the 'essential' person could be found by peeling away the layers of society and culture:

leaving aside everything contingent until, finally, one comes by analysis to the abstraction called natural man.

If one thinks away everything which might even remotely be regarded as particular or evanescent, such as what pertains to particular mores, history, culture or even the state, then all that remains is man imagined as in the state of nature or else the pure abstraction of man with only his essential possibilities.

. . . In 'taking apart' existing society, studying its 'parts', then reconstructing it, Hobbes and Locke have left something out – not something accidental, but the very essence of man's social and political relationships. For this reason their project of grounding human rights in man's pre-political state appeared to Hegel fundamentally mistaken . . .[36]

Leaving the details of Hegel's argument aside, it is enough to show that his critique of liberalism relocates humanity within a communal and cultural context, opening the way for a different way of understanding people – not as beings fulfilled in abstraction and isolation from others, but in fulfilment of their

---

[34] Gerald E. Frug 'The City as a Legal Concept', *Harvard Law Review*, 93, April 1980, p. 1086.

[35] Pinkard, *Democratic Liberalism*, pp. xv-xix. Also Lewis P. Hinchman, 'The Origins of Human Rights: A Hegelian Perspective', *Western Political Quarterly*, 37, March 1984.

[36] Hinchman, *Ibid.*, p. 17. His argument is developed in Cobbah, 'African values'.

identity and selfhood in relation to others. The focus of the critique is made all the more urgent by global political trends that stress the inescapable collective nature of our society and the need to develop more adequate ideological and social structures within which to realise the individual and social needs of contemporary people.

Within this context the African world view emerges as a striking alternative to western individualism. It is at the same time an alternative to ideologies that reduce people to by-products of social and economic forces. This is what makes Cobbah's assessment of the African model so revealing. Individual development and aspirations, he reminds us, are tempered in traditional African society by the needs of the community. He shows the extended family unit and village membership to function as an intermediary between the individual and the state. Each member of these intermediary groupings is endowed by their respective groups with certain rights and responsibilities. At the centre of this membership is *reciprocity*. When someone is in need the community shares the burden, and when someone succeeds it is the community that benefits. Biblical freedom, as already shown, is similarly limited. It is subject to communion with God and the community of other people whose God-given responsibility is also to be free. Personal freedom is only freedom within a free community, and no person is truly free until everyone is free. Although difficult if not impossible legally to enforce, the cultural importance of communal reciprocity is a concept to be promoted rather than minimised in human rights legislation.

The right to choose is inherent to being human. (This cultural/theological emphasis has, of course, important implications for the political decentralisation of state power. It also has significance at an economic level for overcoming the dominant centre–periphery structures which enrich cities at the expense of rural areas.) An incorrect or selfish choice is disruptive to the community, and this ultimately results in the location not only of power, but also of the fullness of humanity in the hands of the few. This, theologically speaking, is sin. The long-term effects of this kind of choice are, enmity, violence and ultimately death – the destruction of oneself, others and life itself (Rom. 6). To choose correctly in response to God's grace is to choose life (Jn. 10:10), which is free from egotism and the domination of others.[37]

This ultimately involves more than a social programme. It is a world view. It means that one's outlook on life and sense of meaning is shaped by being in community with other people – not only the living, but also former members of the living community and generations not yet born. Within this broad sense of community identity and responsibility, western type individual rights, such as the absolute freedom of choice and the right to exclusive forms of dissent, simply make little sense because they isolate the individual from the community.

The psychological and spiritual implications of this understanding of life are extensive. Michael and Lise Wallach show, for example, the extent to which nineteenth-century egocentric Freudian assumptions about the 'healthy self' which continue to influence western psychology should be seen as a counterpart to liberal political ideals. The individual psyche is perceived, they suggest, to be 'a little like the way free market conservatives view the economy . . . We just let everyone do their own thing.'[38] The psychological solution is to rid ourselves of burdensome external stimulation, while exploiting whatever in our environment supports our internal needs. Of course, not all western psychologists share this bias. There is little doubt, however, that individualism has penetrated the social sciences to the point where liberal individualistic analyses and predictions have become self-fulfilling prophecies. And theological notions of humanity and salvation have, under the influence of liberalism and a free-market economy, very definitely come to incorporate non-biblical, individualistic and privatised notions of the self.[39]

African communal ethics has, needless to say, its set of limitations much like any other ethical philosophy. Political elites in Africa have used the African world view to 'mask

[37] Lategan *et al. The Option for Inclusive Democracy*, pp. 10–11.
[38] Michael Wallach and Lise Wallach, 'How Psychology Sanctions the Cult of Self', *The Washington Monthly*, 16, February 1985, p. 49.
[39] C. Villa-Vicencio, 'Protestantism, Modernity and Justification by Faith', *Scottish Journal of Theology*, 38, 1985.

systematic violations of human rights in the interest of the ruling class'.[40] But then the colonial elite at home and abroad have often also abused their highest values as an excuse to exploit the poor. Cobbah is correct. A mutual learning experience needs to take place as a basis for nurturing a human rights culture that does justice to what it means to be human.

The biblical notions of covenant and *koinonia* (community) presuppose by definition the sharing of all people in community building. The body of Christ presupposes the creativity and participation of all people, including the most lowly, in the creation of a community which signifies the presence of Christ in the world (I Cor. 12).

At its most profound, human existence-in-relationship-and-participation is a mirror of God, revealing God as the Word. In His Word God communicates with the world. Furthermore, in the Word made flesh, God participates in the world. Thus community between God and human beings is established, as well as between people themselves. And how could it be otherwise? God Himself is the eternal *relationship* of Father, Son and Holy Spirit; the eternal *communion* of the trinity. It is this God in Whose image all people have been created and in Whose image all people are continuously called to be renewed.[41]

A universal vision

A limited and regional sense of community is important. To love one's neighbour requires relating to those in one's immediate environment (those to whom one has immediate access) in a loving, caring and socially responsible manner. A theological perception of human rights must, however, necessarily be more inclusive. It must give expression to a sense of belonging to a family or community of people that transcends national, sexual, racial and class barriers. Human rights extend to all of humanity.

For the Christian this is a familiar *doctrinal* notion, but one that is not often given practical expression within the context of western individualism. By baptism people are said to be

---

[40] Rhoda Howard, 'Evaluating Human Rights in Africa: Some Problems of Implicit Comparisons', *Human Rights Quarterly*, 6, May, 1984, p. 175. Also Cobbah, *African Values*, p. 326.   [41] Lategan *inter alia*, *The Option for Inclusive Democracy*, p. 7.

incorporated into the one Body of Christ. We are called to bind ourselves in community (*koinonia*) with one another as an expression of our mutual care and strengthening of one another. 'Here there is neither Jew nor Greek, neither bond nor free, neither male nor female; for you are all one in Christ Jesus.' (Gal. 3:28). By analogy and in anticipation of this intimate union a theological reflection on human rights must stress the *universal* nature of human rights. In affirmation of God's love for all of humanity, and Christ's death for the entire world, Christians are obliged to love their neighbours as themselves. This is a teaching that brings Jews and Samaritans and others who live in enmity with one another to the point where they are obliged to recognise the essential needs of all human beings.

This has far-reaching implications for international relations at, for example, a time of war and conflict. At the very least it obliges Christians to support the Geneva Convention (1949) and the two subsequent 1977 Geneva Protocols which prohibit 'direct intentional attacks on non-combatants and non-military targets', arguing for the banning of nuclear arms and the seeking to prohibit torture. In brief a theological–ethical affirmation of human rights insists that it is necessary to love one's enemies in the sense of treating them in the very best possible way. It also has major implications for world hunger and the global economy. The US Catholic Bishops in *Economic Justice for All*, for example, affirm an inter-dependency between nations which 'eliminates the scandal of the shocking inequality between the rich and the poor', over against a world order within which developing nations are thrust into economic dependency on industrial nations.[42] In recognising the need for a revision of the global economy the US Catholic Bishops write: 'We call for a US international economic policy designed to empower people everywhere and enable them to continue to develop a sense of their own worth, improve the quality of their lives, and ensure that the benefits of economic growth are shared equitably.'[43] As

---

[42] US Catholic Bishops, *Economic Justice for All: Pastoral Letter on Catholic Social Teaching and the US Economy* (Washington DC: National Conference of Catholic Bishops, 1986, pars. 252, 253.   [43] *Ibid.*, par. 292.

members of an Eastern European dependent nation, Christians in Hungary make the same point in a more forceful manner.

The equal implementation of equal human rights is rendered impossible by the unjust political, economic, social and cultural differences and conflicts which mark the present world situation of mankind. In the course of historical development not only individuals but whole social strata and peoples have been put to disadvantage against privileged classes, groups and capitalistic interests. For this reason, even on the basis of equal rights, they are not in the position to exercise their human rights in the same and equal manner. On the contrary, on the basis of the principle of equal rights, these social, economic and cultural differences and inequalities, because of the existing differences, instead of being reduced, are actually growing.[44]

A universal vision of human rights, which includes a willingness to address the major structural implications involved, is ultimately the only basis on which Second and Third Generation human rights claims can be adequately considered as a viable part of the human rights agenda.

Needless to say, a universal vision of human rights extends to all people irrespective of race, sex or creed. Given the structures of patriarchal subjugation which characterise contemporary society, it is not out of place to quote here the first article of the *Women's Charter*:

. . . any distinction, exclusion or restriction made on the basis of sex which has the effect or purpose of impairing or nullifying the recognition, enjoyment or exercise by women, irrespective of their marital status on a basis of equality of men and women, of human rights and fundamental freedoms in the political, economic, social cultural, civil or any other field.[45]

In human rights law as in the Christian faith women, however, experience a vast gap between theory and praxis. To quote Denise Ackermann:

It is not surprising that the Church which, on the one hand, affirms the humanity of all as made in the image of God, and on the other hand discriminates against women by denying them full participation in its body at many levels, should, with equal facility, proclaim the values of

[44] 'In Christ – a New Community', in Lissner and Souik (eds.), *A Lutheran Reader*, p. 32.
[45] *Convention on the Elimination of All Forms of Discrimination Against Women*, Article 1.

the reign of God as embodied in the person of Jesus and yet not become involved in the visible practice of these values.[46]

The struggle for human rights at a universal level – extending beyond national borders as well as sexual and racial barriers – is difficult to promote because those discriminated against are often hopelessly under-represented in the body politic. 'We will have to use particular strategies in order to enforce human rights at all levels.'[47] The challenge awaiting the church at this level is extensive. Its work has scarcely begun.

'The image of God', suggests the WARC study, 'is human beings *with* others.'[48] This has significant implications for global politics. The wisdom of this statement needs to be further extended to read, 'the image of God is human beings with others in harmony with nature'.

An ecological vision

A biblical understanding of redemption which restores humankind to harmony with God, making the image of God visible within humanity, is a harmony necessarily manifest and realised only in harmony with others and all of creation. It involves relocating people in their rightful place between God and the natural order. From a perspective of classical theology it anticipates Irenaeus' (Pauline) sense of *recapitulatio* – a recapitulation of the whole of creation to its given order. Theologically this has significant and far-reaching ecological and environmental implications.

The Genesis story sees humankind as a part of the whole creation, requiring women and men to cultivate and care for the earth (Gen 2:15). Dominion over the earth (Gen 1:26) is, in turn, to be exercised by a human race living in harmony with nature. Humankind's God-given dignity, suggests the LWF report, 'obliges [us] to order and maintain the earth for

---

[46] Denise Ackermann 'Women, Human Rights and Religion – a Dissonant Triad'. A paper read at a conference 'Religion in the New South Africa' held at Natal University in September 1991. [47] *Ibid.*
[48] Moltmann, 'The Original Study Paper', in A. Miller (ed.), *A Christian Declaration*, pp. 132. Italics added.

everything living around us also and only to make use of [our] rights in accordance with the life needs of all nature so that the biosphere remains unharmed'.[49] The whole of creation, we are told in the New Testament, 'is groaning in the pains of childbirth' (Rom. 8:22), waiting for the restoration of its integrity. Human beings have a responsibility to share in this process. To plunder and destroy nature is to destroy God's creation. It is also to destroy the possibility of the fullness of human life, and possibly life itself. Because human rights are about what is essential to life, the protection of the earth is such a right.

A similar understanding of humankind's place in the world has, of course, been affirmed with great beauty in native American spirituality. Attuned to nature's rhythm, it challenges the practice of western Christians to rediscover the vision of the scriptures for people to live in harmony with nature. The words of Chief Luther Standing Bear, of the Lakota Indians, makes the point.

[Our] life was attuned to nature's rhythm – bound in mystical ties to the sun, moon and stars; to the waving grasses, flowing streams and whispering winds . . .

The Indian and the white man sense things differently because the white man has put distance between himself and nature; and assuming a lofty place in the scheme of order of things has lost both reverence and understanding . . . And here I find a great distinction between the faith of the Indian and the white man. Indian faith sought the harmony of man with his surroundings; the other sought the dominance of surroundings . . . For one man the world was full of beauty; for the other it was a place of sin and ugliness to be endured until he went to another world.[50]

World-wide environmental concern has, at the same time, become almost the exclusive concern of the more affluent sectors of society. A challenging article makes the point in the glossy Journal of the Botanical Society of South Africa: 'Environmentalists are seen to place the needs of animals above those of the

[49] LWF, p. 24.
[50] Quoted in John Hart, *The Spirit of the Earth: A Theology of the Land* (New York: Paulist Press, 1984), p. 50.

poor.'[51] Printed in the article is the observation of a black person suffering the effects of apartheid:

If I never hear a word about the black rhino and its preservation again, it will be too soon. Here's the country in a mess and all that can be done is to collect *maꞔhepha* [papers] to preserve an animal that to me is as useless as the dinosaur . . . That's the trouble with some people in this land of the Great Divide: they have their priorities upside down. I know that animal life is important for the balance of nature, but for heaven's sake, when the Wildlife Society can find R60,000 to donate to the Save the Rhino Fund, then I ask myself who is cock-eyed.[52]

Albie Sachs makes a pertinent point: 'You do not have to be white to be green.'[53] Conservation is more than a bourgeois concern, it is an essential part of Third Generation rights as they apply to survival, development and empowerment of the poor.

It might appear irreverent to speak of the Maluti mountains and the rolling bushveld when blood is being spilt on our roadways; it would seem inappropriate to lament chimney pollution when the air is thick with teargas. People who have washing machines have no right to condemn others who dirty streams with their laundry; those who summon up energy with a click of a switch should hesitate before denouncing persons who denude forests in search of firewood. It is undeniably distasteful to spend huge sums on saving the white rhino when millions of black children are starving.[54]

Recognising the healing that needs to occur in South Africa, environmental ethics must be located at the centre of the struggle for social reconstruction. The right to unpolluted water, fertile land, safe lighting and environmentally friendly fuel for heat and cooking are rights which are existentially better understood by the poor in townships, squatter camps, 'homelands', 'native reserves' and ghettoes in Third World and degenerated First World cities, than they are by many wealthy and middle-class environmentalists. Those who cling to the margins of the major industrial cities, shut out from their political, economic and social life, can ultimately be enabled to understand the significance of clean air, adequate sewerage, the

[51] Farieda Khan, 'Involvement of the Masses in Environment Politics', *Veld and Flora*, 76:20, June, 1990.   [52] *Ibid.*   [53] Albie Sachs, *Protecting Human Rights*, p. 139.
[54] *Ibid.* pp. 139–40.

proper disposal of waste and adequate drainage, because the very lives of their children are put at risk by these violations. The poor also know that these are issues that cannot be dealt with apart from serious socio-economic and political reform.

The ecological challenge as it relates to socio-economic and political development is perhaps the major issue on the global human rights agenda. It is scarcely an exaggeration to say that the present generation has merely borrowed the land, water and environment it uses from generations yet to be born. An inclusive vision of reality, as seen in native American and traditional African world views, as well as in a biblical focus on the harmony of God's creation, provides a cultural and spiritual incentive which contemporary society can scarcely afford to ignore.

An inclusive vision

A theological understanding of humanity necessitates a broad and inclusive understanding of human rights. Human rights, as the essential conditions which create space within which human beings are able to be fully human and realise their God-given potential, necessarily include the right to life, which presupposes food, shelter, health-care and housing. Life with dignity and purpose, in turn, means the opportunity to participate fully in the affairs of life as a means toward both acquiring the material essentials for life, as well as a means of being a person called to share with God in the creation and recreation of the world of which we are all a part. This presupposes the right to work, education, freedom of speech, the right to assembly and the freedom to dissent. A theological vision of the fullness of life lived in harmony with the natural order further includes the right of access to water, land and an unpolluted environment, without which the future of life on this planet can only become less complete and less conforming to the harmony with which it was once endowed. In brief, all the major theological studies on human rights affirm the right of all human beings to those goods necessary for subsistence and a decent minimum standard of living which protects human dignity (and not merely survival).

Inclusive, all-encompassing concepts of human rights can, as already noted, be dismissed as utopian ideals that do more harm than good to the struggle for a limited, realistic, justiciable notion of human rights. Fanie Jacobs, a Conservative Party member of the South African parliament and a former Professor of Constitutional Law gives expression to this concern in an aggressive manner:

I would like to point to such legally ridiculous provisions as the right that resources be diverted from richer to poorer areas; the right to freedom from hunger, the right to shelter, the right to health and the right to work.

How on earth could one enforce a justiciable right to work against the State when there is widespread joblessness, or the right to health when Aids cannot be cured? The practical application ... will put such strain on the financial and economic resources of any State that it will be financially impossible to implement and enforce them.[55]

Is the theological vision of an inclusive doctrine of human rights then no more than an apocalyptic vision or what Jeremy Bentham called 'nonsense – nonsense on stilts': a set of wishes rather than rights?[56] To this question we return.

A PASTORAL IMPERATIVE

The prophetic proclamation of the church on human rights is imperative. The theological development of human rights objectives is important. A pastoral ministry, structured and designed to realise these goals is, however, indispensable. Without a programme of ministry which translates words into actions, the wise and brave words of prophets and martyrs can be no more than rhetoric. This suggests that the theorising of theologians can be of even less significance!

Within a culture of individualism and self-indulgence, the cost of such a pastoral ministry is inevitably high. Society has become more or less immune to the prophetic words of turbulent

---

[55] Fanie Jacobs, 'What About the Afrikaner?' A review of Albie Sachs' *Protecting Human Rights in a New South Africa* and the ANC's *Draft Bill of Rights* in *Monitor*, December, 1990.

[56] Jeremy Bentham, 'Anarchical Fallacies', in Frederick A. Olafson (ed.), *Society, Law and Morality* p. 347.

priests and accustomed to the high ecclesial ideals found in synod, assembly and conference resolutions. A carefully planned pastoral programme, designed in co-operation with other agencies committed to social transformation based on human rights for people dehumanised by the structures of society, is more difficult to ignore.

A pastoral programme designed to teach people to love one another, respect the human dignity of all people and accept the claim of God on the lives of all people, requiring all people to participate in the shaping of society on a basis of equality and mutual respect must be a priority for the church in the period of reconstruction.

There is a sense in which the context for this ministry is outlined by the papal encyclical, *On Social Concern*, which draws attention to the sinful social structures which shape and influence the attitudes of contemporary people, causing their lives to be conformed to captivating ideologies of power and wealth. The details of a pastoral plan are beyond the confines of this book. Suffice it to say that the call to conversion, which stands central to pastoral ministry 'entails [in the words of the encyclical] a [new] relationship to God, to the sin committed, to its consequences and to one's neighbour'.[57] In other words, pastoral ministry involves commitment to the creation of a social order within which people are judged as people and all people are afforded their essential rights which enable them to live with dignity. In the words of the LWF declaration: 'Human Rights cannot be realised unless social conditions and political structures are justly ordered at the same time.' These structures create 'conditions which lead to innumerable violations of human rights'.[58] The espousing of equal rights within a structurally unjust context is an ineffectual mechanism for promoting the cause of the disadvantaged. More than that, it works in the favour of the strong and powerful to the extent that it supposes that the promotion of human dignity is realistically possible within unjust structures.[59]

[57] *On Social Concern*, par. 38.   [58] LWF, p. 11.
[59] This point is made in the study of human rights by the Lutheran Church in Hungary, 'In Christ – A New Community' in Lissner and Sovik (eds.), *A Lutheran Reader* p. 30.

The burden of *On Social Concern* is that social structures which are motivated exclusively by the twin ideologies of power and profit work against the creation of a just society. The implication is clear. If the church is to take its ministry of pastoral care seriously, it is to share in the process of transforming the dominant socio-economic and political structures of society into more caring and humanising structures. Simply stated, to the extent that structures shape lives and social relations which are not in accordance with the values of the gospel, the transformation of structures is part of the pastoral and evangelical task of the church.

Pastoral concern, in addition to all else, requires the church to share in the struggle for a political economy which ensures the basic requirements for the well-being and functioning of people as free and responsible citizens, able to fulfil their God-given mandate to restore society to its creative purpose. What this means in practice is determined by each different situation. Within a world of limited resources and more especially in western society (which has come to emphasise the right of individuals to possess goods in an unqualified manner) there are, however, certain general challenges facing the church which include the process of facilitating the redistribution and reallocation of basic resources. This means teaching people that the distribution of certain essential goods (for example: food, housing and health care) to all people has in the contemporary world acquired a God-given priority over the absolute right to private property and luxury goods, to the extent that the latter militates against the right of all people to essential goods. While the means of accomplishing this goal are to be worked out (democratically) by each particular society, the task of the church is to contribute towards the creation of a 'popular will' as a basis for this to happen. And in capitalist societies within which the notion of the private ownership of property has become synonymous with personal freedom, this task includes a special moral responsibility to redefine the purpose and function of property in society. The private ownership of property was intended within the evolution of western values as a means of protecting the right to human self-determination and security, while the accumulation of property as an end in itself has come to violate the self-determination and security of an ever increasing number of people.

Recognising, however, (in affirmation of Niebuhrian realism) that the popular will is rarely formed by moral appeal, a primary task of the church concerning human rights involves solidarity with the poor and the provision of theological and material resources as a basis for their empowerment.

More often than not, the powerful in society are able to ignore or circumvent legal instruments. Consequently, any wholistic strategy to protect and extend the human rights of individuals and groups of people involves also a redistribution of power which will enable the underprivileged to protect their human rights through the establishment of a 'balance of power'.[60]

The church is required in a situation of injustice, unequal distribution and political oppression to proclaim the biblical message of liberation in the most concrete terms possible. It is to restore human dignity to the oppressed and a sense of God-given worth to people who, as a result of generations of oppression, have come to allow their own self-perceptions to be shaped by the oppressor's imposition of the less than human categories of who they are. To quote Steve Biko:

All in all the black man has become a shell, a shadow of a man, completely defeated, drowning in his misery, a slave, an ox bearing the yoke of oppression with sheepish timidity . . . The first step therefore is to make the black man come to himself; to pump back life into his empty shell; to infuse him with pride and dignity; to remind him of his complicity in the crime of allowing himself to be misused and therefore letting evil reign in the country of his birth.[61]

Whether in the exodus, the ministry of the prophets or the message of Jesus, God's grace empowers people to rediscover a sense of God-given destiny. The contribution of liberation, black and feminist theologies in communicating this gospel to oppressed and marginalised people is simply immense. The gospel message, which proclaims healing to the broken-hearted, restores the sick and sets captives free in proclaiming an age

[60] LWF, p. 31.
[61] Steve Biko, *I Write What I Like* (London: SCM, 1984), p. 29.

within which justice and peace will dawn, is a gospel heard gladly by the oppressed and often vilified by those, inside and outside of the church, who are responsible for the oppression, or simply benefit from it. It is a gospel which renews and restores what has been denied to oppressed people by sinful people and destructive structures. It is a gospel which also casts the biblical notion of reconciliation in a new light. From the point of view of the oppressed, theological talk of reconciliation can only be understood in the context of self-empowerment. It is in removing the barriers that divide people (cultural, social and material) that reconciliation can realistically take place between the former oppressed and former oppressor.

The church, on the other hand, also has a pastoral obligation to share in the creation of a network of spiritual, psychological, moral and social incentives within which the people and groups who live above the socio-economic median in society can accept the need for diminishing their prospects, interests and even self-perceived rights as a means toward enabling those who are below the level of a decent living to fare better.[62] The economic details of this process are clearly beyond the limits of theology. There are, however, certain values central to a theological anthropology which have direct economic implications. The primary task of the church in this regard is to assist in creating a cultural and social space within which attention can realistically be given to various economic proposals. In assessing these proposals along with all other members of society, theologically the church is obliged to do so with a very specific question in mind: what will best serve the interests of the poor?

Revolution and political transition creates the possibility for change but offers no guarantees. A theology of nation-building is about making change possible. The gospel is about the creation of new people, fully human, living in harmony with the purposes of God for all God's people. This necessitates the creation of integrated structures designed to serve this end. In the same way that purely coercive means to redistribute wealth could produce economic stultification, to make the maximisation of profit the sole end of the political economy could have

[62] Langan, 'Personal Responsibility and the Common Good in John Paul 11', p. 18.

equally disastrous social effects. From a theological perspective, social planning is to take place within the context of all levels of human rights, with the resultant political, social and moral objectives being weighed alongside any economic goals.

A more comprehensive consideration of the encounter between theology and economics is undertaken in the next chapter. Suffice to say for the present, the economic future of most developing countries seems to be no more on track to doctrinaire socialism with centralised planning than it is locked into some form of rugged entrepreneurial individualism. It is more likely to develop along the lines of co-operative endeavours, through both state and non-state owned corporations in economically pluralistic societies, bound together both within nations and between nations on the basis of regional and global networks of trade. In brief the immediate to middle-term chances of anything other than a 'mixed economy' seem unlikely. Theological ideals ultimately, however, have more in common with a distribution of wealth based on socialist ideals than a free-enterprise system within which the strong devour the weak. Theological ideals have also more in common with democratic participatory forms of government than with governments controlled by elitist oligarchies or party machines. For a state to function at essentially a social and democratic level, there need to be certain entrenched constitutional clauses which militate against any one party, tribe or group at anytime grabbing economic or political power for itself. Theology, together with other formative culturally based disciplines, has a special task in sharing in the creation of a culture that serves these ends. It is to share in the creation of a culture of communal sharing and seek to establish incentives which engage people in the creation of a society which does not leave people divided between those who have too much and those who do not have enough.

WHICH RIGHTS WHEN?

The most important human rights are always those which are presently being violated, and the range of reported violations which make it to the media are extensive: newspaper censorship in Thailand, religious discrimination in Ethiopia, the violation of native Indian land rights in Canada, the homeless poor on the streets of American cities, gross neglect of safety precautions at the Chernobyl nuclear plant in the Soviet Union, six Jesuit priests, their housekeeper and her daughter executed by a death squad in El Salvador, routine political detentions in Zaire, children starving in Bangladesh, illiteracy in Sri Lanka, the demolition of Palestinian homes by Israeli soldiers, the destruction of an entire town in Syria, the absence of democracy and aftermath of war in the Persian Gulf, the death of political prisoners and opponents of apartheid in South Africa, the massacre of the Chinese students in Tiananmen Square.

Is human rights docrine expected to address all such atrocities? Are some human rights claims more important than others? How does one choose between claims? A central issue pertaining to these questions is *how to take human rights claims very seriously, without absolutising them.* This, as already noted, is a matter of special concern to theologians who stress the ethical and political importance of relativising all human endeavours before the divine absolute, as a basis for on-going political critique and heightened moral sensitivity. There is also a practical, procedural reason why not all human rights should necessarily be regarded as absolute in the sense of always being implemented without reservation in all situations.

If all human rights were to be regarded as absolute in this sense, the list of agreed rights would necessarily have to be limited, restricted and exclusive of most Second and Third Generation human rights. The argument is a simple one. Certain political or First Generation rights (the freedom of speech, the right to dissent and so on) *can* be protected by legislation and legal enforcement. The provision, for example, of nutritious food and social security for all citizens, on the other hand, requires more than legislation. These are dependent on sufficient food, an adequate economy, resources that most nations in the world simply do not have.[63] Is Iredell Jenkins' argument then not essentially correct? Ought human rights not

[63] Maurice Cranston, *What Are Human Rights?* (New York: Basic Books, 1962), p. 38.

to be restricted to those rights which can be met and enforced? Is the alternative not the beginning of the slippery slope? Does the granting that certain rights are not realisable in all situations not have the effect of undermining all rights?

Joel Feinberg suggests a way through the dilemma. It is to accept a graduated understanding of rights, which at the same time ensures *maximum* fulfilment of all rights. 'Passive negative rights' (rights that protect a person against the behaviour of others) such as torture and denial of free speech can and should, he argues, be regarded as absolute.[64] These are rights which should never be broken, except perhaps in the most extenuating circumstances, such as a defensive war when it might be morally arguable that some 'absolute' rights need to be curtailed or suspended. Positive rights (such as the right to food, housing, health care and social security), he continues, ought on the other hand to be regarded as 'absolute' in a different sense.

[These] must be held to be absolute in the sense that rights to life, liberty, and the pursuit of happiness are most plausibly interpreted as absolute, namely, as 'ideal directives' to relevant parties to 'do their best' for the values involved.[65]

These rights are absolute in the sense of having *prima facie* status, meaning in effect that the burden of justification is on persons or societies who propose to override them. They need to be upheld unless good cause is shown why it is impossible for this to happen. This overriding should at the same time, he argues, not in any sense distract from the *prima facie* obligation of other persons to satisfy these claims. The strength of Feinberg's argument is that it takes socio-economic and political realities seriously, recognising that the right to certain essentials to life, such as food, water and education, simply cannot be guaranteed in all situations. The right to food, shelter and other socio-economic needs are absolute rights in a particular sense only – as 'a valid exercise of rhetorical license'. They are rights in a

[64] Joel Feinberg, *Social Philosophy* (Englewood Cliffs: Prentice-Hall, 1973), p. 88.
[65] *Ibid.*, p. 86. See the discussion of Feinberg's and other views on the absolutising of human rights in 'Defining Human Rights', in Hennelly and Langan (eds.), *Human Rights in the Americas*, pp. 73–81. Acknowledgement of this discussion is given in what follows.

'manifesto sense'.[66] He insists, however, that this sense is politically important, carrying within it certain moral rights which must not be surrendered. These are rights which should be demanded 'not [necessarily] by legal rules – but by moral principles, or the principles of an enlightened conscience'.[67] The affirmation of such rights and values is part of culture-building which becomes the basis of a qualitatively different kind of society.

In summary, pertinent to the debate on socio-economic rights is the axiom *ubi jus, ibi remedium* (where your right is there is your remedy). If, however, a right cannot be enforced the danger is that it is often assumed that it no longer exists. This suggests that if Second Generation rights cannot be enforced through the courts because a particular state does not have the resources to provide housing or food to all its citizens, the declared right can be seen to lose all significance and appeal. Feinberg's argument is that, while the appeal of socio-economic rights is at another level, its claim on society should be not be diminished.

The essential problem is that such rights do not represent valid claims against any particular person or agency. If the government is not *able* to meet the demands, is there any sense, beyond the level of moral ideal, in regarding them as valid claims? Within the context of western individualism this concern is a real one. The validity of social and economic human rights claims acquires a different level of authenticity, however, within the context of a biblical communal ethic and also within the kind of African world view discussed earlier. In a communal situation the existing resources are required to be shared to ensure that everyone has something. The problem is that the complexity of modern society makes this kind of 'voluntary' sharing increasingly difficult, if not impossible.

John Langan, while admitting the difficulties in assigning to specific persons and institutions the responsibilities to meet the basic material needs of others, insists that this does not fundamentally alter the status of the claim. 'I would suggest', he writes, 'that Feinberg's insistence that there must be an assignable individual to be the subject of duty overlooks the

[66] Feinberg, *Social Philosophy*, p. 95.   [67] *Ibid.*, p. 67.

possibility that this duty may fall on the . . . community at large.'[68] He, in fact, sees certain advantages within not assigning the responsibility to a specific agency because it reintroduces into society the need for the kind of intermediary agencies, to which reference has already been made, as a basis for meeting the kinds of needs in question. Allowing that these could take the forms of extended families, churches and community agencies, guilds and/or village co-operatives, the demands on the community could be a basis for reactivating the social conscience of both church and society. Correctly understood and programmatically implemented, this could provide the basis for extensive co-operation between church and state in the nation-building process, as the church relocates social service (*diaconia*) to the poor and needy at the centre of its ministry. In so doing it can rediscover the social role it played before the emergence of secularisation, although in a new and non-triumphal way. More important, it can regain ground lost by the imposition of controls by oppressive regimes designed to exclude all 'interference' in what came to be perceived as the exclusive domain of the state. At the most practical level of nation-building, the church, possibly in co-operation with the state, will need to re-activate its work through clinics, hospitals, schools, crèches, feeding schemes and related social initiatives – while at the same time never allowing the state to abdicate responsibility for such concerns. In so doing it will again be confronted with a new sense of urgency by the challenge of the gospel to feed the poor and minister to those in need.

An openness with regard to precisely who is responsible for meeting Second Generation needs, suggests Langan, 'leaves open the question concerning social organisation and constitutional arrangements which are ideologically divisive'.[69] This he sees as a positive development, if only because a theology of human rights can be seen to reach beyond the legitimate limits of theology when it seeks to prescribe specific forms of government – insisting on a particular political structure to meet a particular need. The church also, however, falls short of its task if it fails to

---

[68] Langan, 'Defining Human Rights', in Hennelly and Langan (eds.), *Human Rights in the Americas*, p. 77.   [69] *Ibid.*, p. 78.

hold all political structures and cultures accountable for providing, where possible, for the social needs of people. The church is obliged as an intermediary organisation vigorously to share in the wider community responsibility to provide socio-economic resources to those in need. As part of this responsibility, however, it is obliged to discern the basic causes which contribute to the impoverishment of people. In so doing the church is continually thrust into making political choices on the basis of disciplined social analysis and awareness.

It is indeed impossible for some poor nations to provide adequate food for all their citizens. This may be a direct result of colonially imposed agricultural practices designed to serve the interests of industrial countries. It may be as a result of arbitrarily imposed national borders during the scramble for colonies. It may also be the result of bad farming practices or corrupt government in the post-colonial era. The fact remains, there are also countries with excess food. Each year, for example, some 15 million people are said to die as a consequence of starvation, while there are programmes within many western countries which pay farmers not to plant and produce all the food of which they are capable. When coupled to the problem of international debt, the likelihood of the poor being fed within as divided a world is very remote.

Because foreign policy is conducted on the basis of national interest rather than moral persuasion it is unlikely that this practice will change before the wealthy nations discover it is in *their own* interests to address this crisis – either because of the regional wars disrupting the global economy, or because of the spread of disease. More tragic, of course, is the situation where similar differences occur within the *same* country! The task of the church and other groups concerned with human rights is at the very least to create an awareness of the essential contradiction which underlies the claim that it is impossible to feed the hungry, and contribute to a global vision of what it means to be a part of the human race.

In brief, human rights need to be seen as an integrated package of rights corresponding to the complexity of human nature. Sensitive to, and aware of, the different contexts within which the struggle for human rights is taking place, the church has shown a particular reluctance to commit itself to actively engaging in the political process of translating human rights into effective and enforceable legal and constitutional demands. In many instances nations have, on the other hand, formally adopted human rights declarations, while in practice showing little regard for the claims contained within the declarations. What this means is that the struggle for human rights finds itself located between two realities. On the one hand it is insufficient merely to proclaim human rights ideals as moral imperatives without concern for the mechanisms of meeting these needs. On the other hand it is necessary to recognise that the formal and/or legal adoption of human rights declarations is insufficient to ensure their implementation. The task of the church is, in this regard, important. Nationally it is to share in the creation of a new national culture which evokes the kind of communal awareness and commitment being asked for in the social–democratic manifestations of liberalism, in the communal ideas of the African world view, in some socialist economic models and in biblical communal ethics. In brief, there is room for a broad consensus among the different human rights constituencies to emerge. Internationally this obliges the church to share in the creation of a world view based on mutual co-operation and humanitarian concern.

HOW BROAD IS TOO BROAD?

The question has already been asked and partly answered. Is it possible to take a human rights agenda seriously which includes Second and Third Generation rights?

In a situation where the larger part of the economic, social and material power is disproportionally located in the hands of a minority, the affirmation of First Generation rights to the exclusion of Second and Third Generation rights can have the most negative implications. To ensure oppressed people basic political rights, without some kind of affirmative action designed to restore the basic resources denied or taken from them during the period within which they were without political rights or due process to protect themselves, is likely to unleash an extended and embittered period of enduring political and social conflict. A simple vote without food, shelter and health care is to use First Generation rights as a smoke screen to obscure the deep underlying forces which dehumanise people. It is to create an appearance of equality and justice, while by implication socio-economic inequality is entrenched. To protect individual rights which include the abuse of the private ownership of property located almost exclusively in the hands of the few, to allow major business concerns to continue disproportionately to serve the interest of the shareholders, and not to affirm the right to education and work as a means of redressing social imbalances, can only broaden rather than narrow the gap between the rich and the poor. To entrench First Generation rights to the neglect of other rights is to ignore the fundamental problem of poverty which characterises western societies. To the extent that the fulfilment of the basic human rights to the material necessities of life is inherent to what it means to be human, the denial of such rights can only perpetuate conflict and revolution.

Mindful of this possibility, and building on the traditional teaching of the church, which affirms the right of all people to have access to the material goods of the earth, in 1967 Paul VI in *Populorum Progressio (On the Development of Peoples)* addressed the problem of world hunger. 'Private ownership', he stated, 'confers on no one a supreme and unconditional right.' 'The right of ownership is never to be used to the detriment of the common good.'[70] This, suggests the Pope, means that if those who own property do not use it for the benefit of other members of the human family, expropriation *is* an option to which the state may be required to resort.

The common good . . . at times demands the expropriation of an estate if it happens that some estates impede the common prosperity either on

[70] Paul VI, *On the Development of Peoples (Populorum Progressio)* (Washington DC: United States Catholic Conference, 1967), par. 23. For the traditional position of the church on property ownership, see St Thomas Aquinas, *Summa Theologica* (London: Burns Oates and Washbourne, 1929), Part 2 (Second Part), Q. 57, art. 2–3 and Q. 66, arts. 2, 7.

account of their vast size, or because of their small or negligible cultivation, or cause extreme poverty to the population or bring serious harm to the country.[71]

In his speech to the Indians of Oaxaca, Mexico, during his trip to the Latin American Bishops' Conference (CELAM III) in 1979, John Paul II declared:

The Church does indeed defend the legitimate right to private property, but she also teaches no less clearly that there is always a social mortgage on all private property, in order that goods may serve the general purpose that God gave them. And if the common good requires it, there should be no hesitation even in expropriation, carried out in the due form.[72]

Central to a theology of the land is the Leviticus 25:8–13 teaching on the jubilee year, reaffirmed in the teaching of Jesus in Luke 4:17–21. However strictly or loosely interpreted, it has to do with preventing the heritage of an entire people from falling into the hands of the few. The jubilee year was a year within which the Israelite economy was reorganised to the advantage of the poor.

The year of God, then, (said Paul VI) was also the year of Man, the year of the Earth, the year of the Poor, and upon this view of the whole human reality there shone a new light which emanated from the clear recognition of the supreme dominion of God over the whole of creation.[73]

Theologically renewal begins with redistribution. In the South African situation where productive land is (whatever the implications of scrapping the notorious 1913 Land Act) *de facto* almost exclusively in the hands and at the disposal of whites, a future dispensation which prevents the realistic transfer of property to blacks constitutes a social order at variance with this basic theological insight. The question of compensation for landowners is essentially a political or procedural matter, which needs to be pragmatically worked out to the maximum benefit of society as a whole, mindful of the need for the affirmation of

---

[71] Paul VI, *ibid.*
[72] *John Paul II in Mexico: His Collected Speeches* (London: Collins, 1979), p. 96.
[73] Paul VI, 'Bull of Indiction of the Holy Year 1975', par.34. *Ibid.*, p. 109.

social stability. Precisely *how* land is to be returned to those from whom it has been forcibly taken, and what use is to be made of this land in the future, involves complex political, economic and agricultural issues. There are, nevertheless, sound theological and political incentives for property law to promote the need for the use of agricultural land for the benefit of the entire nation. The rights of workers to have the security of a home, future contractual relationships regarding land tenure and need for just labour relations is, at the same time, a dimension of nation-building theology which the churches will be obliged to promote.[74]

The privatisation of state owned land in Eastern Europe presents similar problems. Theologically the private ownership of land should not result in the land simply passing into the hands of those with the financial resources to purchase what land is available, leaving the poor without a land base. First Generation and Second and Third Generation human rights are theologically two sides of the same coin.

HUMAN RIGHTS BY WHAT PROCESS?

Bhakti Hinduism teaches the intricacies of the constant inter-relationship between 'cat doctrine' and 'monkey doctrine'. When the mother cat wants to save her kittens from the threat of danger, she takes them by the scruff of the neck and relocates them in a safe place. By way of contrast, the baby monkey, sensing the imminence of danger in the cries of its elders, clings of its own accord to the mother as she moves towards safety. In the process the baby monkey is 'graciously saved'.[75] In a time of social renewal both movements occur. The demands of human rights are today being forced on countries and regions undergoing transition in places like Eastern Europe, the Soviet Union and South Africa. Global and internal events have taken these regions and countries by the scruff of the neck, dragging them into a space within which justice and peace is at least a

---

[74] See Sachs, *Protecting Human Rights*, pp. 104–38.
[75] Max Stackhouse, 'The Theological Challenge of Globalization', *Christian Century*, 3 May 1989, p. 469.

possibility. Under this pressure some of the most ardent opponents of reform in earlier years are coming to rediscover the neglected resources within their own religious and secular traditions, allowing themselves, 'baby monkey-like' to be carried into the new age.

The church is not a foreign body required to work out its salvation in isolation from the world. Nor is it an elitist body able to confer salvation on the world. It is a body of people called to humbly share in the human task of humanising the world. In so doing it brings to this task its theological insights to be blended with the insights and contributions of others. For this to happen it must be prepared to share in both cat and monkey operations to expedite this process. The tragedy is that, despite the important theological insights uncovered in its many theological studies on human rights as a part of its heritage, few churches have seen the need to make the human rights issues an integral part of their liturgy, preaching and practice. Arend Van Leeuwen in his important work *Christianity in World History*, suggests that in the modern world democracy and human rights, grounded as they are in biblical prophetic presuppositions, are spiritual forces in secular garb which the church can simply no longer afford to ignore.[76]

[76] Arend Van Leeuwen, *Christianity in World History* (London: Edinburgh Press, 1964).

CHAPTER 6

Theology and political economy

Gar Alperovitz, president of the National Center for Economic Alternatives in Washington DC has observed: 'Perhaps the most important lesson of recent developments in Eastern Europe and the Soviet Union is that fundamental problems in any society – despite misleading appearances of superficial calm – are very difficult to "paper-over" forever.'[1]

There is little doubt that the social experiment inaugurated in the Russian Revolution in 1918, and imposed on other eastern bloc countries in the wake of World War II, has failed. The gloating response of western imperialist opinion concerning the 'failure of socialism' is, at the same time, misleading. The cracks within predominantly capitalist societies seem to grow wider, reaching almost daily ever deeper into the social fabric of the West. For some this is owing to government interference with market forces. For others it is because government has not guided the economy firmly enough. Whatever the cause, the enormous gap in income and wealth between the rich and poor in many western countries ought to be enough to persuade those who rejoice in the failure of Eastern European socialism of the flaws within the western economy.

In the United States, Britain and elsewhere accumulated private wealth has been used to subvert the democratic process in a variety of different ways. Economic privatisation has frequently denied the poor access to adequate social services. The private funding of special interest candidates has skewed the electoral process, while the promotion of acquisitive material values has often been successfully used to distract public opinion

[1] Gar Alperovitz, 'Building A Living Democracy', *Sojourners*, July 1990, p. 21.

away from crucial social and economic issues. In Scandinavian countries, social democratic ideals (tending more towards welfare capitalism in recent years) have successfully led to a greater sense of egalitarianism. Materialism, individualism and a loss of communal concern has at the same time characterised the Scandinavian value system in ways not dissimilar to those of the United States and Britain. This raises the question, of course, whether successful industrialisation can ever exist without an increase in material greed. Be this as it may, the West is today faced with the consequence of a brand of individualistic spirituality reducible to the worship of money, materialism and seemingly endless greed. A consequence of this is a failure to facilitate the fullest democratic participation in the economic and political management of society.

The disastrous failure of the economic and political life of Eastern Europe, living with the Stalinist legacy of bureaucratic–authoritarian statism, has collapsed into what has been called a form of 'socialism without democracy'.[2] Thoughtful conservative and social democratic opinion in the West, in turn, suggests that when both economic and political power is exclusively located in one institutional structure, the destruction of individual rights, democracy and the human spirit is an inevitable consequence. Freidrich von Hayek, whose book *The Road to Serfdom* has become a conservative bible, points to the implications of monopoly control.

The most important change which extensive government control produces is a psychological change, an alteration in the character of the people . . . The will of [people] is not shattered but softened, bent, guided; [people] are seldom forced by it to act, but they are constantly restrained from acting. Such a power does not destroy, but it prevents existence; it does not tyrannize, but it compresses, enervates, extinguishes and stupifies a people, till each nation is reduced to be nothing better than a flock of timid and industrial animals, of which government is the shepherd.[3]

[2] Joe Slovo, *Has Socialism Failed?* (London: Inkululeko Publications, 1989), p. 3.
[3] Friedrich A. von Hayek, *The Road to Serfdom* (Chicago: Chicago University Press, 1980). Quoted in Alperovitz, 'Building a Living Democracy'. p. 12.

The deep and relentless drive of people to realise their full potential is, however, also such that in the absence of alternative channels through which to realise their humanity, people eventually rise up in rebellion. The dancing in the streets of Berlin, Prague, Warsaw, Budapest and Bucharest, as one dictatorship after another fell in the closing months of 1989, was a celebration of the human spirit that no state can ever afford to ignore.

A cursory consideration of the social fabric of both East and West, emphasises the need to transcend both the uncompromising greed-centred individualism of free-market capitalism and the loss of individual worth associated with eastern bloc statism. Is it possible for an alternative system to emerge within which *both* individual liberal democratic freedoms (classic First Generation rights) *and* socio-economic and economic rights (Second and Third Generation rights) are a reality? This question is focussed in the political–economic debate as probably nowhere else. It concerns a vision which affirms the legitimate concerns within both more responsible presentations of liberal democracy and the realistic concerns of socialism.

An attempt is made in what follows, from a theological perspective, to harness the essential concerns of the 'two once-great traditions' (Alperovitz) with a view to reaching towards an alternative, more compassionate, democratic, just and efficient economy.

RHETORIC AND DISCONTENT

There are few debates as marred and polarised by the exchange of slogans and rhetoric as those on the political economy. This outrage cannot be ignored. It gives expression to a reality which must be addressed. The use of socialist and Marxist–Leninist slogans by exploited workers and the unemployed in Third World countries, together with the socialist aspirations of many workers in established western countries reflects *real* discontent by the under-class within free-market capitalism. The majority of Soviet and Eastern European workers, together with large sections of the membership of the ruling parties in these countries have, on the other hand, initiated a sweeping rush away from a state controlled economy to the only alternative with which they are vaguely acquainted, which is free-market capitalism. The war of rhetoric and slogans suggests that those who know each system best – *those who suffer its consequences on the margins of its structures*, are looking for both viable and qualitatively different solutions.

These solutions are likely to be found only as the ideologues on both sides step away from their dogmatic preconceptions and accept the emergence of more innovative praxis-based policies. This requires a careful analysis of the legitimate discontent among the poor in the East and West, as a basis for discerning realistic alternative programmes which meet the particular needs of each specific society; a task beyond the scope of this particular study. It is also beyond the skills of this author, who is a theologian and not an economist. The focus of the study must therefore be more limited. It is to identify only such ethical principles which emerge from a theological understanding of the political economy. For such principles to be related to contextual needs, however, they must emerge from a theological reading of existing economic systems and engagement in existing secular debate on the economy. In other words, theological ethics must be located within the context of the *actual* struggle for a transformed society. In so doing, it is on occasions likely to be quite specific in making concrete proposals, while in other situations less than concrete in keeping alive a vision of what a particular society may not regard as realistically possible at a particular time in its history – having to live with the accusation of being too visionary and idealistic.

Two summary comments: the first is that this particular theoretical study is undertaken within the context of what can be broadly defined as a western-style capitalist economy, marred by apartheid. It is written in response to the challenge facing a South African economy which struggles to throw off the effects of apartheid-based capitalist exploitation and stagnation. This necessarily results in critical attention being given to problems faced by workers and the unemployed within *capitalism* rather than socialist alternatives. The second, a point already emphasised, is that the gospel requires Christians to promote the interests of those who suffer most in any society, while always being concerned for the welfare of the whole family of God. This means that Christians are required to challenge, push and reshape most of the basic assumptions of the free-enterprise system. This, it is argued in what follows, predisposes a theological understanding of political economics in the direction of what is broadly understood as social democracy or democratic socialism.[4]

OWNERSHIP AND USAGE

Theologically central to this focus, as already made clear in the earlier chapters on human rights, is the need for people (as agents of God in history) to participate in the creation of their own future, both economically and politically. This has far-reaching practical implications for the political economy. One aspect of this needs to be noted before considering the broader interface between theology and economics.

Recognising and affirming the emotional and real significance of the *ownership* of the means of production, *democratic control* over the use of land and factories, for the benefit of those who work them and the poor who are dependent on them, is equally important. The failure to recognise this sometimes causes debate on private ownership as the dominating issue in projected plans for economic redistribution to exclude concern over the democratic right of the populace to control the way in which the means of production is used, *whether owned privately or by the state.*

Pieter le Roux somewhat provocatively (for the left) argues that social democrats have with some success shown that political control over the means of production (by whoever it is

---

[4] A brief historical and contemporary description of these two options is provided in James Leatt, 'Neither Adam Smith nor Karl Marx', in Michel Albeldas and Alan Fischer, *A Question of Survival: Conversations with Key South Africans* (Johannesburg: Jonathan Ball Publishers, 1987), pp. 87–99.

owned) is more important than *collective ownership*.[5] Marxists, on the other hand, usually criticise social democracies for failing to bring economic exploitation to an end in allowing for the continuation of private ownership. Leaving this particular debate aside, theologians recognise the need to emphasise the obligation of all people to attain their full God-given potential through active engagement in life. This obliges theologians to emphasise the need for maximum participation in economic institutions by all people. It involves, by whatever specific economic strategy available, the 'democratisation of capital' or, alternatively, the 'socialisation of capital'. However conceived, it involves more than the nationalisation of industry, which does not necessarily lead to the redistribution of wealth nor the transfer of the control of economic enterprise.[6]

The latter point requires the charge of *statism* levelled against social democracy by Nicos Poulantzas to be taken very seriously. He criticises social democracy precisely where it is commonly regarded to be strongest:

social democracy and Stalinism . . . exhibit a fundamental complicity: both are marked by statism and profound distrust of mass initiatives, in short by suspicion of democratic demands.[7]

The extent of Poulantzas' accusation against social democrats seems at one level quite absurd. Le Roux at the same time allows that the emphasis on proportional representation characteristic of some social democracies, the dominant role of trade unions in negotiating working conditions, together with the need for compromise between trade unions and the business sector often takes the decision-making process away from the direct representatives of the people. Social democratic parties are (like other dominant parties) able to implement legislation that does not necessarily reflect the views of the electorate, while relying

---

[5] Pieter le Roux, 'The Case for a Social Democratic Compromise', in N. Nattrass and E. Ardington (eds.), *The Political Economy of South Africa*, (Cape Town : Oxford University Press, 1990), p. 25.

[6] Johann Maree and Liv Torres, 'Democratisation of Capital in South Africa: Wage-Earner Funds'. A paper presented at the Association for Sociology in South Africa, Twentieth Annual Congress, University of Stellenbosch, 1–4 July 1990.

[7] Nicos Poulantzas, 'Towards a Democratic Socialism', in D. Held (ed.), *States and Society* (Oxford University Press, 1990), p. 25.

on pre-election antics to regain the popular vote. An alternative is the Swiss system of regular referendums for testing government decisions.[8] At the level of local government in South Africa's black townships, the notion of street and area committees (for all their structural weaknesses) is intended to serve a similar process. Whatever the exact model employed, participatory democracy requires maximum participation in the major decision-making process by all people concerned. It is an ideal which theologians are compelled to support, while taking account of the management difficulties and 'paralysing' effect this process can have on economics and politics.

Implying that a social democracy is likely to be the outcome of a negotiated settlement in South Africa, Albie Sachs, in turn, comes closer than most supporters of 'radical' redistribution to allow for the possibility of the political control over the usage of farm land as an alternative to *nationalisation*, at least as a possible interim solution to the present impasse.[9] The debate of such matters is, of course, far from over, and the burden of the long history of land exploitation in South Africa is likely to be a decisive factor in settlement of the question concerning who should own the means of production. Ultimately it is likely to be the practical dimension of what is involved in a system of democratic control over the land and industry, as much as the level of the mix between private and public ownership of these, that will determine its economic success or failure.

Land is a category of theological significance. The biblical tradition opposes the accumulation of property in the hands of the few, making the 'landless poor' a focus of prophetic concern. Theological realism requires, however, that the 'mix' between the different kinds of ownership be determined by the changing needs of each particular society, recognising that there are few economies in the world which are not mixed at one level or another. A theological assessment of any particular political economy requires an assessment concerning the level at which the mix best meets the needs of the populace – and more especially the poor and marginalised people of society, *both in the present and in the future*. Ideological considerations aside, it is a

[8] *Ibid.*   [9] Sachs, *Protecting Human Rights*, pp. 114–16.

concern to empower the poor economically (and in other ways) which deserves the support of Christians.

Accepting the conservative dimensions inherent to aspects of traditional theological teaching concerning land ownership, it is important to note that this tradition places the onus on whoever owns property to use it for the common good. Papal statements already quoted in Chapter 4 identify the theological argument in favour of a 'social mortgage of all private property in order that goods may serve the general purpose that God gave them'. John Paul II reiterates this point: 'If the common good requires it, there should be no hesitation even in expropriation.'[10]

In South Africa these words take on special significance:

5 per cent of South Africa's population own 80 per cent of the personally owned wealth.

Whites effectively own in excess of 70 per cent of the land in South Africa and 95 per cent of the 'means of production'.[11]

As far as control of industry goes, six corporations ultimately control companies whose shares account for more than 85 per cent of the total value of shares quoted on the Johannesburg Stock exchange.

Suffice it to say the redistribution of the ownership of land and the means of industrial production is as much a remedial ingredient to this situation as is any talk of democratic and political control over the use to which it is put in a new South Africa. *Theologically*, the ownership and the use of God's creation is to be used for the benefit and well-being of all God's children, especially those who are at any point in time in most need of empowerment.

THEOLOGY AND POLITICAL ECONOMY

Douglas Meeks recaptures the meaning of the word *economy* (*oikonomia*) by tracing its etymological roots to the Greek words

---

[10] *John Paul II in Mexico*, p. 96. See also Paul VI, *On the Development of Peoples*, par. 23.
[11] It is usually accepted that 86 per cent of land is owned by whites. The 'in excess of 70 per cent' is estimated by some economists as a result of deducting such land that is taken up in national parks, roads and railways, 'coloured rural areas' amounting to approximately 1.5 per cent of the surface area, and urban centres to which black people have some access.

oikos (household) and *nomos* (law or management). Economy means literally 'the law or the management of the household'. Theologically this means not the modern household or nuclear family, but the 'public household'. It concerns the management of national and global economies as part of the household of God, which is a household of justice.[12] This understanding of the economy requires Christians to regard the political economy, in the words of the US Catholic bishops, as 'one of the chief areas where we live out our faith'.[13]

Defending the title of his book, *God the Economist*, Meeks shows that in antiquity it would have been problematic to refer to God as Economist, since the *homo economicus* was qualitatively inferior to the *homo politicus*, whose prerogative it was to rule over the economy. This has, however, changed in the complexity of the modern world. 'To call God the economist means that the God of Israel and of Jesus Christ is fundamentally identified through what God does in relation to household building and management.' It is to 'express God's life and work with biblical concreteness'.[14]

The foundation of Meeks' analysis is so basic and self-evident that it is too often overlooked by people who have forgotten what it means to be without the necessities of life: In order for people to live, they must have the basic means of subsistence. The basic necessities of life are, however, simply not available to the majority of the world's population. This is not primarily because they are truly scarce, but because they are unevenly allocated. In Britain, the United States and South Africa some simply have too large a share of the economic resources of their respective societies, while many (in South Africa, the majority) cannot afford the most basic requirements of life.[15] Few critics or friends of capitalism would dispute the 'relative' discrepancies between

---

[12] M.Douglas Meeks, *God the Economist. The Doctrine of God and Political Economy* (Minneapolis: Fortress Press, 1973, pp. 3, 36, 40.

[13] *Economic Justice for All. Pastoral Letter on Catholic Social Teaching and the US Economy* (Washington: DC: National Conference of Catholic Bishops, 1986), Pastoral Message, par. 6.   [14] *Ibid.*, pp. 76–7.

[15] A recent United States Congressional Budget Office study, for example, showed the following statistics for 1988: The top 5 per cent of American families received almost as much income as the bottom 60 per cent of American society – roughly 150 million people. The top 10 per cent received roughly the same income as the bottom 70 per

the rich and the poor where distribution is left to unfettered market forces. An increasing number of people are, in turn, now showing a growing concern about 'absolute' poverty that seems to have become a central feature of an unfettered free-enterprise system.

The extent of poverty is massive and in many instances it is increasing, affecting specific groups of the community – women, children, the elderly and other marginalised groups – in a way that requires a thorough gender and age analysis of the problems of poverty.[16] Economic and social structural prejudices which support white adult males, at least to the extent of giving them a wider range of choices, constitutes an ingredient of capitalist society that needs yet to be fully investigated and radically transformed. The Report for the Second Carnegie Inquiry into Poverty and Development in Southern Africa concludes:

Women are discriminated against in all aspects of life – in the home as girls being brought up and educated; in the allocation of resources at school and institutions of higher learning; at work; and in society in general. African rural women are at the bottom of the economic pyramid in this country because of the added problem of paucity of resources and more rigid sexist practices in these areas.[17]

cent – roughly 175 million people. A mere 1 per cent of American families at the very top had more income than the bottom 40 per cent – roughly 100 million people.

According to official definitions, 13 per cent (32 million people) of the American society lived in poverty in 1988. Statistics at the same time showed that poverty does not extend equally to all sections of society. Racism and sexism are entrenched. Only 12 per cent of all whites were offically classified poor, while 35 per cent of blacks and 28 per cent of Hispanics were described as poor. Fifty-three per cent of all poor families were headed by women. More than 44 per cent of all black children were living in poverty, while the estimates for the homeless and hungry range from several hundred thousand to more than 3 million.

A 1989 research paper by the National Union of Metalworkers of South Africa, in turn, noted that while official statistics put the unemployment figure at 800,000, other estimates range from 1 to 3.5 million. Fifty per cent of wage earners earn less than the calculated minimum subsistence levels. The housing shortage is officially put at 1 million required units, while unofficial figures put the figures at probably 3 times as many. There is a critical shortage of health care facilities for the black rural population, adjacent to the sophisticated facilities available in cities, especially for those able to pay for them. The abysmal shortage of black schools in contrast to under-occupied and closed-down white schools again emphasises the disproportionate allocation of resources within South Africa, where the inequities of capitalist classism is exacerbated by entrenched and legislated racism.

16 See Francis Wilson and Mamphela Ramphele, *Uprooting Poverty: The South African Challenge* (Cape Town: David Philip, 1989), pp. 169–85.   17 *Ibid.*, p. 179.

A theological understanding of human rights obliges Christians in the West to be deeply concerned about this and other specific dimensions of poverty. The church is, however, theologically obliged not merely to minister to the victims of poverty and deprivation, but to redress the causes of this situation. The place to begin is to understand the enormity of the task at hand. Theologians and others who wish to engage economists in discussion are, however, also faced with varying degrees of ideological purity from economists (to the 'left' and 'right') who insist that economics is determined by a set of laws internal to itself. Some *laissez-faire* capitalists, for example, believe they have discovered the laws of motion which make for indefinite economic progress and prosperity, while many Marxists teach a brand of 'scientific socialism' which claims to have exposed the inherent flaws of capitalism and the inevitability of an alternative socialist order.[18] There are also, of course, an infinite number of less ideological approaches to economics, drawing on both 'capitalist' and 'Marxist' insights, that are far more flexible in such matters.

The less ideologically based scepticism with which both capitalist and socialist economists frequently respond to theologians as they address economic problems is, on the other hand, not entirely ill-founded. The meddling and 'easy answers' offered by theologians, who passionately (but often with splendid economic ignorance) insist on simple solutions to the burning economic problems of the day, warrants dismissal by economists who often share both the passion and the vision of these theologians, while being forced to grapple with realities that undercut the easy solutions which theologians seek to promote. 'Religion cannot produce grain, nor does it build houses!' is the legitimate reminder of such economists to theological enthusiasts. Theologians who, on the other hand, seek to respond to the magnitude of the economic crisis more thoughtfully would do well to ponder the stubborn choices

---

[18] Meeks, *God the Economist*, p. 9; J. Philip Wogaman, *The Great Economic Debate: An Ethical Analysis* (Philadelphia: Westminster Press, 1977), p. 15. Wogaman's helpful study is acknowledged outlining the discussion on capitalism and socialism that follows.

which face economists, as well as the overwhelming power of the economy to shape the destiny of humankind.

The history of economic systems is well documented in many useful and clarifying studies.[19] In the words of Wallerstein, a 'fundamental break' and 'significant rupture' in western society gave rise to capitalism. He suggests three dates around which the transition happened:[20] 1500 which marks the beginning of a world market; 1650, with an emphasis on Britain and the Netherlands as the first 'capitalist' states and the emergence of key 'modern' ideas with Descartes, Leibnitz, Spinoza, Newton and Locke; and 1800, as the height of the industrial revolution. Marxian scholarship tends to see the rupture as occurring over the entire period. Etienne Baliber, for example, identifies the period between 1500 and 1750 as the period of 'transition to capitalism' and the period after 1750 a 'capitalism proper', while Paul Sweezy simply speaks of these two phases of capitalism.[21]

However conceived, one of the most significant outcomes was the emergence of the *modern market*. It unleashed a process which, in the words of Karl Polanyi, 'showed its staggering capacity for organizing human beings . . . into industrial units under the command of private persons mainly engaged in the buying and selling for profit'.

Man's ultimate dependence on nature and his fellows for the means of his survival was put under the control of that new fangled institutional creation of superlative power, the market . . . [it] then gave rise to yet

[19] Eric Roll, *A History of Economic Thought* (London: Faber and Faber, 1987); Immanuel Wallerstein, *The Modern World System* (New York: Acadamic Press, 1980, 3 vols.; *Historical Capitalism* (London: Verso, 1983; New York, Charles Scribner's Sons, 1958); Karl Polanyi, *The Great Transformation* (Boston: Beacon Press, 1967); Alexander Gray, *The Development of Economic Doctrine: An Introductory Survey* (London: Longman, 1980); Richard Rosecrance, *The Rise of the Trading State: Commerce and Conquest in the Modern World* (New York: Basic Books, 1987); R. H. Tawney, *Religion and the Rise of Capitalism* (New York: Harcourt, Brace and Co., 1926); Max Weber, *The Protestant Ethic and the Spirit of Capitalism* (New York: Charles Scribner's Sons, 1976). J. Philip Wogaman, *The Great Economic Debate: An Ethical Analysis* (Philadelphia: Westminster Press, 1977).
[20] Wallerstein, *The Modern World System*, pp. 5–7.
[21] Etienne Baliber, 'Sur les concepts fondamentaux du materialisme historique', in Louis Althusser and Etienne Balibar (eds.), *Lire Le Capital* (Paris: Maspero, 1968) vol. II; Paul Sweezy, 'Karl Marx and the Industrial Revolution', in *Modern Capitalism and Other Essays* (New York: Monthly Review Press, 1972), pp. 127–46. Both authors quoted in Wallerstein, *The Modern World System*, pp. 5–6.

another, even more extreme development, namely a whole society embedded in the mechanism of its economy – a *market economy*.[22]

So powerful and dominant are market forces that they soon came to be seen as controlling 'economic laws', functioning in the market place in much the same way as physical laws were seen to control the physical universe and natural laws were said to be part of reality itself. 'What before was merely a thin spread of isolated markets was now transmuted into a self-regulating *system* of markets', with economic laws (so-called *economic reality*) making the 'marketing mind' part of the western 'habit of thought'.[23] This is a socio-economic and mental reality, suggests Polanyi, which represents a formidable obstacle to anyone seeking to address the essential economic problem within western society. If these forces cannot be democratically controlled, the only option for those who would be free is indeed, as Marx held, the destruction of the market economy! The fundamental right of people not to be reduced to the mere consequence of economic and material forces is theologically non-negotiable.

Without being able to discuss all the elaborations of capitalist and socialist theory, it is helpful to identify (at what Weber called a *typological* level) what is at the heart of each set of perceived 'laws' which are said to be governing the political economy.

'Laissez-faire' capitalism

Linked to the emergence of liberalism and the growth of democracy, capitalism came to be seen by some as a 'guarantor of liberty', a position championed by radical free-enterprise ideologues like von Hayek and Milton Friedman. Born within the struggle against despotism and poverty, liberalism went a long way towards achieving an escape from political domination and economic impoverishment for at least a section of the population of democratic, industrialised nations. Few were not impressed by the 'spectacular' successes. Even Marx and Engels

---

[22] Karl Polanyi, *The Livelihood of Man*, edited by Harry W. Pearson (New York: Academic Press, 1977), p. 9.   [23] *Ibid.*, pp. 5, 10.

acknowledged the successes (while oblivious of the ecological implications) of early capitalism:

The bourgeoisie, during its rule of scarce one hundred years, has created more massive and more colossal productive forces than have all preceding generations together. Subjection of nature's forces to man, machinery, application of chemistry to industry and agriculture, steam navigation, railways, electric telegraphs, clearing of whole continents for cultivation, canalisation of rivers, whole populations conjured out of the ground – what earlier century had even a presentiment that such productive forces slumbered in the lap of social labour?[24]

Almost a century before the *Communist Manifesto* was written, however, Adam Smith, Thomas Malthus, David Ricardo and others already discerned what they thought to be certain self-regulating laws within the capitalist system. Malthus, in his *Essay on Population* pessimistically saw disease, famine, poverty and death as the only means of keeping the population from outdistancing food supplies, regarding any attempts to lessen the impact of such events by interfering in the economic process as a sure recipe for disaster.[25] Ricardo spoke of the 'Iron Law of Wages' (with positive and negative implications) as a central ingredient of the emerging science of economics.[26] It was Smith's optimistic discernment of 'an invisible hand' in the capitalist system in *The Wealth of Nations* in 1776, however, that set the stage for *laissez-faire* capitalist ideology that was to follow:

Every individual is continually exerting himself to find the most advantageous employment for whatever capital he can command. It is his own advantage, indeed, and not that of society, which he has in view. But the study of his own advantage naturally, or rather necessarily, leads him to prefer that employment which is most advantageous to the society . . . In this case, as in many other cases, he is led by an invisible hand to promote an end which was no part of his

[24] *The Communist Manifesto*, in Robert C. Tucker (ed.), *The Marx–Engels Reader*, (New York: W.W. Norton and Co., 1978), p. 477.

[25] Thomas Malthus, *An Essay in the Principle of Population* (New York: A.M. Kelley, 1965).

[26] *The Works of David Ricardo*, edited by P. Sraffa (Cambridge: Cambridge University Press, 1951), vol. I, pp. 93–109.

intention . . . I have never known much good done by those who affected to trade for the public good.[27]

After two-hundred years Smith's 'principled selfishness', although often differently explained, continues to be an essential ingredient in capitalism, with ideological *laissez-faire* capitalists continuing to believe that the market fares best when left to market forces, free from all forms of government interference and/or moralistic meddling.[28] In brief, it is argued that there are simply too many unknown factors in the complexity of modern economics for these to be co-ordinated in any centrally planned economy. The genius of the free market, on the other hand, is that no one is required to make such momentous decisions. Through each person and economic agency attending to their own business, promoting their own interests, the laws of supply and demand will ensure that all resources (material and labour) and finished goods are made use of to the best advantage of all concerned. When prices of certain raw materials rise owing to short supply it is, for example, to the advantage of suppliers to increase the supply. If prices fall, on the other hand, because of excess supply, the opposite message is sent. In this way it is not only resource allocation that is controlled; indication is also given as to where viable investment should be made. This generates jobs and income which, in turn, creates the necessary market for the (manufactured) goods produced. This, in brief, is then seen to be the 'miracle' of the self-regulating market.

In one sense *laissez-faire* capitalism is quite utopian. The essential assumption of capitalism is that, left alone, the market will generate more or less full employment and workers will receive sufficient wages to create an adequate market for the goods which they produce. Those who fall through the cracks of the system need, in turn, to be taken care of through welfare and income assistance – something allowed by most free-enterprise theorists to the extent that it does not materially reduce the efficiency with which resources are employed. In reality *laissez-*

---

[27] Adam Smith, *An Inquiry into the Nature and Causes of the Wealth of Nations* (New York: The Modern Library, 1937) Book IV, Chapter 11, pp. 421 and 423.
[28] Wogaman, *The Great Economic Debate*, pp. 17–19; 84.

faire capitalism soon, however, came to realise that even its self-adjusting machine required periodic guidance from the state in the form of monetary and fiscal interventions.

Mike de Klerk shows that such interventions sometimes quite invidiously promote the interests of a particular section of society, recognising that no market operates in a political or social vacuum.[29] The miracle of the 'self-regulating' market, it might be argued is, in fact, socially and politically induced. A variety of factors, technological developments, individual and group preferences and political actions, manipulate and determine the supply and demand of the market. Changes in these forces cause prices to change, signalling to the market the need to re-allocate resources. This much is clear, argues de Klerk from, for example, the changes in the political and social environment that influenced the markets for land, labour and capital in South Africa. The most obvious and relevant example here is the passing of the 1913 and 1936 Land Acts which, by changing the patterns of land ownership and use, gave the market in rural areas its racially exclusive character. It gave white farmers (at the expense of blacks) a once-off subsidy on land purchases and an ongoing subsidy on wage labour. 'A cynic might argue that manipulating markets is what politics is all about.'[30] Reconstruction in South Africa requires at the very least that these social and political factors be changed, in order to facilitate economic change.

For the present it is enough to acknowledge that linked to the 'utopian' ideals of *laissez-faire* capitalism is a measure of fatalism. Recognising that the system often fails to fulfil the ambitions of all sections of society, the bravest of capitalist theorists tell us that this does not really matter. What is important, they insist, is not the equal or even fair division of the pie as much as an increase in the size of the pie which, it is argued, is to the benefit of all concerned. Equality, the strict free-marketeer would argue, is both impossible and economically undesirable. Ludwig von Mises, for example, argues that 'men are unequal; individuals

---

[29] Mike de Klerk, 'Addressing Land Hunger: Choices for Supplying the Land'. To be published in R.A. Schrire, *Critical Choices: Beyond the State and Market* (Cape Town: Oxford University Press, 1991).   [30] *Ibid.*

differ from one another. They differ because their prenatal as well as their postnatal history is never identical'.[31] Supporting equality under the law and recognising that absolute poverty constitutes a moral problem, von Mises insists that this should not be confused with economic inequality. Milton Friedman has, on the other hand, suggested that in the long run *laissez-faire* capitalism will be an equaliser.[32] He suggests, 'capitalism leads to less inequality than alternative systems of organization and . . . the development of capitalism has greatly lessened the extent of inequality'.[33] Joseph Schumpeter, a less ideological proponent of capitalism, has come to a more nuanced conclusion, suggesting that capitalism eliminates both absolute poverty and relative poverty by making mass-produced goods available to an increasing constituency of people. The illustration he employs points to both the successes and the limitations of capitalism.

Queen Elizabeth owned silk stockings. The capitalist achievement does not typically consist in providing more silk stockings for queens but in bringing them within the reach of factory girls in return for steadily decreasing amounts of effort . . . the capitalist process, not by coincidence but by virtue of its mechanism, progressively raises the standard of the life of the masses.[34]

Social and economic justice is, of course, about more than silk stockings. The acquisition of such commodities can be a form of diversion and political pacification. There are many instances of people being reduced to destitution by spending their meagre wages on non-essential goods. Others have been left in absolute poverty through the destruction of old trades and farming methods, requiring Schumpeter to speak of the 'destructive creativity' of capitalism. Capitalism has, however, also produced

---

[31] Ludwig von Mises, *The Ultimate Foundation of Economic Science: An Essay on Method* (Princeton: D. Van Nostrand Co., 1962), p. 59. See also *The Free and Prosperous Commonwealth: An Exposition of the Ideas of Classical Liberalism* (Princeton: D. Van Nostrand Co., 1962), p. 29.

[32] Accepting that 'middle order' developing or industrialising economies may well show vast inequalities, where industrialisation succeeds fully these discrepancies will disappear or at least significantly decline.

[33] Quoted in J. Philip Wogaman, *The Great Economic Debate: An Ethical Analysis* (Philadelphia: Westminster Press, 1977), p. 87.

[34] J.A. Schumpeter, *Capitalism, Socialism and Democracy* (New York: Harper and Row, 1962), p. 64.

food and other essential goods. It has, in fact, succeeded like no other economic system in the production of commodities. Marx, as noted, recognises this and certainly the capitalist economy of South Korea, aided by an authoritarian government, has prospered where socialism in Tanzania, for example, has failed. Wogaman's comment is well taken: 'The miraculous market mechanism may be a good servant, but it is almost certainly a bad master.'[35] The essential problem with free-market capitalism is the unequal distribution of its fruits, the price exacted from those entrapped within its structures and the inability of people to act creatively against the dominant structures in shaping their own future.

Capitalism does not always create more jobs. Unemployment *and* inflation make the market a grim and depressing place for people who have nothing to sell except muscle and sweat – with little bargaining power as a basis for getting a decent rate of exchange. Despite what is suggested by free-market capitalist theory, profits are not always reinvested to the benefit of general economic growth. Money is often invested in ways that benefit workers very little. The creation of border industries in South Africa and cross-border industry in the United States has, for example, left organised workers unemployed and those who do obtain employment exploited – without the backing of strong unions. Not only are these workers compelled (and willing) to receive low and inadequate wages, but profits are largely channelled away from the local economies from which their communities could benefit, enriching the economic centre at the expense of the periphery. International trade and investment is, in turn, often undertaken on a basis which benefits primarily the richer rather than poorer nations.[36] The International Monetary Fund (IMF) and World Bank, are (contrary to what was originally intended) systematically removing money out of Third World economies. Poor borrowing nations have simply not been able to repay the borrowed capital, and spiralling

---

[35] Wogaman, *The Great Economic Debate*, p. 97. See his discussion on what precedes, pp. 77–97.

[36] An informative study on multi-national corporations is provided in Richard J. Barnet and Ronald E. Muller, *Global Reach: The Power of the Multinational Corporations* (New York: Simon and Schuster, 1974).

interest payments are often too high to allow a rise in the living standards of the average citizen in the borrowing countries. In many cases standards are in constant decline, and when farmers are forced to plant crops capable of generating foreign currency in First World industrial markets, in order to repay the interest on loans, under-nourishment and starvation is a frequent consequence. Captive to the regulations which govern global trade, individual nations and people increasingly lose control over their own lives and surrender their ability to shape their own futures – a matter that ought to be of the greatest concern to theologians.

Outwardly offering an opportunity to everyone to improve his or her position in life on the basis of free choice, a little thoughtfulness shows the extent to which the 'free' contenders (those who own and those who work the means of production) within capitalism are all too often drastically mismatched from the start. Frequently workers (many of whom in South Africa have as a result of the notorious Land Acts no option but to sell their labour to industry, often at exploitive wages) in order to stay alive, are required to accept the exploitation imposed on them by those who own and control industry. Again it needs to be theologically stated that *if* this process is an inevitable part of the capitalist process and best left untampered with by democratic participation (as free-marketeers imply), then these structures need to be destroyed.

Robert Nozick's important study, *Anarchy, State and Utopia*, nevertheless offers a serious and formative defence of capitalism based on the freedom of choice. His theory is built on three premises: The *principle of acquisition*, the *principle of transfer* and the *principle of rectification*. His argument is that provided the processes of acquisition and transfer of goods are just (without coercion and with free, agreed compensation) ownership is legitimate. 'Whatever arises from a just situation by just steps is itself just.'[37] This means that even gross inequality, if properly generated, is morally protected. Nozick goes further to argue that any distribution of goods according to some other principle

---

[37] Robert Nozick, *Anarchy, State and Utopia* (New York: Basic Books, 1974), p. 151.

pattern, allowing for example for the equal distribution of wealth, without the free consent of all, is unjust. 'For each as they choose; to each as they are chosen.'[38]

The problem is that the complexity of the modern capitalist society makes it almost impossible to analyse and weigh economic transactions according to Nozick's principles. Bruce Ackerman argues, for example, that Nozick's principles only make sense in some idealistic world where all forms of constraint and market superiority of one agent over another have either not yet emerged, or have been done away with.[39] Given the long history of conquest, colonialism and domination, the unjust acquisition of property and the compulsion of the poor to sell their labour in the capitalist system, it could be argued that Nozick's theory excludes the very possibility of just exchange.[40] Two consequences follow: To declare the history of acquisition and transfer in the existing capitalist system just, ignoring the scars of domination and exploitation which mar this history, is to provide a form of legitimation to capitalism which no theologian can afford to confer on any economic structure.

Nozick's failure to realistically face the historical complexity of capitalist formation is further compounded by his failure to address the actual implications of the rectification principle in society. He does not, for example, suggest how far back one is to trace the history of acquisition and transfer, making no attempt to discuss the transactional advantages of the rich over the poor or the ultimate consequences of unrestrained 'just' acquisition. Michael Walzer suggests that 'a radically *laissez-faire* economy would be like a totalitarian state, invading every other sphere, dominating every distributive process'.[41] In a just society certain human rights ought to be protected against all forms of exploitation or appropriation by others.

Nozick's theory could, of course, be used as a moral principle for arguing that much of the land in South Africa, Zimbabwe and elsewhere should be given back for peasant and/or co-

[38] *Ibid.*, p. 160.
[39] Bruce Ackerman, *Social Justice in the Liberal State* (New Haven: Yale University Press, 1980), p. 186.
[40] Lebacqz, *Six Theories of Justice* (Minneapolis: Augsberg, 1986) p. 62.
[41] Michael Walzer, *Spheres of Justice* (New York: Basic Books, 1983), p. 74.

operative farming. In South Africa, parts of this land were taken from blacks as recently as the late 1980s. The same reading of Nozick would require land in the United States and Canada to be returned to the native Indian people, as well as to peasants in Central and South America and other colonial situations. Charles Simkins is quite unambiguous in suggesting that from a Nozickian point of view 'the South African distribution of income and wealth is unjust'.[42]

This is not, however, the use which Nozick makes of his own theory. Simkins uses Nozick's theory to undermine the very system he sets out to defend. Arguing for minimum government, there only to protect the rights of individuals, he opposes all forms of taxes which are paid for the benefit of others (such as welfare and communal services) as a form of forced labour![43] Nozick believes that such rectification which might be necessary in certain situations can be carried out within the confines of his own scheme, while implying that in no situation is there need for extensive rectification. Says Simkins:

[This] is an assumption that is questionable in any industrial society; it is one of the major defects of Nozick's argument that a lacuna exists at this point. The evidence of extensive injustice in the South African case makes the programme of rectification a dream, but without it the distribution of holdings cannot be reconstructed in a justifiable form.[44]

A definite ingredient of the free-market system is 'free choice'.[45] 'As liberals', writes Friedman, 'we take the freedom of the individual, or perhaps the family, as our ultimate goal in judging social arrangements'.[46] Unless the long history of exploitation and domination in capitalism is ignored, it is impossible to speak of either free choice or just transactions in a market economy. It is this that prompts Cohen, in his radical critique of Nozick, provocatively to ask whether the acquisition

[42] Charles Simkins, *Reconstructing South African Liberalism* (Johannesburg: South African Institute of Race Relations, 1987), p. 48.
[43] Nozick, *Anarchy, State and Utopia*, p. 169.
[44] Simkins, *Reconstructing South African Liberalism*, p. 48.
[45] Meeks, *God the Economist*, p. 53. Polanyi, p. 25.
[46] Milton Friedman, *Capitalism and Freedom* (Chicago: University of Chicago Press, 1962), p. 12.

of private property is not theft.[47] To ignore the history of property acquisition, while arguing that the economics be defined at the level of every transaction being decided in terms of 'free' choice, raises serious ethical questions. To the extent that a transaction involves an exchange of cash for a luxury item, the process need presumably not be regarded as a major ethical issue. Where bread and other *essential* requirements are involved, however, the nature of the transaction becomes ethically more serious. And where, in its most callous and individualistic form, the market economy reduces the labour of people to a commodity to be traded at the best price available, ethicists and theologians are necessarily concerned. In a word, personal worth cannot and must not be reduced to an exchange value. To suggest that socio-economic human rights (such as the right to eat, receive education and have health care) are available only to those who have something to trade, if not money and goods then muscle and sweat, comes dangerously close to implying that people who have no marketable resources at their disposal are without worth in a consumer society. Intrinsic human worth cannot be decided by what people own.

And yet this is what stacks the deck against some and in favour of others in many contemporary societies. Freedom requires realistic alternatives. Those who have resources have alternatives. Those who have no resources have no alternatives. They are obliged to sell their labour (sometimes at any price) in order to survive, and some do not survive at all. This in a word is what constitutes the masked domination and exploitation that is inherent to free-market capitalism. There *is* no free choice for the poor.

A conflict between economics and theology is inevitable when it is argued that this situation is best left untampered with and that market forces should be allowed to take their toll, except for minimum forms of welfare. When an economic system denies Christians the opportunity and the right to live for the sake of God's *universal household* (Meeks) it strikes at the very basis of a Christian understanding of what it means to be a person created by God to be in community with other people. Christian ethics

[47] G.A. Cohen, 'Nozick on Appropriation', *New Left Review*, 150, 1985, pp. 89–105.

takes the freedom of choice very seriously. It is not prepared to concede, however, that because a contract involves choice it is necessarily right. If parties to a contract of sale or labour 'freely' agree to the contract, it does not necessarily mean they have chosen rightly. The story of the market economy is a story of labourers often being required to sell their labour for less than a just price. It is the task of the church to share in correcting this process. Ronald Dworkin notes (in a different context) that the free choice to sell a painting for $100 on Monday does not make it a fair price on Wednesday when I discover it is a masterpiece.[48] Workers are becoming increasingly aware that their labour is worth more than they have for generations been compelled to accept.

Theologically, economic management is about ensuring the best possible livelihood for everyone. It is about liberating economic structures to ensure that no one is exploited or treated as 'strangers and aliens', incorporating everyone into the 'household of God' (Eph. 2: 19–22). It has to do with the establishment of a household within which the goods necessary for survival and for functioning as free and equal citizens take priority over such goods that are not included in this basic core. In John Langan's words: '*A fortiori*, it is morally and religiously unacceptable, indeed sinful, to deprive people of these goods.'[49] The complexity of such decision-making requires, however, that attention be given not only to what is immediately required for survival, but also for the creation of an economy able to provide *future* essential goods. This requires the production of investment (capital) goods as well as what is immediately needed for survival – compelling society to look beyond mere satisfaction of the *immediate* demands of the poor.

This all requires justice-making actions in a world of injustice. Drawing on the teaching on the sabbath and jubilee years (Lev. 25) and Jesus' proclamation of the dawning of this age (Luke 4: 18–19), Karen Lebacqz argues that this involves the reclamation of land, economic restructuring and the freeing of the

---

[48] Ronald Dworkin, 'The Original Position', in Norman Dawicks (ed.) *Reading Rawls* (New York: Basic Books, n.d.), p. 19.
[49] John Langan, 'Personal Responsibility and Common Good in John Paul II,. p. 14.

oppressed to share fully in society.[50] The exact economic form which these actions should take is not, however, found in the Bible! Theologically it involves the development of structures inspired by the biblical vision, but shaped by the economic context within which they are required to operate; addressing the specific needs of a particular society.

Central to the biblical vision is also restoration. This involves *restoration* which is more than a calculated and reluctant act of giving to each what is his or her due. From a Christian perspective it involves the joyous sharing in the restoration of the covenantal basis for 'a genuine human community of liberty and equality'.[51] It has to do with the emancipation from servitude and dehumanising dependency, which involves economic reconstruction and a sense of communal belonging. This is what, from a theological perspective, gives socialism a certain instinctive appeal – with the insistence that it includes the democratic right of people to share in the shaping of their own future. Theological realism further demands that an economy be efficient and effective, as a basis from which each is realistically able to receive and to which each is effectively able to contribute.

Scientific socialism

The problem, from a theological perspective, is that scientific socialism, like *laissez-faire* capitalism, also discerns a set of self-regulating laws within the economy, which, in effect, makes human action subordinate to socio-economic forces. It discerns self-regulating principles which are seen to predetermine the ultimate outcome of the political economy. Friedrich Engels in *Socialism: Utopian and Scientific* argues that where the *means of*

[50] Karen Lebacqz, *Justice in an Unjust World: Foundations for a Christian Approach to Justice* (Minneapolis: Augsburg, 1987), p. 122. Hans Jochen Boecker, *Law and the Administration of Justice in the Old Testament and Ancient East* (Minneapolis: Augsburg, 1980) (quoted in Lebacqz, p. 125) using Isaiah 61, as a base within which the jubilee traditions emerge, suggests the jubilee images include three elements: the announcement of the reign of God, good news for the poor in the form of the restoration of land and the forgiveness of debt, and a declaration of release to captives. In 4: 18–19 Luke combines Isa. 61 and 58:6. See also Sharon Ringe, *Jesus, Liberation and the Biblical Jubilee* (Philadelphia: Fortress, 1985), pp. 36–38.

[51] Lebacqz, *Justice in an Unjust World*, p. 128.

production ('the instruments of labour – land, agriculture, implements, the workshop, the tool . . .') are in conflict with the *mode of production* (the social structures) rebellion and social change is inevitable.[52] The process is best described in Engels' own words:

The mode of production peculiar to the bourgeoisie, known, since Marx, as the capitalist mode of production, was incompatible with the fuedal system, with the privileges conferred upon individuals, entire social ranks and local corporations, as well as with the hereditary ties of subordination which constituted the framework of its social organisation. The bourgeoisie broke up the feudal system and built upon its ruins the capitalist order of society . . .

Now modern industry, in its more complete development, comes into collision with the bounds within which the capitalist mode of production holds it confined. The new productive forces have . . . outgrown the capitalist mode of using them.[53]

What, according to Engels, is the more precise nature of the clash between the new productive forces in the industrial society and the capitalist mode of production? Briefly stated it is that:

Hitherto, the owner of the instruments of labour had himself appropriated the product, because, as a rule, it was his own product and the assistance of others was the exception. Now the owner of the instruments of labour always appropriated to himself the product, although it was no longer *his* product but exclusively the product of the *labour of others*. Thus, the products now produced socially were not appropriated by those who had actually set in motion the means of production and actually produced the commodities, but by the *capitalists*.[54]

Herein, suggests Engels, is the 'germ of the whole of the social antagonisms of today'.[55] The contradiction between socialised production and capitalist appropriation of the products and profits must inevitably (according to Engels) lead to a confrontation between the workers and the owners of industry.

Marx and Engels suggest that, because workers, constituting the exploited under-classes within the existing social structures, fail to receive sufficient remuneration for their work, they are

[52] Friedrich Engels, 'Socialism: Utopian and Scientific', Part III, in *The Marx–Engels Reader*, pp. 700–17.   [53] *Ibid.*, p. 701.   [54] *Ibid.*, p. 704.   [55] *Ibid.*

driven into confrontation with those who own and profit from owning the means of production. The crisis point is reached when owners are no longer able to realise a profit because production has expanded beyond its market, partly because workers are insufficiently paid to generate an adequate market. Recession and/or depression sets in and workers are retrenched. This means there is even less purchasing power in the market, leading to a vicious circle within which an increasing number of people are left unemployed.[56]

Marx describes the crisis in relation to two key concepts: the *industrial reserve army* and the *accumulation of misery* theory.[57] It is a crisis, Marx argues, which occurs on the one hand as the employed part of the work force is overworked and exploited, while on the other hand the ranks of the reserve army of unemployed grows ever larger. The result is the accumulation of misery and suffering until the very system which capitalists seek to maintain collapses. Arguing with the moral fervour of a Puritan preacher, Engels insists that human relations are reduced to no more than 'cash payment'. Crimes increase, trade is reduced to cheating and marriage becomes a cloak for prostitution and adultery. Boredom and asocial behaviour set in, and money becomes the sole purpose for living. 'Fraternity', Engels insists, is replaced with 'the chicanery and rivalries of the battle of competition'.[58] In brief, the Marxian critique of capitalism is as much a moral critique as it is economic. It is, at heart, a rebellion against exploitation and human alienation. Deprived of the larger share of the surplus value (profit) realised by their labour, workers are alienated from one another as each individual and each class struggles for survival against the other. Yet, because in Marxian thought people realise themselves not only in communion with others but also in creative work as an extension of themselves in the world, by being alienated from the fruits of their labour people are alienated from themselves. It is a system, says Marx, within which 'the worker sinks to the level of a commodity and becomes indeed the most wretched of

---

[56] See discussion in Wogaman *The Great Economic Debate*, pp. 20–2.
[57] Karl Marx, *Capital*, vol. I, part v, section 3, in *The Marx–Engels Reader*. pp. 422–8.
[58] Engels, 'Socialism: Utopian and Scientific', *ibid.*, p. 686.

commodities', a form of wretchedness that exists 'in inverse proportion to the power and magnitude of his production'.[59] Trapped within an economic system that reduces all to 'cash value', the owners of the means of production, workers and unemployed alike, are all reduced to cogs in a machine that manipulates and controls their lives and destiny.

> The worker becomes all the poorer the more wealth he produces, the more his production increases in power and range. The worker becomes an ever cheaper commodity the more commodities he creates. With the *increasing value* of the world of things proceeds in direct proportion the *devaluation* of the world of men. Labour produces not only commodities; it produces itself and the worker as a *commodity* – and does so in the proportion in which it produces commodities generally.[60]

These kinds of economic crises (of an excess of supply over demand) will occur, suggests Engels, on a regular basis, forcing capitalists to resort to a variety of measures to moderate and control the situation. Joint-stock companies and trusts will be formed and even state ownership considered; but 'workers will remain wage-owners – proletarians'.[61] The outcome is a temporary suspending of the ultimate confrontation, while the majority of the population are transformed into proletarians and a power which 'under penalty of its own destruction' is forced to rise in revolution. 'The proletariat seizes political power and turns the means of production into state property (now under the control of the workers).'[62] This becomes the first step towards the process of creating a qualitatively different kind of economic system, within which people (all people) share in the fruits of their labour, participate in the creation of their own future and affirm their dignity as people.

This crisis, suggests Marx, may also occur via a different route. He describes this under the rubric of 'the falling tendency of the rate of profit'.[63] Briefly stated, he argues that the same amount of labour working with more elaborate and efficient equipment is capable of producing a greater volume of

---

[59] Karl Marx, 'Economic and Philosophical Manuscripts of 1844', in *The Marx–Engels Reader*, p. 70.   [60] *Ibid.*, p. 71.
[61] Engels, 'Socialism: Utopianism and Scientific', *ibid.*, p. 711.   [62] *Ibid.*, p. 713.
[63] Karl Marx, *Capital*, vol. III (London: Lawrence and Wishart, 1974), pp. 211f.

manufactured goods than was the case before the acquisition of this equipment. The problem is that, while the productivity of labour has grown, the outlay of capital on equipment and machinery has also increased. This results in a tendency marked by a falling rate of profit. Leaving aside the many related factors which Marx sees this tendency giving rise to, the consequences are essentially the same as those mentioned above. Workers are laid off, wages are depressed, the market stagnates or goes into depression and this precipitates the kind of crisis that ultimately results in worker revolution.

In brief, concerned with the plight of workers in a (nine-teenth-century) capitalist society, Marx seeks an alternative to what he regards to be the inevitable predicament of workers. This is a concern that leaves the avowed Christian economist Denys Munby arguing: 'If modern Marxism gives the wrong answers, at least it asks the right questions.'[64]

Marxian economic speculation has produced a variety of different socio-economic experiments by way of suggested 'answers'. It is now history that the centrally controlled economies of the Soviet Union and Eastern Europe, inspired by a Marxist–Leninist philosophy (although not always executed accordingly), have failed hopelessly. Scientific socialist experiments elsewhere seem, in turn, (for whatever reasons) not to have fared vastly better.

CHRISTIANITY AND MARXISM

Many Third World Christians, in isolation from direct Soviet and Eastern European influences, at the same time continue to affirm both Marxian and socialist ideals in protest against exploitative capitalism. The use of Marxian social theory by some liberation theologians as a way of under-cutting the identification of Christianity with capitalism has, in turn, raised the question concerning the legitimacy of the use of Marxian analyses and theory by Christians.

Marxism, suggests Douglas Hall, is a non-religion to the extent that it denies any transcendental framework or guarantee

[64] Quoted in Wogaman, *The Great Economic Debate*, p. 55.

of meaning outside of the material universe. 'It is a quasi-religion, however, insofar as it finds meaning built into the historical process as such.'[65] Marx was an atheist. It has, however, frequently been argued that his understanding of history does not necessarily exclude the possibility of the Judeo-Christian God as an instrument of historical interpretation. For theists, God is necessarily other than and not reducible to the product of human thought and imagination. The question, asks Nicholas Lash, is whether 'belief in the reality of such a God [is] compatible with the conviction that all that occurs, in nature and history, is explicable, in so far as it is explicable at all, without direct reference to the reality or agency of God?' His tentative answer is as thought-provoking as his question: 'If it is, then there would seem to be at least a *prima facie* case for supposing that "religious materialism" is not necessarily a contradiction in terms.'[66] This is not the place to reopen the complex debate concerning the manner within which God operates in history. Nor is it the place to discuss Bonhoeffer's 'secular talk' of God. Lash argues that to limit divine activity to a function of rigid (Marxian) dialectical materialism limits human initiative in history, leading to ethical quietism. On the other hand, suggests Lash, the limiting of God to suprahistorical intervention surely constitutes the essence of theological–ethical quietism.[67] Called actively to participate in the creation of a society of justice (the reign of God), Christians are obliged to turn away from both interpretations of the historical activity of God.

It is enough for our purposes to accept that the Marxian affirmation of this-worldly humanism provides an essential critique of other-worldly religion which contradicts the historical vision of prophetic biblical religion. Milan Machovec, the Czechoslovakian philosopher, makes the point in his book, *A Marxist Looks at Jesus*, in asking whether Marxists are not the true inheritors of the social vision of prophetic Judaism and the

---

[65] Douglas Hall, *Thinking the Faith: Christian Theology in a North American Context* (Minneapolis: Augsburg, 1989), p. 214.
[66] Nicholas Lash, *A Matter of Hope: A Theologian's Reflections on the Thought of Karl Marx* (Notre Dame: University of Notre Dame Press, 1981), p. 136.   [67] *Ibid.*

early Christian Church. The German title of his book is perhaps more appropriate, *Jesus für Atheisten*:

One may even wonder whether the disciples of Karl Marx, who 1800 years after Jesus set in motion a similarly far-reaching and complex process with as yet quite unforeseeable consequences but similar aspirations to a radical transformation of social relationships and a future conceived in a radically different way, have not in fact the greatest right to regard themselves as the authentic perpetrators of Old Testament messianism and early Christian desires for radical change. Many Marxists, but also many self-critical modern theologians, are aware of the fact that concern for the future – that longing for liberation and radical change once found in Christianity – has been taken over in the modern period almost exclusively by Marxism.[68]

Christianity, suggests Machovec, has spiritualised the message of Jesus to the point of leaving a 'shocking disproportion' between 'the ideal which brought Christianity into existence and the results'. It is a discrepancy, suggests Machovec, which 'ought to disturb Christians more than it does'.[69] Arguing that dogmatised Christian theology represents a victory for Docetism, he sees it as being instrumental in destroying the radical historical message of the prophetic tradition. Douglas Hall suggests that a more aggressive critic might well argue that the dominant theology of the church has indeed *prevented* Christians from grasping the true message of Jesus.[70]

Mundy's response to the challenge of Marxism and the growth of Communism is a sobering one for western Christians:

The emergence of Communism as a world force threatening the values we cherish is not merely the result of the plotting of a few evil men; it is the inevitable offshoot of a materialistic world, in which the poor are despised, the peasants neglected, the workers exploited, and the victims of the colonial powers uncared for. It is not for those, who have been satisfied with a world in which power and riches have ruled, to object when those they have oppressed proceed to use power and riches against them.[71]

---

[68] Milan Machovec, *A Marxist Looks at Jesus* (London: Darton, Longman and Todd, 1977), p. 193.   [69] *Ibid.*, pp. 194–5.

[70] Douglas Hall, *Thinking the Faith: Christian Theology in a North American Context* (Minneapolis: Augsburg, 1989), p. 215.

[71] Quoted in Wogaman, *The Great Economic Debate*, p. 64.

For Wogaman, despite the gross misunderstandings of Marxian 'materialism' 'the Christian cannot find anything to quarrel with directly concerning the Marxist idea of the human spirit'.[72] The Marxian vision of humanity rises in rebellion against all forms of economic and political exploitation, finding common cause with the social teaching in the prophetic message of the Old Testament and the teaching of Jesus. At the same time it evokes the Christian objection that it is God who gives the oppressed strength to rebel and ultimately to build a qualitatively new and different kind of society. The flip-side of this theological critique of Marxism is a questioning of the confidence with which Marxism views post-revolutionary humanity. Social and economic structures do shape the character and attitudes of people. This point is clearly made by John Paul II in the encyclical, *On Social Concern (Sollicitudo rei Socialis)*. Theology also insists, however, that the reality of sinfulness and the abuse of power resides in *all* humanity.[73] Wogaman's argument is a strong one:

If human alienation has its source *only* in structural problems of exploitation in a class society, *then* the overcoming of those problems will finally rid us of human selfishness, sinfulness, and evil *forever*. Why forever? Because once the sources of class conflict have been destroyed [in the Marxian utopia] nobody would *ever* be motivated to exploit or harm a fellow human being again. If we can truly believe this to be so, then that belief would go a long way toward justifying almost any actions designed to bring on the revolution and, with it, the final destruction of the shackles of human oppression. But if we cannot believe this, then that may have much to say to us about the need to make *continuing* provision for the sinfulness in human life.[74]

In brief, from a theological perspective, the Marxian understanding of humanity is left wanting. Neither capitalists nor workers are as single-minded, resolute or devoted to their respective causes as Marxian doctrine suggests. Capitalism has survived for centuries despite gross injustices and exploitation. Economic stagnation has, in many situations, survived for decades. Yet economic and political collapse, with few excep-

---

[72] *Ibid.*, p. 65.   [73] John Paul II, *On Social Concern*, paragraphs 36–40.
[74] Wogaman, *The Great Economic Debate*, p. 66.

tions, has not occurred in the form that Marx and Engels predicted. This for a variety of reasons.[75] Not least of all has been the resilience and flexibility of capitalism in dealing with worker demands, inspired by the willingness of capitalists to compromise and even show a sense of human compassion. Alternatively, the flexibility could be attributed simply to a capitalist capacity to *manage* the market. But this too points to a human resourcefulness and skill which Marx failed fully to appreciate. Workers have, in turn, also been much more wayward in their dedication to revolution than Marx anticipated. Capitalist economies have stagnated, unemployment has intensified and misery accumulated, but revolutions of the proletariat have been slow in coming. The South African sociologist Fatima Meer has correctly observed: 'Revolution, though dependent on the populace, is not a popular cause. The security of the familiar system, even if limiting, is invariably preferable to the risks of change.'[76] History shows that discontent and latent rebellion seethes just below the surface among the poor and oppressed of any generation, but it has also been slower in exploding into revolution than Marx realised, not least because of the depth of oppression and total dependency of the exploited on the limited resources made available to them by their masters.[77] Revolutionaries have in some situations also become the hangmen of a new

---

[75] V.I. Lenin, for example, argues that industrial nations have managed to postpone the ultimate collapse of the capitalist economy through industrial imperialism. Industrial workers in the developed countries are left relatively well-off by being employed in skilled jobs, while peasant workers in underdeveloped countries are exploited – explaining why revolutions have tended first to occur in Third World countries. See *Imperialism, the Highest Stage of Capitalism* (Moscow: Foreign Languages Publishing House, 1917). The American Marxist Paul Sweeney, in turn, refers to monopoly capitalism and militarism as a basis for explaining the postponement of the ultimate confrontation between those who own and those who work the means of production, while pointing to the evidence of increasingly acute contradictions within capitalism. See Paul A. Baran and Paul M. Sweeney, *Monopoly Capital: An Essay on the American Economic and Social Order* (New York: Monthly Review Press, 1966). Also Paul M. Sweeney, *Modern Capitalism and Other Essays* (New York: Monthly Review Press, 1972). Discussion in Wogaman, *The Great Economic Debate*, pp. 22–6.
[76] Fatima Meer, 'African Nationalism: Some Inhibiting Factors', in Heribert Adam (ed.), *South Africa: Sociological Perspectives* (London: Oxford University Press, 1971), p. 150.
[77] See, for example, Shula Marks, 'The Ambiguities of Dependence: John L. Dube of Natal', *Journal of Southern African Studies*, 1:2, 1975, pp. 162–80.

society.[78] Material and financial resources have also not always been expended to the maximum benefit of workers in post revolutionary socialist situations. Sin is no respector of persons, making the Marxian vision of humanity at once both too romantic (people's highest ideals are tarnished by waywardness) and too Promethean (people seldom have the resourcefulness to realise their ideals).

Socialist ideals and Marxian intentions aside, the essential question is whether any person or group of persons (political party) should ever be entrusted with unlimited power. Reinhold Niebuhr's famous dictum remains true: 'Man's capacity for justice makes democracy possible; but man's inclination to injustice makes democracy necessary.'[79] Niebuhr did not deny the human capacity for fairness. He argued that such values are mixed up with more selfish emotions. If human nature were more benign, he observed, the benevolent ruling class would be a realistic political possibility. But because human beings are selfish and corrupted by the attainment of power, democracy is essential. The utopian Marxian notion which suggests that the corruption of human power will be eradicated with the transcendence of class divisions and the private ownership of property, does not correspond to the radicality of a biblical understanding of human sinfulness.[80] Theologically, this is what makes legal safeguards against the abuse of power imperative.

A theological critique of the political economy is at the same time ultimately a critique of theology. Karl Barth's critique of liberal theology as a legitimation of the dominant cultural trends of the nineteenth century is well established. As theology drifted deeper and deeper into synthesis with the dominant ideological trends of the period, so it became increasingly willing to leave ever larger sections of society to the specialised control of others. Politics became the domain of politicians, education was left to educationalists and the economy became the exclusive responsibility of business leaders and economists. This is nowhere more vividly portrayed than in an article published by Andrew

---

[78] Albert Camus, 'Neither Victims Nor Executioners', *Politics*, July-August, 1947.
[79] Reinhold Niebuhr, *The Children of Light and the Children of Darkness* (New York: Scribner's, 1944), p. 19.   [80] Wogaman, *The Great Economic Debate*, p. 69.

Carnegie, American business tycoon and sometime 'theologian' in the late nineteenth century. It is not the task of the Christian faith, he insisted, to comment in any way about *how* money is made since (in Douglas Meeks' paraphrase) 'the process of producing wealth is determined by inexorable natural laws, such as the laws of the survival of the fittest and the competition of tooth and fang'. The Christian religion, Carnegie argued, only becomes pertinent after the production process is completed, money is generated and reinvested. The surplus should then, he argued, be disposed of in such a manner as to include charitable donations to the *deserving poor*.[81] John Wesley, a century earlier, provided similar counsel in suggesting that Christians earn all they can, save all they can and give all they can. The only restraints he saw fit to mention at the level of acquisition pertained to moralistic concerns with gambling, smuggling and alcohol.[82]

There is, of course, an alternative and more critical vision of theological responsibility *vis à vis* the political economy. In addressing the Evangelical Commission for Advancement and Social Responsibility in Nicaragua in October 1989, during the build up to the election that brought Violetta Chamora's coalition government to power over the Sandinista revolutionary party four months later, a local pastor, Reynaldo Teffel, observed:

A true reading of the Gospels leads to democracy and socialism. I say democracy and socialism because historically they occur as separate trends, which the Stalinists as much as the capitalists have tried to present as antagonistic trends, as dichotomies, impossible to synthesize. In reality socialism is a culmination of democracy, so much so, that a true democracy leads to socialism and a true, profound, humanistic socialism can only develop from a democracy.[83]

The implication being – neither dogmatic *laissez-faire* capitalism nor dogmatic scientific socialism. A theological understanding of the political economy demands more than either can deliver.

---

[81] Meeks, *God the Economist*, p. 20.
[82] John Wesley, 'The Use of Money', in Edward H. Sugden (ed.), *Wesley's Standard Sermons* (London: Epworth, 1956), vol. II, pp. 309–27.
[83] Reynoldo A. Teffel, 'Evangelical Perspectives on Faith and Democracy in Nicaragua', *Amanecer*, 11, January–March, 1990, p. 32.

CHAPTER 7

Theology and economic justice

Central to a theology of reconstruction is economic transformation. Recognising the weaknesses and failures of the dominant economic systems of both East and West, a commitment to economic democracy and social well-being requires a determined global effort aimed at the emergence of an economic order that transcends the weaknesses of both systems.

TOWARDS AN ALTERNATIVE VISION

The World Council of Churches had already defined the challenge facing the churches at its first Assembly in 1948:

The Christian churches should reject the ideologies of both Communism and *laissez-faire* capitalism, and should seek to draw men away from the false assumption that these extremes are the only alternatives. Each has made promises which it could not redeem. Communist ideology puts the emphasis upon economic justice, and promises that freedom will come automatically after the completion of the revolution. Capitalism puts the emphasis upon freedom, and promises that justice will follow as a byproduct of free enterprise; that too, is an ideology which has been proved false. It is the responsibility of Christians to seek new, creative solutions which never allow either justice or freedom to destroy the other.[1]

John Paul II has, in turn, insisted that both liberal capitalism and Marxist collectivism 'are imperfect and in need of radical correction'. Facing the implications of his own words, the Pope ponders the question 'in what way and to what extent are these two systems *capable* of changes and updatings such as to favor or

[1] *The First Assembly of the World Council of Churches*, edited by W.A. Visser 'T Hooft (New York: Harper and Brothers, 1949), p. 80.

promote a true and integral development of individuals and people in modern society?'[2] At the same time he insists that 'the church's social doctrine is not a third way between liberal capitalism and Marxist collectivism'.[3] It constitutes rather a vision which transcends both, while affirming the strengths and turning away from the weaknesses of both systems.

It is clearly not the task of the church to conjure up some alternative to both capitalism and socialism. This would be for the church to irresponsibly dabble well beyond the confines of its theological domain. It is the task of the church, however, to subject economic systems to the demands of the gospel which affirm the dignity of all people and their obligation to work for a more just social order. It is the task of the church to keep alive a social vision in support of such economic initiatives which shape, bend and redirect the world economic order as well as individual national economies towards the benefit of those who suffer most in society – with a view to addressing both their *present* needs and their future demands.

This involves the identification and utilisation of contradictions within the liberal culture which sustain capitalism, as well as of the inconsistencies within Marxist ideology used to sustain socialism. Briefly stated, the church is obliged to support the ideals of *democratic* liberalism, to the extent that it allows all members of society to be equally free to fulfil their capacities in society, over against such dogmatic forms of liberalism which function as an ideological justification of individualistic notions of the freedom of choice and an unfettered market system. It is at the same time obliged to support the goals of *democratic socialism*, to the extent that it promotes economic sharing and decision-making, over against a ruling elite in state-controlled economies. In brief, *theologically the appeal must be for democratic intervention in the economy*. Theologically speaking, ethics and human rights must take precedence over economics. To leave the political economy to market or social–scientific forces is to turn away from the God-given calling to participate in the transformation of society. It is to abdicate the human spirit to impersonal and manipulative

---

[2] John Paul II, *On Social Concern*, para. 21. Italics are added.   [3] *Ibid.*, para. 41.

forces which destroy and confine the capacity of people to share in the shaping of their own destiny.

At one level this intervention could result in no more than a 'mixed economy', drawing on capitalist *and* socialist economic institutions to produce the correct mix for a given society. At another, suggests Karl Polanyi, *'not for the first time in history may makeshifts contain the germs of great and permanent institutions'*.[4] Whether the quest for economic justice ultimately transcends both capitalism and socialism or mixes the two is not theologically important. Economic justice is!

The collapse of Soviet and Eastern European economies and the growing contradictions within western capitalism have given rise, among a small but growing community of economists, concerned democrats, political activists and theologians, to a perceived need to move beyond economic ideological warfare which leaves large sections of workers in the East and West alienated, excluded and often exploited. The concern for a managed economy which is able to address the welfare of this stratum of society is something that few economists can afford to ignore.

There is a sense, of course, in which the capitalist political economy has always been shaped in *praxis* (it is a consequence of actual struggle). Advocates of free-market capitalism have, for example, been forced by circumstances and worker struggles to make concessions which benefited workers, such as workers' compensation and pensions. Trade union laws and antitrust regulations emerged in a similar manner, coming to be seen by capitalists as expedient for the maintenance of the self-regulating market. This kind of intervention in the political economy, argues Polanyi, ultimately separates the social democratic side of economic liberalism from *laissez-faire* capitalist theory.

The height of the battle, he suggests, was fought in the late nineteenth century when Herbert Spencer and others charged liberals with deserting their principles for the sake of 'restrictive legislation'.[5] Polanyi's list of industrial related social legislation

---

[4] Karl Polanyi, *The Great Transformation: The Political and Economic Origins of our Time* (Boston: Beacon Press, 1967), p. 251. Italics are added.   [5] *Ibid.*, p. 145.

(ranging from the prohibition of child labour to health laws and employer liability for injuries suffered by employees) is, in turn, enough to suggest that pure (hands-off) *laissez-faire* capitalism is 'inapplicable to advanced industrial conditions'.[6] Differently stated, the self-regulating ingredient of *laissez-faire* capitalism came to include such regulations which were demanded by workers. The key to the emergence of further developments to a more just and participatory economy is to be found here. It is indeed in the actual struggle for justice that lies the seed of future economic structures and social transformation.

John Rawls' *A Theory of Justice*, provides a theoretical framework for political–economic renewal so important that it must be mentioned in a discussion of this kind. His concern is the defence of liberty while making every effort to ensure that no one benefits at the expense of anyone else. For him 'justice is fairness'.[7] His argument is familiar to many. In brief, if a group of people were projecting values on which to build a future just society from behind a 'veil of ignorance' (not knowing where they would fit into the resulting socio-economic matrix), while having some knowledge as to how society operates, they would decide on two principles:

First Principle: Each person is to have an equal right to the most extensive total system of equal liberties compatible with a similar system of liberty for all.

Second Principle: Social and economic inequalities are to be arranged so that they are both: (a) to the greatest benefit of the least advantaged ... and (b) attached to offices and positions open to all under conditions of fair equality of opportunity.[8]

He further argues that the first principle ought to have 'lexical priority' over the second.[9] In other words, any attempt to adjust inequalities ought to take place without violating the basic liberties of others. 'Liberty can be restricted only for the sake of liberty.'[10] The second principle, in turn, allows that whatever inequalities exist in an economic system ought to be to the benefit of the least advantaged members of society. This

[6] *Ibid.*, p. 150.
[7] John Rawls, *A Theory of Justice* (Cambridge, Mass: Harvard University Press, 1971), p. 12.   [8] *Ibid.*, p. 302.   [9] *Ibid.*, p. 242–51.   [10] *Ibid.*, p. 302.

situation could arise, for example, if the payment of a higher wage to a particular factory worker resulted in a greater overall surplus divided between all the workers to the benefit of all, including the least advantaged workers.[11] 'Social and economic inequalities . . . are just only if they result in compensating benefits for everyone, and in particular for the least advantaged members of society.'[12] Finally, Rawls argues that the difference between the most and least advantaged members of society should not necessarily be a permanent feature of society. Hence his insistence in part (b) of the second principle that 'offices and positions be open to all under conditions of fair equality of opportunity'.

Assessments of Rawls' theory have been varied and extensive.[13] Comment here is limited to five observations which have direct theological implications:

1 Rawls' theory is clearly a compassionate and persuasive presentation of liberalism. It must be accepted as such. Concerned to be fair to all, Rawls does so within the context of each individual weighing his or her position in society against that of other individuals. What he fails to do is verify his assumption that everyone behind a 'veil of ignorance' would necessarily want to structure a society with a focus on individualism. His liberal assumptions are in fact the focus of debate among those committed to a new political economy. They cannot merely be assumed. Differently stated, Rawls' principles are not as neutral as they might appear to be. The communal or covenantal understanding of humanity, discussed in Chapter 5 would, for example, provide a different set of principles.

2 The lexical priority given to basic liberties over the fair distribution of goods leaves David Hollenbach arguing 'if push were to come to shove it would appear that social and

---

[11] See Lebacqz, *Six Theories of Justice*, p. 36.   [12] *Ibid.*, p. 15.

[13] See, *inter alia*, Norman Daniels (ed.), *Reading Rawls* (New York: Basic Books, n.d.); Robert P. Wolff, *Understanding Rawls: A Reconstruction and Critique of a Theory of Justice* (Princeton: Princeton University Press, 1977). Charles Simkins, *Reconstructing Liberalism*; Lebacqz, *Six Theories of Justice*. A useful Marxist response is found in Allen E. Buchanan, *Marx and Justice: The Radical Critique of Liberalism* (Totowa, New Jersey: Rowman and Littlefield, 1982), pp. 101–61.

economic claims are not claims at all'.[14] Rawls nevertheless allows that basic liberties may, in certain circumstances need to be restricted in order to 'prepare the way for a free society'.[15] Hollenbach's point is that in this concession Rawls identifies the fundamental problem facing a liberal theory of rights. The tacit recognition by Rawls, that sometimes a trade off is required between liberties and goods, is not adequately developed in his theory.

Rawls' theory of justice fits a society within which there is a more or less equal distribution of wealth better than it does situations that show vast discrepancies between the rich and poor, which is a dominant feature of South African society and an increasing number of contemporary capitalist countries. In brief, Rawlsian theory does not explicitly address the complexity of a global economy with the urgency that is needed.

3 'Equal liberty without equal worth of liberty is a worthless abstraction', writes Norman Daniels.[16] Rawls is not unaware of the problem, but ultimately concludes that although the 'worth of liberty' is affected by economic inequality, liberties can still be distributed equally.[17] Rawls' reluctance to face the contradiction between basic liberties and economic inequality with sufficient concern ultimately leaves his theory without the insight required to reshape the existing contradiction within western societies. Alperovitz's observation that 'democracy dies when equality grows' presents a challenge which Rawls cannot afford to ignore.[18]

At the heart of Rawls' theory seems to lie the assumption that the normal functioning of the market, with those at the top better off than those at the bottom, will have a trickle down effect to the benefit of everyone. Brian Barry dismisses this assumption as a 'living fossil'.[19] Contradictions presently

[14] David Hollenbach, *Claims in Conflict* (New York: Paulist Press, 1979), p. 17.
[15] Rawls, *A Theory of Justice*, p. 152.
[16] 'Equal Liberty and Unequal Worth of Liberty,' in Daniels (ed.), *Reading Rawls*, p. 204.   [17] Rawls, *A Theory of Justice*, p. 204.
[18] Alperovitz, 'Building a Living Democracy', p. 13.
[19] Brian Barry, *The Liberal Theory of Justice: A Critical Examination of the Principle Doctrines in a Theory of Justice by John Rawls* (Oxford: Oxford University Press, 1973), p. 111.

tearing at the heart of capitalism suggest that this Rawlsian assumption needs radical reassessment.

4 Robert Wolff tellingly concludes that Rawls' theory is ultimately a theory of distribution rather than justice.[20] It suggests that an increase in income will necessarily result in an increase in self-respect. There is sufficient empirical evidence to show that this is not the case.[21] What Marxists refer to as the alienation of labour (as discussed in the previous chapter) within capitalism has not been addressed by Rawls. Will a mere increase in wages in itself eliminate the alienation of workers?

5 Rawls' theory which seeks the welfare of the least advantaged members of society, while protecting the basic liberties of all citizens, presents a challenge which cannot be dismissed. The challenge has to do with bending, stretching and transforming the existing economic structures until they function 'to the greatest benefit of the least advantaged' (first part of his second principle). Charles Simkins argues that Rawls' concern is not to compare capitalism and socialism as ideal types, but rather to enquire which system would in a given situation best serve the least advantaged.

> The fruitful approach for South Africans (writes Simkins) is to start from an analysis of existing South African society and to ask whether the successive introduction of more capitalist elements or more socialist elements or even a coherent mixture of both would lead to a more just society in the sense of improving the position of the least well-off.[22]

E.P. Thompson, by implication, comes close to the position affirmed by Simkins. Addressing the ideologically loaded matter of law (as already noted in Chapter 3) he argues that while law is by definition an 'instrument of the *de facto* ruling class', it 'cannot simply be reduced to class power'. In actual struggle it becomes 'less an instrument of class power than a central arena of

---

[20] Wolff, *Understanding Rawls*, p. 210.
[21] R. Sennett and J. Cobb, *The Hidden Injuries of Class*, (New York: Knopf, 1973), especially pp. 4–8, 18, 22, 28–9, 53.
[22] Simkins, *Reconstructing South African Liberalism*, p. 47.

conflict'.[23] These insights apply equally to economic institutions. Economic realism requires more than a simple repudiation or walking away from the existing order. The moral claims of this existing order, suggests Roberto Unger, need to be pushed to their logical conclusion and exploited to the advantage of the poor.[24] This demands rigorous analysis of all available options in the service of the poor, and forceful participation in the existing order to gain maximum benefit from it for the disadvantaged. It also, where necessary, requires participation as a basis for subverting and eventually transforming the existing order.

Compelled to give expression to its most essential belief in human worth, the church is obliged to serve those whose dignity is being destroyed by the structures of society. This requires the discernment of gospel values in secular dress within the struggle for economic justice. It is this that makes the nexus between theology and economics a focal point of any theology of reconstruction.

A THEOLOGICAL CHECK LIST

The social history of the church in the West has to a significant degree been the struggle for power between church and state. The rise of the market economy, suggests Meeks, has shifted the locus of power away from the state to capital. This does not mean that state power is no longer an authoritarian threat to human dignity, but it does mean that theology is obliged to be more focally concerned with economic domination as it shares in the struggle for a society within which the fundamental human rights are affirmed.[25]

The point has already been made. It is not the task of theology to provide a blue-print for an alternative economy. It is not competent to do so. There are, however, biblical and theological teachings on economic values pertinent to the struggle for economic justice. It is the task of the church to affirm these and

---

[23] E.P. Thompson, 'Class Rule', extracted in Piers Beirne and Richard Quinney (eds.), *Marxism and Law* (New York: Wiley, 1982), p. 133.
[24] Unger, *Social Theory*, pp. 169–90.   [25] Meeks, *God the Economist*, p. 49.

related ethical values, and therefore to measure all economic systems against them. These would need to include:

1 An affirmation of the fundamental values inherent in a Christian understanding of human dignity. As discussed in Chapter 5 these constitute a broad and inclusive set of rights which affirm the truth about what it means to be a human being created in the image of God. They include individual rights such as the freedom of speech and the right to vote together with such socio-economic rights as the right to eat, shelter, health care and education. They further include the right for each person to claim these with dignity and to realise his or her full potential when sharing in the creation and maintenance of society. In other words, rights and responsibilities are inherently related.

2 The insistence on political and economic democracy. This means that First Generation human rights cannot be separated from Second and Third Generation rights. Alperovitz, as already noted, argues in his powerful article in *Sojourners* magazine that, 'democracy dies when inequality grows'.[26] The growing gap between the rich and poor, in many countries in the world, results in increasing numbers of people being socially marginalised. Apart from the suffering and loss of human potential involved, a political consequence is the growing power of the economic elite in society. In recognising the capacity of all people to promote the ends of justice, and at the same time to show a seemingly inevitable inclination toward injustice and the abuse of power (Niebuhr), theologians are obliged to fight for the fullest democratic participation in society. A theological understanding of humanity and politics instinctively works against ruling elites whether before or after any revolution. Structures which militate against the fullest participation in society by all people, must also be perceived theologically as a violation of the opportunity for people to fulfil their God-given obligation to share in the creation of a better world. This means that an economic system which systematically excludes people from

[26] Alperovitz, 'Building a Living Democracy', p. 13.

sharing fully in the shaping of economic and other forms of life must inevitably face theological censure.

3 Preference for the provision of the basic necessities which enable all people to share fully in life over against the *absolute* protection of all property rights and the endless accumulation of wealth. As discussed in Chapter 4, this requires the church to be engaged in pastoral ministry designed to promote the orderly redistribution of resources to the benefit of the poor – recognising that there are no 'polevaults to equality'.[27]

The appeal does not imply statist paternalism. Material handouts often do more harm than good to the poor. An economic system which, on the other hand, leaves the poor destitute while the rich go joyfully about their business is destructive to the humanity of both the rich and the poor. Economists concerned to promote the interests of the poor are at the same time increasingly aware that the indiscriminate nationalisation of property ultimately fails to serve the interests of the poor, primarily because it undermines the vibrancy of the economy. The task of the religious sector is not to promote any particular proposed economic solution to the needs of the poor, but to thoughtfully test all such proposals against the ethical demand that all people have access to such resources that enable them to attain the fullness of life.

4 An ecological concern. There is a growing awareness that the exploitation of natural resources for immediate profit, without regard to the needs of future generations or the effects of pollution on the natural order, is already beginning to have the most disastrous effects on life potential. A theology which sees humanity to be a related and integrated part of the entire created order, as discussed in the Chapter 5, cannot but be committed to economic development only within the confines of ecological concern.

5 Actual economic reconstruction, rather than the promotion of any particular economic ideology. If there is ever to be a

---

[27] See Langan's discussion on John Paul II's encyclical *On Social Concern*. Albie Sachs discusses some models for redistribution in 'A Bill of Rights for South Africa: Areas of Agreement and Disagreement', *Columbia Human Rights Law Review*, 21:1, Fall, 1989, pp. 23–6; 33–6.

way forward to a living democracy, it will almost certainly
have to involve the transformation of society beyond what is
conceptually embodied in either revolution or reform. Revolution, in the form of the complete rejection of the existing
order of things, is becoming more and more difficult in the
complexity of the modern world. *There are perhaps no more
opportunities to start again, given the all encompassing nature of the
world economic order.* Revolutionary attempts to do so in the
West, often end (for a variety of conflicting reasons) in
consequences that contradict the values of the proponents of
change. Reform, on the other hand, tends to seek to attain
changed goals without changing the underlying structures of
society. Writing on the American experience, Alperovitz'
comment is a telling one:

> If 20th-century experience teaches us anything, it is that despite the
> gains of the civil rights movement, the feminist movement, the New
> Deal, and the Great Society, progress toward reducing real world
> inequality of fundamental economic circumstances has been vir-
> tually nil.[28]

Without suggesting that reform initiatives ought to be
abandoned, Alperovitz' concern is rather that the gains made
and opportunities won within the reform process be pushed to
where existing structures are stretched and transformed to the
point where they give way to *alternative institutions*. Martin
Buber, Alperovitz reminds us, employed the notion of
reconstruction, long before the word *perestroika* made its way
into the modern vocabulary of the West, in order to suggest
this option. It involves a slow (by comparison with cataclysmic revolution) but resolute and effective commitment to the
transformation of the existing order. This includes 'building
"within the shell of the old society" step by step until enough
experience, vision, moral energy, and political organizing has
occurred – enough social and political momentum has been
built up – to allow a more general *perestroika* to take place'.[29]
Roberto Unger, as already shown, addresses the same need in
arguing that the Marxist notion of revolution, within modern

---

[28] Alperovitz, 'Building a Living Democracy', p. 22.   [29] *Ibid.*

society, is both too radical and not radical enough. He argues for an option somewhere between the total rejection of the existing order and conservative tinkering with the existing order. This is a position, he suggests, more radical than revolution primarily because of its commitment to the sometimes tedious and always less romantic task of reconstruction. At the same time it necessitates a commitment to ensure that people are not left defeated and exhausted, but, rather, equipped for continuing struggle beyond political transformation.[30] In brief the notion of 'revolutionary patience' (Dorothy Solle) needs to be rediscovered as an ingredient in the ongoing struggle for a new economic order.

The theological commitment to the realisation of the values of the gospel involves this subversive commitment to a positive long-term future. It involves too the promotion of what Barth calls 'God's revolution', demanding more than the highest ideals of the revolution, without ever using this as an excuse not to support the best alternative options available at a given time, or what John Bennett has termed 'the next steps that our own generation must take'.[31] Grateful for the limited victories won through reform, rebellion and revolution, and supportive of those which promote the interests of the oppressed and create the possibility of a more egalitarian culture, the theological task is also to agitate and work for goals beyond immediate attainment. The desire to keep alive the highest ideals of social justice and egalitarianism is what lies at the heart of the prophetic and messianic teaching of the scriptures, whilst requiring Christians to support the best economic options that a society can come up with at a given time in history.

6 Support for the creation of structures of socio-economic renewal. The Christian debate on socialism in the West has been as firmly grounded within the context of democratic liberalism, as it later became influenced by the thought of Karl Marx. In many instances it has been content to adopt a reformist position, and in recent times rarely concerned itself

---

[30] Unger, *Social Theory*, p. 151.
[31] John Bennett, *Christian Ethics and Social Policy*, p. 77.

with the overthrow of the existing economic structures. It has nevertheless sought to emphasise democratic participation and a broadening of the economic base, over against the unrestricted economic freedom of the individual. The history of these developments is extensive and varied, and need not be reviewed here.[32]

7 The promotion of programmes of socio-economic renewal, designed to mobilise and incorporate grassroots people in reconstruction and social development. These would need to include technical and other forms of education and training initiatives, the promotion of urban services designed to reintegrate the poor into the structures of society, rural and land development, and support for intermediary structures in society, intended to enable the fullest democratic participation in the nation-building process.[33]

DAMN YOUR CHARITY — WE WANT JUSTICE

Karl Marx disparagingly observed: 'Christian socialism is but the holy water with which the priest consecrates the heart-burnings of the aristocrat.'[34] Building partly on the early roots of the Christian socialist movement, with some adding a dash of Marxism, Walter Rauschenbusch, William Temple, Reinhold Niebuhr, Karl Barth, Paul Tillich and others have expanded the values of economic democracy without ever becoming locked into an ideological attack on the market system. Temple is reported to have insisted that his own inner feelings were summed up in the banner frequently carried at parades of workers and the unemployed: 'Damn your charity — we want justice!'[35] It has, nevertheless, largely been Third World liberation theologies that have inserted a 'revolutionary fervour' into the Christian debate on socialism, and in many ways it is liberation theology that has thrust the socialism debate back

---

[32] John C. Cort, *Christian Socialism* (Maryknoll: Orbis Books, 1988).
[33] See proposals on such developments in post-independent India in Thomas, *Christian Participation in Nation-Building*, pp. 125f, 178f, 188f.
[34] Quoted in Bernard Murchland, *The Dream of Christian Socialism: An Essay on its European Origins* (Washington: American Enterprise Institute for Public Policy Research, 1982), 'Preface'. [35] Quoted in Cort, *Christian Socialism*, p. 171.

into prominence on the theological agenda. Liberation theologians have at the same time been criticised, from the left and right ends of the theological and political–economic spectrum, for failing to develop specific strategies of reconstruction (as asked for by Unger, Buber, Alperovitz and others) designed to transform the existing order of things, without destroying the socio-economic infrastructure required to build a new society. Two brief comments must suffice:

The first concerns *collective capital sharing*. Gary Dorrien in his article 'Economic Democracy', in *Christianity and Crisis*, shows that Archbishop William Temple (in *The Hope of a New World*) promoted the idea of a decentralised economic democracy in such a way that he anticipated a movement for worker participation in management which found growing support in Europe and elsewhere at the time. He proposed an 'excess profits' tax which could be used to create a series of collective, worker-controlled funds, that would eventually enable workers to attain a controlling share in major economic enterprises. Today (fifty years later), worker participation in industrial management has become a major policy proposal of many democratic socialist parties in Europe.[36] Dorrien draws on the work of Rudolf Meidner, a pioneer economist in the field of collective capital sharing and control whose proposal, in a modified form, was accepted several years back by the Social Democratic government of Sweden. The plan, accompanied by built-in wage restraints, provided for a 20 per cent tax on major company profits to be paid in the form of shares into a mutual fund controlled by workers. As the amount of the mutual fund grew, so workers would be collectively entitled to representation on company boards, with a ceiling of 40 per cent on worker-owned shares – a further compromise of the Meidner plan. Details of the specific plan aside, 'the overriding importance of the plan', suggests Dorrien, '. . . is that it offers a way beyond the welfare state, by expanding the base of economic power, while saving the social and political gains of liberalism.' In brief, the plan offers an alternative to the welfare state as well as an

---

[36] Gary J. Dorrien, 'Economic Democracy: Common Goal For Liberation Movements', *Christianity and Crisis*, 50:12, 10 September 1990, pp. 271–4.

alternative to state-owned industry – both of which deny/limit the participation of workers in the shaping of their own economic future. The four original goals of the Meidner plan deserve the attention of all who are concerned with the democratisation of economic structures. They are:

1 to provide employees with a share in the benefits accruing from excess profits;
2 to counteract the increasing concentration of capital in the Swedish economy;
3 to give workers a greater say over their working lives;
4 to contribute to collective savings for productive investment.[37]

As important as the Swedish vision, is the reason why the Swedish Social Democratic government was ultimately obliged to turn away from it. This was because the scheme did *not* ultimately give individual workers a sense of personal fulfilment and control over industry. It transferred a measure of control away from management to the trade unions. Workers chose a simple increase in wages as a better alternative. Worker expectations, material aspirations and demands for radical participatory democracy constitute a challenge that trade unions, no less than democratically elected governments, are obliged to unravel and address. The consideration of the relevance of the Meidner plan to South Africa (accepting the vast difference between the Swedish and South African economies), undertaken by Maree and Torres, opens the way to creative options beyond both the concentration of ownership in the hands of the few and the nationalisation of industry.[38]

Unrelated to the Meidner project, an alternative scheme has emerged in Alaska as a basis for compensation to the inhabitants of the region by the oil industry. The entire Alaskan community receives a payment of almost $1,000 per resident per year from oil royalties, with equal amounts being allocated to publicly determined uses.[39] The Malaysian government's 'Bumiputra'

---

[37] Maree and Torres, 'Democratisation of Capital in South Africa', paper delivered at *Association for Sociology in South Africa*, Twentieth Annual Congress, July 1990, p. 10.
[38] *Ibid.* [39] Alperovitz, *Building a Living Democracy*, p. 19.

policy, in turn, ensures a gradual transfer of share ownership in Malaysian companies from Chinese investors to the indigenous Malaysian population.[40] Looking at related options, Albie Sachs raises a variety of models of economic reform in South Africa which could allow workers and others to benefit more fully in the economic resources of the country.[41]

The options for broadening the bases of ownership of the means of production are wide and extensive. European countries, Britain and the United States can all point to joint ownership ventures, and South African history in the 1930s provides numerous co-operative ownership schemes designed to promote Afrikaner participation in what was largely an economy owned by English speakers. Steve Biko's promotion of the Black Peoples' Convention created to co-ordinate and promote black political and economic well-being, until it was banned in 1976, is a further example. Laurence Harris (professor of economics at the Open University in London) has, in turn, spoken of options for redistributing wealth through antitrust legislation, the implications of nationalising what are often referred to as the 'commanding heights' of the economy (which are those industries whose products and services affect the running of virtually every other sector of industry) and the promotion of private and co-operative ownership in other areas.[42] To debate these and other proposals for enabling broader participation within the economic wealth of society is beyond the limits of this study.

This brief mention of different initiatives is enough to show that there are options for redistribution which lie between *laissez-faire* capitalism and state-controlled industry. Pieter le Roux interestingly investigates some of these options with regard to South African state pensions, characterised by the gross discrepancies inherent in the apartheid system. His

---

[40] Donald Leyson, 'Sachs: a Visionary with Resentments', *Monitor* December 1990, p. 71.
[41] Sachs, 'A Bill of Rights for South Africa', *Columbia Human Rights Law Review*.
[42] Laurence Harris, 'The Mixed Economy of a Democratic South Africa'. A paper delivered at the Lausanne Colloquium of the Institute for Social Development, University of the Western Cape, under the auspices of the Institut De Hautes Etudes en Administration Publique, Université de Lausanne, Switzerland, 8–13 July 1989.

concern is not only with workers' democracy regarding the administration of the funds, but also with the very significant investment contribution made by the funds.[43] Suffice to say yet again, from a theological perspective, all specific economic proposals need to be investigated and tested (as difficult as this process may be, because there is no laboratory!) to determine to what extent they benefit the poor and least advantaged members of the community.

The privatisation and deregularisation policy presently being adopted by some western governments, notably in Britain and South Africa, of course, raises problems for the implementation of these kinds of proposals. Certainly this development must be of the greatest concern to black South Africans as they watch the South African government *selling off the family silver* just as they are about to take their place at the table. This fear is perhaps nowhere more clearly seen than in the cutback of medical services for the poor and the further privatisation of medicine.

The second comment on structures for socio-economic renewal is directly related to the importance of *intermediate political structures* such as trade unions and other 'middle level' structures (between people and government). The imposition of centralised state control over all sections of society was a hallmark of Soviet and Eastern European statism. The point has already been made; oppressive regimes around the world, South Africa among them, have repeatedly interfered with Trade Union and other intermediary structures. In so doing they have undermined worker participation in the shaping of the economic system. Theologically these structures can function as channels (even 'means of grace') through which people can realise their God-given calling to share in the creative process of renewing society. They are part of the intermediary structures of civil society which new wisdom is recognising to be essential buffers between the political elite and the people – as already discussed in Chapter 5.

The significance of the civil society for initiating and maintaining options of the kind proposed in the Meidner plan,

---

[43] Pieter le Roux, 'Whither With Pensions in a Post-Apartheid South Africa', *Monitor*, December, 1990, pp. 90–6.

the Alaskan agreement, the Malaysian scheme and the goals envisaged by Biko and others is immense. The re-emergence of the trade union movement with broad-based black participation in South Africa has, in turn, become perhaps the major influence for change both in national politics and industrial relations in the last decade. It has contributed to the political organising of the working class, provided an effective base for collective bargaining with management and become the major influence for improved worker conditions and management accountablility.

WHAT IS TO BE DONE?

What then are the general demands that the church is obliged to make on a future political economy in South Africa?

1 The economy would need to be strong, vibrant and growth-oriented to enable the upliftment of the poor. Redistribution is probably the most important item on the political agenda of a new South Africa, much in the same way that it dominates the reconstruction agenda of Eastern Europe. Apartheid involved the deliberate and systematic redistribution of land and resources from blacks to whites, and reconstruction must necessarily involve some measure of redistribution of wealth from whites to blacks. This, it is argued, is an exercise in levelling the playing field. The moral persuasion of such an argument, provided the redistribution process is fairly executed with some form of compensation, is overwhelming. The economic and political equation involved is, at the same time, a delicate one. Anything short of economic empowerment of the poor is likely to be politically impalatable. There are at the same time limits to the redistributive capacities of any economy – not least a sluggish South African economy. A 1991 publication by a group of South African economists committed to redistributing economic resources to the poor entitled, *Redistribution: How Can It Work In South Africa*, provides useful resource material which has a sobering effect on anyone committed to the welfare of the poor. Turning

away from nationalisation as a solution to the problem, the authors of the study identify a range of alternative options ranging from tax reforms to labour market interventions, education initiatives and economic growth proposals.[44] However committed we may be to improving the economic status of the poor, or narrowing the gap between the two extremes of the political economy, this is simply not possible without an economy capable of sustaining the exercise.

To ensure sufficient immediate redistribution to meet the political demands of the expectant poor, while allowing for sustained economic growth to facilitate the long-term benefit of the under classes, the church is obliged to support a 'managed economy' designed to serve the interests of those hitherto excluded from the wealth of the nation. Accepting that the economy has, since the beginning of the colonial period, been designed to serve the interests of whites (and poor whites since the inter-war years), it is insufficient merely to deregulate the economy allowing 'market forces' to determine future economic development. The dispossession of blacks needs to be reversed, with affirmative economic actions designed accordingly.

2 Given its bias in favour of the poor, the church cannot allow market forces to marginalise and/or exclude those whose resources make them unable to compete in a market economy with those who own or dominate the means of production.

3 The church would be required to consider providing moral support for the renationalisation of those sectors of the infrastructure of the country that have been privatised as a means of preventing certain resources from passing into the hands of a democratic government. This applies especially to the privatisation and semi-privatisation of schools, medical services and other social services.

4 A theological concern for the economic well-being of the poor would further require the serious consideration by economists of the effects of relocating key sectors of the economy in the hands of the state, joint-ownership schemes and/or a broad

---

[44] Peter Moll, Nicoli Nattrass and Lieb Loots (eds.), *Redistribution: How can it Work in South Africa?* (Cape Town: David Philips, 1991.

spectrum of share-holders as a possible means of redistributing the wealth of the nation to the maximum benefit of the least advantaged members of society. Alternatively regulations would need to be explored as a means of ensuring that the present ownership of the 'means of production' serves the interest of the poor.

5 The huge concentration of economic wealth in the hands of the few conglomerates, controlled by a small sector of the white population, would need to be broken up as a basis for creating a fairer and more level economic playing field which allows more participation by more people in the economic decision-making of the nation.

6 The church would need to support the generation of funds to redress the desperate consequences of the unequal distribution of resources under apartheid. These funds could be partially provided through the scrapping of wasteful, duplicated facilities and bureaucracies required to implement apartheid in schools, government services, legislative councils and related structures. A meaningful 'peace dividend', arising from a scaling down of the military and politically related police services, could also make its contribution. The church (a vast land-owning institution) would itself, in turn, need to investigate ways of facilitating economic redistribution. Ultimately, however, it would take the injection of a massive amount of foreign aid and investment to rebuild a war-torn apartheid economy. This would require a profit-oriented economy to realistically meet the expectations of western, capitalist-oriented governments and business corporations.

7 Services and economic resources would need to be extended to areas ignored or underserviced by the apartheid regime. This would mean the upgrading of the infrastructures and basic services available in rural areas.

8 The energy of all people and resources in the private and public sectors would need to be harnessed to meet the challenge of reconstruction. This would require innovative ways of relating the private and government sectors in a mixed economy. The degree to which this is likely to emerge in

the future could determine the extent to which economic reconstruction is a realistic possibility.

9 Recognising the need for all people to realise their full human potential through participation in all facets of life, the democratisation of the economy, aimed at promoting a shared solution to the economic challenges of reconstruction, is ultimately a theological priority.

BY WHAT POWER?

A theological check-list as inclusive as the one mentioned, together with the general demands stated immediately above, could be perceived as overbearing – if not unrealistic. It can be little more than romantic rhetoric, if not grounded in a progressive cultural renaissance which sustains the nation in its long-term quest for renewal. The goals can only be considered options to the extent that society is inspired by ideals, and can only be attained through a culture that allows this process to happen. This constitutes an important unfulfilled task, which stands at the centre of the quest for an alternative economic system. It has to do with the probing of cultural and religious traditions and moralities as a basis for projecting new goals and empowering people. Cornel West writes:

The prophetic elements of religious traditions that sustain communities, preserve universal values, and project international visions may well constitute the most credible agents for progressive political hope in the new epoch.[45]

He suggests that alternative traditions, such as liberalism, social democracy and other secular initiatives have failed to generate the necessary breadth of sacrifice and commitment required to create this alternative vision. This failure has given rise to a predominance of nationalisms and sectarian interests that militate against the very communal vision that is needed. This, West provocatively argues, 'means that the grand

---

[45] Cornel West, 'Sustained by Prophetic Vision', as part of the series of responses to Alperovitz, 'Building a Living Democracy', *Sojourners*, October 1990, p. 22.

enlightenment linkage of progressive politics to secular ideologies has been damaged, and may even be severed'.[46] West's concern in his *The American Evasion of Philosophy*, is a reconception of philosophy (and no doubt theology) as 'cultural criticism that attempts to transform linguistic, social, cultural, and political traditions for the purpose of increasing the scope of individual development and democratic operations'.[47] Drawing on Antonio Gramsci, his goal is a form of *prophetic pragmatism* capable of engaging in 'a cultural battle to transform the popular mentality'.[48] West's own prophetic pragmatism is located in the prophetic Christian tradition and democratic socialism. Others approach a similar goal from within different religious and political traditions, meaning that, ultimately, the empowering source of renewal is necessarily culturally and religiously pluralistic, complementing and mutually enriching of different traditions.

New visions are not easily born and the forces weighing against their realisation are massive. Without a new vision, however, there is likely to be an intensification of the existing political and economic contradictions; a widening of the gap between the rich and the poor (with a few becoming very rich and many more becoming poor) and a greater level of authoritarianism required to contain the conflict. The medium-to long-term consequence for national, regional and global social stability is terrifying, making the quest for an alternative vision all the more urgent. For West, Alperovitz, Unger and others it involves radical democratic participation in life, grounded in cultural renewal. Larry Rasmussen makes the sobering point. 'Perhaps it is not . . . whether democracy nurtured by a considerably different culture is up to the task. Perhaps the question is whether human nature is.'[49]

It is this that links questions of political economy to theological concerns about the nature and renewal of humanity. Given the human propensity for selfishness and personal gain,

---

[46] *Ibid.*
[47] Cornel West, *The American Evasion of Philosophy: A Genealogy of Pragmatism* (Madison: The University of Wisconsin Press, 1989), p. 230.   [48] *Ibid.*
[49] Larry Rasmussen, 'A Task for Generations', *Sojourners*, October 1990, p. 23.

although also for justice and community, theological reflection reminds us that we cannot hope to live in a world without exploitation. To borrow a phrase from Camus – we can, however, at least fight for a world in which exploitation is no longer legitimate.[50] To proclaim the gospel in today's world means in addition to all else ensuring that justice, essentially for the poor and those hitherto excluded from the economic heritage of society, gains priority over the selfishness of others. Above all it means the right of people to participate in the shaping of their own destiny and future. This theologically is a 'lexical priority' (Rawls) and 'imperative of grace' on which the church can never afford to renege.

Writing four years after Algerian independence, which came in the wake of savage war, the expulsion of a million *pieds-noirs*, the estimated death of a million Algerians (out of a population of 12 million people) and an extensive destruction of the infrastructure of the country, Frantz Fanon wrote:

The fundamental duel which seemed to be that between colonialism and anti-colonialism, and indeed between capitalism and socialism, is already losing some of its importance. What counts today, the question which is looming on the horizon, is the need for a redistribution of wealth. Humanity must reply to this question, or be shaken to pieces by it.[51]

This is a lesson which ideological cadres of both *laissez-faire* capitalism and scientific socialism would do well to learn as nations, old and new, edge towards reconstruction. The church, to the extent that it is concerned about socio-economic justice, has a special obligation to facilitate this learning process because, when all is said and done, the gospel is about concrete expressions of good news to the poor. It has no interest in promoting any particular ideological perspective on the economy.

50 Albert Camus, *Neither Victims Nor Executioners*, (Chicago: World Without War Publications, 1972).
51 Quoted in Wilson and Ramphele, *Uprooting Poverty*, p. 357.

CHAPTER 8

The right to believe

At the centre of the struggle for human rights is the right to the freedom of conscience, freedom of speech and the consequent right to social or political organisation as a basis for defending and promoting one's views. These fundamental rights constitute the heart of the democratic process, on which all other human rights are built, maintained and promoted – whether individual or socio-economic.

The freedom of religion, rather than mere toleration, is an integral and indispensable part of this right and process; not merely at the bourgeois level of each person having the right to hold and promote his or her most essential values whether idiosyncratic or of social value, but more especially as an important ingredient of democratic participation, human solidarity and open debate. This is clearly not to suggest that these social practices are dependent on religion, or that they do not occur without religion. History is cluttered with instances of religious authoritarianism, while many noted democrats and political activists do not choose to regard themselves as 'religious'. To affirm the importance of the freedom of religion is simply to make two distinct, though related, observations about social engagement.

The first is the *sociological* claim that (most) people need solidarity groups for the mutual sustaining and care of one another, as a basis for promoting social concerns and, where necessary, as a basis for criticising and opposing the abuse of power. Where this right is protected by law and practice, the democratic process in greatly enhanced. While acknowledging the authoritarian manifestation of religious belief in history, it is also necessary to acknowledge that religion (especially in times of extreme repression) has also provided a basis for social engagement. This is witnessed, *inter alia*, in the seventeenth- and eighteenth-century Puritan movements in England and the American colonies, in the social engagement of the Dutch Reformed Churches in South Africa in the 1930s and in the role of the churches in the struggle against apartheid in the late 1980s when all secular resistance and liberation movements were either banned or restricted. History making religions (notably Christianity, Islam, Judaism and many indigenous African religions) promote the obligation of believers to sustain one another in commitment to the sacrificial promotion of social values through participation in the political order.

The second is the related *theological* claim that commitment to the realisation of the ideals enunciated in earlier chapters cannot come about through rational argument and persuasion alone. It comes from encounter and experience out of which cultural, moral and spiritual insight emerges. Solidarity groups, linking people across racial, economic and sexual divisions, can serve as an important corrective to people living in isolation from the opinions and needs of others, helping to transcend the fragmentation of society and the selfishness of people. For all the failure of the non-racial churches (the so-called English-speaking Protestant churches and the Roman Catholic Church) in the struggle for a new South Africa, the exposure of their members to the immediate suffering and needs of one another has contributed to an amelioration of the harsh divisions of the apartheid society in a way that racially divided churches were never able to accomplish. From this milieu has come a motivating and sustaining culture that has united Christians, people of other faiths and of secular culture into a community of struggle.

THE SOCIAL SIGNIFICANCE OF RELIGION

Karl Marx's concern was that religion misdirected the attention of the proletariat away from the socio-economic causes of their misery to the empty and non-existent heavens. This perception did not, however, prevent him from realising that 'religious suffering [of the oppressed] is at the same time an expression of real suffering'.[1] He argued that the early Christians 'lost their chance of the kingdom of heaven on earth because they rejected and neglected engagement in overt political action'.[2] From this malady, at differing levels of intensity, the church has suffered ever since. Religion has at the same time been a significant part of the process of social transformation in western society. It is perhaps not insignificant that one of the most noted celebrations of direct human participation in the historical process came with the birth of the Protestant and Catholic Reformations and the emergence of the industrial age. Bracketing out the debate on the complex relationship between religious ideas and the socio-economic or material base, it is important to note that the bourgeois leadership in both industry and church needed to act quickly to suppress the poor who, inspired by religious ideals, thought that they too were entitled to share in the fruits of this new-found liberatory process. The growth of technological political control and the loss of individual initiative in human history, in turn, emerged at a time when religion was being driven out of the political arena, into the ghetto of privatisation.

The advantages of the secularisation process and modern technological inventions are too obvious and too numerous to discuss here. Modernity has at the same time driven more than one society, and perhaps western culture itself, into what Max Weber has aptly described as an iron cage.[3] Marked by rationalisation, bureaucratisation, systematisation and control, it has held people (with the exception of the brave and rebellious!) mentally and culturally captive to an all-absorbing, all-controlling bureaucratic organisation that excludes dissident ideas, dysfunctional behaviour and rebellious tendencies. The outcome is the loss of self- and community control over life,

---

[1] Karl Marx, 'Contribution to the Critique of Hegel's Philosophy of the Right', in *The Marx–Engels Reader*, edited by Robert C. Tucker (New York: W.W. Norton and Co. 1978), p. 54.
[2] Karl Marx, *The First International and After: Political Writings*, III (New York: Vintage Books, 1974), p. 324. Also Jose Miranda, *Marx Against the Marxists* (Maryknoll: Orbis Books, 1978), pp. 277–8.
[3] Arthur Mitzman, *The Iron Cage: An Historical Interpretation of Max Weber* (New York: Kopf books, 1970), pp. 181–92.

decreased democratic participation in life and ultimately social indifference. All too often the Orwellian Big Brother and Ministry of Truth is not even required in the modern world. Like the characters depicted in Huxley's *Brave New World*, humankind comes to enjoy its captivity, infatuated by the mechanical orderliness of it all.[4] We are ready to accept the official version of truth, sometimes out of fear and sometimes because there are certain dubious social benefits to be derived from so doing. The outcome is blunted imagination and domesticated hope, while religion becomes little more than the spiritual legitimation of the dominant ideology which teaches people to accept 'what is' as being without a realistic alternative.

Steve Biko depicts the reality of this attitude towards life for black South Africans, in writing:

All in all the black man has become a shell, a shadow of a man, completely defeated, drowning in his own misery, a slave, an ox bearing the yoke of oppression with sheepish timidity . . . The first step therefore is to make the black man come to himself; to pump back life into his empty shell; to infuse him with pride and dignity, to remind him of his complicity in the crime of allowing himself to be misused and therefore letting evil reign in the country of his birth.[5]

The alarming decline in the level of actual democratic participation in western societies has emerged in a different, but not unrelated, manner. In discussing state legitimation, Jurgen Habermas sees the modern state being increasingly held captive to the demands of the economy, while finding it increasingly difficult to justify its actions to an ever increasing section of society.[6] The only thing the state can do in this situation, suggests Habermas, is to pacify its citizens with consumer goods. But this too can only work to a limited extent. Unable to avoid the impoverishment of more and more by fewer and fewer, the state is inevitably confronted with a legitimation crisis. In order to survive it is compelled to resort to increasingly exclusive or undemocratic forms of government, if not simple repression.

---

[4] Neil Postman, 'Amusing Ourselves to Death'. Address to 36th. Frankfurt Book Fair, October, 1984.
[5] Steve Biko, *I Write What I Like* (London: Heinemann, 1978), p. 29.
[6] Jurgen Habermas, *Legitimation Crisis* (Boston: Boston Press, 1971).

Nicholas Wolterstorff takes issue with Habermas at this point, perceptively suggesting that in an increasing number of situations the crisis does not materialise.

> In North America and the Western world in general, I find citizenry more and more acquiescent in the face of these developments. Perhaps those who shape ideology in our societies have succeeded in persuading the public that these developments are something like unfortunate facts of nature about which nothing can be done. If that is what is going on, then it appears to me that, for the time being, at least, the ideologues have been successful – assisted, no doubt, by the obvious difficulties of the socialist economies.[7]

If there is any hope amidst the gloom of such total control and submission it is to be found, in the words of Paul Tillich, in the fact that:

> Human beings cannot renounce being human. They must think; they must elevate being into consciousness; they must transcend the given . . . When this has happened, there is no way back.[8]

It is the beginning of a restless sense of discontent; a precious and essential ingredient of democracy to be nurtured, sustained and promoted by all freedom-loving people. Grounded in what it means to be human, it is sustained by a variety of different world views and cultures – and, for a significant part of South Africa, Eastern Europe and many Third World situations, by prophetic religion.

Prophetic biblical religion (and there are many pathological brands of religion) is about the quest of people to rise above the limitations of their captivity. St Augustine gives expression to this religious incentive in defining theology as a response to a restlessness buried within the question concerning what it means to be human. 'Do you not believe', he asked, 'that there is in [the human person] a "deep" so profound as to be hidden even to that person in whom it is?'[9] Whether understood psychologically, socially or theologically, this kind of religion is about the

---

[7] Nicholas Wolterstorff, 'Theology, Law and Legitimate Government'. Occasional Paper No. 2, published by the Theology in Global Context Association. 1989, pp. 4–5.

[8] Paul Tillich, *The Socialist Decision* (New York: Harper and Row, 1977), p. 44.

[9] St Augustine, *Expositions on the Book of Psalms*, vol. II (Oxford: A Library of Fathers, 1848), p. 194.

need to transcend the real or imaginary limits imposed on the human condition.

Freud, Marx and Nietzsche argue that the *religious* quest for fulfilment of the Augustinian 'deep' was misdirected. They suggest that all manner of social ills can be cured if the victims of religious neurosis would only 'withdraw their expectations from the other world and concentrate all their liberated energies into their life on earth'.[10] Despite their too optimistic preoccupation with their own solutions to life's dilemmas, they were essentially correct in their response to the distorted and anti-human brand of state-sponsored religion with which they were confronted. Julian Huxley reminds us that the notion of God 'out there' is neither adequate nor broad enough to describe or account for the 'feeling of the sacred' which he too sees as innate to the human condition.[11] Martin Heidegger, in turn, insists that to live religiously is not necessarily to be a Christian, a Muslim or a Jew. It is simply 'to dwell poetically' and to be open to the challenge of life beyond the existing order of things.[12] Paul Tillich, seeking to bridge the gap between Christian theology and secular society, spoke of a 'God above God', and the need to transcend theism, as basis for discovering what it means to be human and realise our full potential as humans in the face of the oppressive and alienating structures of life.[13]

Karl Barth, of course, rejects this kind of human-centred religion as rebellion against God. For him it is an exercise in anthropology rather than theology. God, he insists, is radically and wholly 'other', while many anxious theists instinctively rush to affirm at least this bit of Barthian dogmatics! It was precisely the identification of God with humanist ideals, he argues, that led to notions of an Aryan superman (the masculine emphasis is appropriate here). He suggests that the very desire of humanists to affirm a restlessness within humanity, is ultimately destroyed

10 Sigmund Freud, *The Future of an Illusion* (Garden City, New York: Anchor Books, 1964), p. 82.
11 Julian Huxley, *Religion Without Revelation* (New York: Harper and Bros, 1957), pp. 47–50.
12 Martin Heidegger, *Existence and Being*, edited by Werner Brock (Chicago: Regnery Gateway, 1968), p. 280–90.
13 Paul Tillich, *The Courage to Be* (New Haven: Yale University Press, 1952), p. 186.

by reducing God to an ideal or ultimate form of who *we* are. For Barth, God 'must never be identified with anything which we name, or experience, or conceive or worship as God'.[14] God is the source of human restlessness precisely because God is beyond human conception (except that God is revealed in Jesus Christ), always demanding that we be more than we are at any time in history. As such God is seen as the source of the correcting, disturbing and challenging dynamic within the human endeavour, drawing it forward to ever greater achievements, enabling it 'to be and to stay human in the world', preventing it from 'devouring its own children'.[15]

There are significant differences between the God-centred kind of theology of Barth and the social humanist tradition of religious thought of people ranging from Huxley to Tillich. There are also similarities. Leaving aside the differences, and turning away from the theological and philosophical debate that has for so long characterised the encounter between these traditions, it is clear that the notions of religion and faith employed in both traditions are concerned with motivating people to break out of socially and ideologically imposed images of who or what they are or can become.

Mikhail Bakunin warned that 'whenever a chief of state speaks of God . . . be sure that he is getting ready to shear his flock'.[16] Attempts to exclude or limit the influence of religion in society ought to be viewed with equal concern. Religion has bedevilled many a political situation, while at best it is a source of human restlessness and potentially a source of continuing social renewal. Without this dynamic the democratic process is impoverished. Turbulent priests and other troublesome people motivated by a belief in the fundamental right of the freedom of conscience and/or religious belief can be socially bothersome but they are important 'disturbers of the peace' within the democratic process. The litmus test for democracy is ultimately: *where are your dissidents?*

[14] Karl Barth, *The Epistle to the Romans* (London: Oxford University Press, 1960), p. 330.
[15] Paul Lehmann, *The Transfiguration of Politics* (New York: Harper and Row, 1975), p. xiii.
[16] Quoted in Nicholas Lash, *A Matter of Hope* (Notre Dame: Notre Dame University Press, 1981), p. 167.

Rosa Luxembourg had cause to observe in a polemic with Lenin:

Freedom only for the supporters of the government, only for the members of one party – however numerous they be – is not freedom at all. Freedom is always and exclusively freedom for the one who thinks differently . . . its effectiveness vanishes when 'freedom' becomes a special privilege.[17]

Luxembourg's words were not regarded by all democrats as immediately appropriate in the special conditions that prevailed immediately after the October revolution. Whether deliberately deceptive or simply naïve, Lenin's argument that the social and political repression which he deemed necessary at the time would be short-lived was palpably wrong. His assumption that the state and its traditional instruments of repression would wither away was even further off the mark. The outcome, writes Slovo, was 'the narrowing of democracy for the majority of the population, including the working class'.[18] Unless individual freedom and the right dissent is incorporated in society from the outset, it is unlikely to become an ingredient of that society without immense struggle and conflict.

The costly and well-known words of Martin Niemoller exist as a perpetual reminder of the alternative to the right to believe and proclaim one's beliefs:

The Nazis came for the communists and I didn't speak up because I was not a communist.
Then they came for the Jews and I did not speak up because I was not a Jew.
Then they came for the trade unionists and I didn't speak up because I wasn't a trade unionist.
Then they came for the Catholics and I was a Protestant, so I didn't speak up.
Then they came for me . . . by that time there was no one to speak up for anyone.[19]

---

[17] Rosa Luxembourg, *The Russian Revolution.* Quoted in Joe Slovo, *Has Socialism Failed?* (London: Inkululeko Publications, 1990.), p. 14.   [18] *Ibid.*, pp. 14–15.
[19] Quoted in Paul Lehmann, 'Piety, Power and Politics: Church and Ministry Between Ratification and Resistance'. A lecture delivered at the Divinity School, Vanderbilt University, February 1982.

LEARNING FROM OUR PAST

The most important human rights in any situation, it was earlier argued, are those being violated at the time. This requires a Bill of Rights protecting human rights to address the *de facto* social ills of the society for which it is being written.

If South Africa is to be given a new lease of life, the designers of the new social order would do well to enquire which were the fundamental causes of the collapse of the old order.[20] These, as discussed in earlier chapters, include the systematic interference in the rights of individuals to dissent from state ideology and engage in democratic actions designed to change the dominant ideology. The point has already been made. The outcome was a form of totalitarianism (or 'state interference in matters that ought not to be the subject-matter of political control'), resulting in interference in academic freedom, the closing down of newspapers, the indiscriminate banning of books, restrictions on the freedom of speech and interference in the freedom of religion.[21]

The latter, being the focus of the present chapter, has roots extending back to the arrival of the first white settlers and the Dutch East India Company in South Africa, 1652, and the establishment of the Nederduitse Gereformeerde Kerk (NGK) as the religious centre of that community. When almost a hundred years later (1738) the Moravian missionary George Schmidt established a mission station at Genadendal he was forbidden by the civil authorities from administering the sacraments – ostensibly because his evangelical piety clashed with the Calvinist orthodoxy of the established church. In 1744 Schmidt was forced to close his mission and return to Europe, primarily because his work was a threat to the social life of the settler community, with the 'good burghers' of the white settlement in Stellenbosh (a hundred kilometers away) com-

---

[20] See the approach to constitutionalism adopted by Johan van der Vyver in commenting on the South African Law Commission's provisional report on 'Group and Human Rights' in the *South African Law Journal*, 106, 1989, pp. 539–40.

[21] The definition of 'totalitarianism' is that of Johan van der Vyver, 'Constitutional Guidelines of the African National Congress', *South African Journal of Human Rights*, 5, 1985, p. 139.

plaining that the sound of the mission bell disturbed their services of worship! Roman Catholics were, in turn, prohibited by both successive Dutch and English colonial rulers from public worship in the Cape until 1804, while the rallying call of the Afrikaner church–state alliance, well into the present era, has traditionally included a warning of a *'Roomse gevaar'* (Roman danger) along with the paranoia of a 'black danger' and 'red peril'.

The most notorious direct act of interference in religious freedom in the modern period came in 1957 when Hendrik Verwoerd, Minister of Native Affairs, introduced what came to be known as the 'church clause' designed to impose racial segregation in the worship services of the non-racial churches, despite the fact that black worshippers in so-called 'white' congregations were (and still are) extremely few. The churches protested and the outcome was modified legislation allowing the state to prevent black Christians from worshipping with white Christians should anyone complain that they were a 'nuisance' or worshipping in 'excessive numbers'![22] Then, when as recently as 1983 the Eloff Commission was appointed to investigate the affairs of the South African Council of Churches, it condemned all forms of political theology, whether 'for the state' or 'against the state', arguing that the true gospel addresses 'only truly spiritual purposes' and that politics should be left to the secular forces of 'national interest'.[23] And in 1987 the Commissioner of Police introduced regulations making it illegal for churches to call for the release of political detainees. Seeing this as a violation of religious freedom, church leaders organised an ecumenical service in St George's Cathedral in Cape Town, calling on Christians to pray for the release of those in prison. 'The state', said Stephen Naidoo, who was Roman Catholic Archbishop at the time, 'is trying to take away our right to decide for whom we

---

[22] This legislation is discussed in my *Trapped in Apartheid: A Socio-Theological History of the English-Speaking Churches* (Maryknoll: Orbis. Cape Town: David Philip, 1988), pp. 18–19.

[23] For an analysis of the Eloff Commission see, C. Villa-Vicencio 'Theology in the Service of the State: The Steyn and Eloff Commissions', in C. Villa-Vicencio and J.W. de Gruchy (eds.), *Resistance and Hope: Essays in Honour of Beyers Naude* (Grand Rapids: Eerdmans. Cape Town: David Philip, 1985), pp. 112–25.

shall pray. With regard to public prayer, we will not accept it.'[24]

The state had, of course, recognised the political significance of religion and the claimed right to worship God. Non-racial worship could (with more organised commitment by the churches) have become an important act of resistance against the feverish attempt by the zealous Verwoerd to segregate South African society. The political content of worship, however, became most clearly obvious in the latter part of the 1980s when the vacuum created by the restrictions placed on political resistance groups was being filled by the churches and other religious groups. The distinction between what the state judged as worship and political engagement had grown extremely thin. Churches and mosques were providing hospitality to political activists whose organisations had been crushed by state oppression. The activists, in turn, helped sensitise church and mosque to the obligation to resist repression and affirm the God-given right of people to be free. From a Christian perspective they provided the context within which the church was reminded of the ministry of Jesus, who resisted the domination of the state and affirmed a gospel which proclaimed good news to the poor and liberty to the oppressed (Luke 4: 18–19).

Essentially, the right of people to affirm and proclaim their most fundamental beliefs, which lies at the heart of all religions, constitutes a vital contribution to society. It cannot be turned away from without destroying the democratic process.

THE SEPARATION OF RELIGION AND STATE

The freedom of religion and conscience, as part of the democratic process, presupposes the existence of the secular state. Free from the constraints of both theocracy and atheism, the secular state which is tolerant and accepting of conflicting and different individual views and social values, ultimately accepts that there is only one tribunal for dealing with the pluralism of modern society, and that is the political process. Religion which is, in turn, committed to the affirmation and

---

[24] C. Villa-Vicencio, *Trapped in Apartheid* (New York: Orbis Books, 1988), p. 94.

proclamation of truth cannot afford to settle for anything less than the truth as it emerges from the encounter with other truth claims from different religions and secular philosophies.

We return to the notion of 'sovereignty' as discussed in Chapter 3, recalling that it was at the height of the sixteenth-century European religious wars that Jean Bodin perceived the need for a notion of sovereignty which enabled people of different religious and ideological persuasions to live together in harmony. His solution was a sovereign under the laws of God and the constraints of a constitution.[25] The state, he argued, should at one and the same time transcend the sectarian demands of any one particular group while subjecting itself to an authority higher than itself. In a traditional homogeneous religious sense this has been seen to require submission by the state to the will and demands of God. In a situation of religious pluralism this immediately raises the question, whose God? Within a particular religion related questions emerge concerning the correct interpretation of what the will of God might be for a given nation. In the same way that people need to be protected from state dictatorship, the history of religious authoritarianism is enough to convince us of the need to be protected against religious tyranny.

The separation of religion and state protects not only the state from sectarian interests and perceptions of the truth, it also protects religion from becoming captive to the dominant interests and values of the state. The alliance between the Afrikaner churches and the Afrikaner state, from which the Dutch Reformed Churches have found it almost impossible to distance themselves, is only one example of this malady which has cost both state and church dearly in South Africa. The role of the English-speaking churches in British colonialism has been an equally hazardous example of the church ultimately becoming the spiritual aroma of the dominant political ideology of the time. Indeed the mention of the name of the Christian God within the South African constitution has probably done more to alienate exploited black people from the church than any

[25] Bodin, 'Sovereignty', *Encyclopedia of Philosophy*, (New York, Macmillan Publishing Co. 1967). vol VII, p. 502. Pinkard, *Democratic Liberalism*, p. 58.

secular or atheist state philosophy could ever have accomplished. To separate religion from the state allows scope for a prophetic witness, on the part of churches, mosques, synagogues and temples, which contributes to the democratic process and enables religion to take its own teaching seriously.

The European Convention on Human Rights of 1970 has probably come as close as is required to meet the needs of religious freedom:

Everyone has the right to freedom of thought, conscience and religion; this right includes freedom to change his religion or belief and freedom, either alone or in community with others and in public or private, to manifest his religion or belief, in worship, teaching, practice and observance.

Freedom to manifest one's religion or beliefs shall be subject only to such limitations as are prescribed by law and are necessary in a democratic society in the interests of public safety, for the protection of public order, health or morals, or for the protection of the rights and freedoms of others.

In summation, religion is obliged to accept certain limitations which ultimately serve its own interests in a secular state:

1 No one section of society can impose its beliefs on others. The separation of religion and state guarantees the freedom of belief and practice. One religion protects its right to believe by protecting the right of others to believe differently. Alternatively one religion is likely to dominate others, promoting a kind of religious classicism that can only undermine the quest for national unity.

2 No particular religion can utilise the machinary of the state to impose its views or social norms on others. This enables religion to escape the temptation to succumb to the temptation to which it has so often submitted; the resort to coercion and legal censure to attain its ends. The only valid religious means of persuasion are rational debate, patient teaching and the challenge of a good example. If Christians do not wish to fish on a Sunday, Jews refuse to use public transport on a Saturday and Muslims insist on attending mosque on a

Friday, these are religious rights to be promoted by religious means and democratically respected. They cannot be imposed on those who do not wish to observe them. Theologically it is wrong to ask the state to do what a particular religion is unable to do for itself.

3 There ought to be sufficient space within the separation of religion and state to allow for mutually beneficial co-operation between government and religious institutions. Especially in developing nations church-based schools, clinics, child-care centres and other social services may well warrant government funding, provided these do not function in a proselytising or discriminatory manner. The absolute or rigid separation of church and state in emerging nations is likely to generate more social problems than it can solve by persuasion.

4 The separate organisation of different religions promotes intermediary social structures which (as indicated in earlier chapters) can help address the growing need for social services at a community level, while helping to overcome both collectivist and individualistic worldviews. Individuals need to cultivate the art of living in relation to one another, while preserving the richness of diversification in contributing to the larger structure of the nation without conforming to some notion of statism imposed by the ruling elite. Edmund Burke once spoke of the 'little platoons' of life, which he defined as church, family, neighbourhood and party. Whether these be religious, cultural, vocational or voluntary communities it is within and through these kinds of 'accessible' structures that democratic participation in life, mutual caring and spiritual/cultural sustenance is most likely to be found. Outside of these groups individuals, and more especially those individuals who are economically or socially marginalised, are likely to drop out of society. This point has already been made regarding economic participation in Chapter 6.

5 The right for each religious group to meet and promote its views and values on an equal basis with others preserves a sense of diversification and pluralism in society which sustains

ongoing debate and the challenge of new perspectives. Rather than relativising the search for truth, the challenge of competing faiths promotes the complexity of truth.

6 There are, of course, a variety of specific religious issues to be faced in affirming the separation of religion and state. These include religious holidays, the oath of government office, religious education in schools, religious services on radio and television and a variety of related issues. Dialogue between religions and with the state is the only basis for a satisfactory solution to these concerns. The only proviso being that no specific religion be allowed to enjoy domination over others (as is the case in South Africa and many other western countries).

THE POLITICAL RESPONSIBILITY OF RELIGION

F. Scott Fitzgerald once argued that it is the mark of a first rate intelligence to be able to live with two contradictory ideas and still function. Such wisdom aside, a sound doctrine of religion–state separation presupposes the affirmation of both secularisation and religion in the political arena.[26] In brief, the separation of church and state does not amount to religious quietism. The issue is not the right of believers to influence public policy, but *when and how they ought to do it.*

Religious and political judgment are both needed in structuring society – and they are not the same thing. Religious and conscientious opinion and conviction are often the driving force behind moral and social renewal. The imposition of these ideals on all other members of society by way of legislation, however, constitutes a violation of a central tenet of both the democratic process, as well as an enlightened understanding of religious identity which presupposes the thoughtful and free acceptance (or rejection) of the demands of a particular religion. From a

---

[26] Martin E. Marty makes the point that the separation of church and state in the United States emerged in response to two social movements, religious pietism and secular enlightenment. See *Faith of Our Fathers: Religion, Awakening and Revolution* (Wilmington, North Carolina: Consortium Books, 1977), p. 137. See also William Lee Miller, *The First Liberty: Religion and the American Republic* (New York: Paragon House Publishers, 1988).

democratic perspective, the religious person (like anyone else) is free to use the political process to persuade his or her fellow citizens that the behaviour which he or she proposes in a given situation is to the benefit of the entire society. Such a person may firmly (and religiously) believe that the proposed behaviour should not only be promoted on a parochial or sectarian basis but, because it is promotive of order, peace, justice, kindness and love should be for *everyone* concerned. The limits of democracy require, however, that the believer (like everyone else) is obliged to accept that some may disagree with such views, or merely stubbornly resist them. Some battles are won and some lost. Tolerance, mutual co-existence and democracy always carry within themselves the option of defeat. The words of Thomas Jefferson in this regard point to the power and the weakness of democratic rule: 'We set up government by consent of the governed, and the Bill of Rights denies those in power any legal opportunity to coerce that consent. Authority here is controlled by public opinion, not public opinion by authority.'[27]

Speaking on his responsibility as both a Roman Catholic and governor of the state of New York (in dealing with the difficult issue of abortion) Mario Cuomo argues that, while believing he has a 'salvific mission as a Catholic', this does not mean he is conscience bound to do everything he can as governor to translate all his religious views into the laws and regulations of the state of New York.[28] In order to be free to practice his own beliefs, he sees himself duty bound to defend the right of those who disagree with him, not to be bound by his views. Recognising that society is made up of people of many different religions and cultures, holding different moral values he argues:

Our public morality, then – moral standards we maintain for everyone, not just the ones we insist on in our private lives – depends on a consensus view of right and wrong. The values derived from religious belief will not – and should not – be accepted as part of the public morality unless they are shared by the pluralistic community at large, by consensus.

27 Quoted in Miller, *The First Liberty*, p. 68.
28 Mario Cuomo, 'Religious Belief and Public Morality', an address delivered at the University of Notre Dame on 13 September 1989. Published in *Origins*, 14:15, September 1989.

That values happen to be religious values does not deny them acceptability as a part of this consensus. But it does not require their acceptability, either.[29]

Rather than excluding religion from the public arena of political debate, the secular state encourages religious people and organisations to enter the debate with fervour and commitment in order to promote their particular views – with one proviso, and that is that they play by the same democratic rules as anyone else. In a heterogeneous society this is the only viable basis for promoting a public morality. There may well be some absolute 'rights' and 'wrongs' for society, as many religious people and groups would argue there are. In public morality these are to be defined, defended and promoted on the basis of reason and political process rather than revelation.

From a theological perspective, a viable, practical, political ethic emerges on the basis of both theological principles and contextual demands. Driven and challenged by the former, we are obliged to restlessly strive for a morality higher than what any particular society is able to attain at any particular time of its history. Constrained by the obligation to challenge and motivate society by teaching, example and argument rather than by coercion and imposition, we are obliged to accept (although sometimes not to condone) the less than ultimate moral values that characterise a given society at a given time. The one demand which no person supportive of democracy can compromise, is the right to participate in the democratic process through which to change these norms. History shows that where these structures do not exist, revolution is inevitable.

Cuomo reaches to the heart of the right to the freedom of religion in a democratic state in posing the question: 'Are we asking government to make criminal what we believe to be sinful because we ourselves can't stop committing the sin?' Applying this to the proliferation of abortions in the United States, he argues: 'The failure is not Caesar's. This failure is our failure, the failure of the entire people of God.'[30] Bishop Joseph Sullivan, a man whose life is dedicated to work among the poor in New York

---

[29] *Ibid.*, p. 236.   [30] *Ibid.*, p. 239.

City and who is resolutely opposed to abortion, supporting the call of the Catholic bishops for a change in the abortion law, ultimately argues:

The major problem the church has is internal. How do we teach? As much as I think we're responsible for advocating public-policy issues, our primary responsibility is to teach our own people. We haven't done that. We're asking politicians to do what we haven't done effectively ourselves.[31]

Obviously the church's responsibility regarding abortion goes beyond teaching, as Sullivan himself insists. It is to provide counselling clinics, to provide funds and opportunity for pregnant women to rationally (and spiritually) face the options of abortion and childbirth, and to enable society to debate and resolve what is involved in the affirmation of the sanctity of life.

In brief, the task of the religious institutions in society is to be accomplished through persuasion and participation in the democratic process, not by coercion nor by special privilege. Accepting the implications of this challenge Kyril, Archbishop of Smolensk and Kaliningrad, in his address (referred to earlier) to the Council of Bishops of the Church of Russia spoke of the need for the church in the Soviet Union to move away from what had earlier been perceived as her destiny: 'to exist on the periphery . . . [without] usefulness to society'.

A new model for the relationship between the church and the socialist government is coming into existence [suggests the Archbishop]; the revolutionary principle of freedom of conscience is genuinely being proclaimed.[32]

Insisting that while within the Soviet context this means that Christians are no longer regarded as second-class citizens, it does not imply a privileged status for the church in society. Recognising that Christians are theologically obliged to co-operate with nonbelievers, he stresses the need for a form of participation by the church in society which makes sense to the

---

[31] *Ibid.*

[32] Kyril, Archbishop of Smolensk and Kaliningrad, 'The Church in Relation to Society Under "Perestroika".' A report given to the Council of Bishops of the Church of Russia, held at St Daniel's Monastery, Moscow, on 9–11 October 1989.

community beyond the confines of the church. In so doing, it is the task of the church, he states, to address and surmount the problems faced by the Soviet people in their present crisis. In South Africa this is a lesson which the Christian church still needs to learn. Given the immense privileges with which it has traditionally lived (although clearly certain sections of the church more so than others), it is likely to learn this lesson only with difficulty. To do so will, however, serve the cause of democracy. It will also enable the church to rediscover its biblical mandate to be the servant of the people under the will of God. It is the only basis on which the religious groups will be able seriously to engage in a theology of nation-building.

THE RIGHT TO RESIST

The ultimate spiritual and social obligation of all religions is resolute and simple obedience to God. Called to work as the leaven in the dough, the church in a post-exilic age is obliged to find creative and positive ways in which to work with a democratically elected government. Theologically it is required, however, to do so with one proviso. This is never as a result consciously to disobey God in so doing. The biblical mandate, to obey God rather than a human agency where the one contradicts the other, constitutes an enduring ingredient of the gospel which the church can only deny at the peril of its very identity. In his *Letter from Birmingham City Jail*, Martin Luther King wrote: 'In no sense do I advocate evading or defying the law . . . This would lead to anarchy. One who breaks an unjust law must do so openly, lovingly . . . and with a willingness to accept the penalty.'[33] In facing a democratically elected government, given to the welfare of all the people of the country, even King's 'gentle' resistance ought to be a last resort. In certain situations, however, the church is obligated to exercise this option. This is ultimately the highest service the church can render the state. To fail to do so timeously, boldly and decisively could precipitate a situation within which the tyranny and

---

[33] Martin Luther King, *Why We Can't Wait* (New York: New American Library, 1963), pp. 76–95.

oppression from which nations in Eastern Europe, South Africa and elsewhere are struggling to escape, could happen all over again. In a similar way the church in established western democracies is required to learn again how to resist evil and support the common good.

As a Christmas gift for Colonel Oster and Hans von Dohnanyi (both of whom were executed on the same day as Bonhoeffer), Bonhoeffer wrote his celebrated essay from prison entitled 'After Ten Years'. 'Are we still of any use?' he asked.

We have been silent witnesses of evil deeds; we have been drenched by many storms; we have learnt the arts of equivocation and pretense; experience has made us suspicious of others and kept us from being truthful and open; intolerable conflicts have worn us down and even made us cynical. Are we still of any use? Will our inward power of resistance be strong enough, and our honesty with ourselves remorseless enough, for us to find our way back to simplicity and straightforwardness?[34]

This is the question that faces the church in established countries in the West. History suggests it is also the question which churches facing the opportunity to share in the process of reconstruction will do well to ponder as they face the challenges and temptations inherent to the nation-building process that lie ahead.

[34] Dietrich Bonhoeffer, *Letters and Papers from Prison* (London: Fontana Books, 1964), p. 148.

CHAPTER 9

An unconcluding postscript

A theology of reconstruction is about facilitating, promoting and supporting such actions that make and sustain human life in the best possible manner. The point has already been made. It is a positive and constructive theology, concerned with social, economic and political structures. It is more than a theology of resistance.

It is a theology which is obliged to say 'No' to all that distracts from or counteracts the life giving and sustaining process. As such it, in turn, needs to say 'Yes' to that which promotes social justice and human dignity. In some situations the 'No' will need to be bold and unequivocal. In others the 'Yes' will need to be decisive and without compromise. In most cases, however, concrete proposals, social programmes and actions involve neither an unqualified 'No' nor an uncompromising 'Yes'.

A theology of reconstruction is not an exact science. It is a creative and imaginative art, grounded in the hard realities and inevitable contradictions of human life and political manouverings. It involves an ethic which goes beyond slogans, while refusing to be dogmatically prescriptive. It cannot, however, afford the luxury of taking refuge in generalities and principles with which few take issue and most will have no dispute – primarily because such generalities are devoid of specific content. The complexity of issues central to reconstruction are at the same time such that there is no unqualified and detailed 'Christian' directive, arrived at on the basis of the Bible or a textbook of moral rules. A theology of reconstruction is obliged to keep alive the biblical (eschatological) vision which draws society beyond what can be accomplished at a given time, to new

274

ideals and better goals. It is a theology committed to continuous social renewal and revolution.

At the centre of this theology is the integration of an ultimate vision which disturbs the status quo that emerges at any given time, while promoting concrete proposals which provide the best possible solution to the specific needs of the time. Such a theology can only emerge from a thorough and careful understanding of the nature of the society it is seeking to address. In this sense, it is marked by contextual particularity, while drawing on historical and global insights as a basis for providing a thoughtful and critical social ethic. Standing within the methodological designs of liberation theologies, the quest for positive and practical alternative proposals constitutes (in a cautious manner) a new way of doing theology.

A METHODOLOGY IN OUTLINE

In what follows the essential ingredients of this 'new' kind of liberating theology are identified. The exercise is not intended to provide a theological or ethical conclusion (much less an answer) to the preceding chapters. It is rather an 'unconcluding postscript' which will hopefully contribute to the practical endeavour to find a new basis for living together.

Analysis

For theology to be contextually grounded it must emerge from, and in relation to, the actual, prevailing situation which it seeks to address. For this to happen an ethic which is seriously committed to concrete forms of social renewal must necessarily be committed to social analysis. Its concern is to discover, clarify and explain 'what is going on' in a given context. It is to engage in critical, non-ideological analysis, given to uncovering the power relations, socio-economic structures and cultural values which are responsible for suffering, exploitation and social conflict. While concerned to deal with and heal the painful symptoms responsible for these social maladies, an ethic of renewal is obliged to help identify the underlying *causes* of suffering.

Without this kind of rigorous commitment to *telling the truth* (despite who it may offend), an ethic of renewal will inevitably fall prey to a political power game, within which the concern for social renewal may be no more than an ideological mask for sectarian gain aimed at the subordination of one or another section of society. In pursuit of the common good, it is necessary clinically to discern the causes that militate against this end. Such clinical concern must however, as already made clear in early chapters, be located in the midst of life – where the cut and thrust of the necessary and real searching for alternatives is taking place. Theologically, truth and renewal are measured in terms of *praxis*, not ivory-tower perceptions of what suffering and renewal are perceived to be.

Theory

Theoretical debate often acquires a bad press in the struggle for social renewal. Frequently not without good cause. Theological work, grounded in *praxis* is, at the same time, by definition the creation of a conceptual framework within which political struggle, ethical endeavour and social renewal can and ought to be promoted. Without a *praxiological* foundation, theology is no more than abstract idealism. Without a theoretical framework for reflective critique and conceptualisation (grounded in the struggle for justice) *praxis* can be no more than thoughtless, reflexive and goalless activism – a kind of frantic running around in circles.

Interdisciplinary

Social analysis and a theoretical framework of reflection necessarily involves interdisciplinary work. A theology of reconstruction, required to address legal, political and economic concerns must be undertaken at the interface of the social sciences. As such a theology of reconstruction is by definition an interdisciplinary exercise. 'Theology', suggests Duncan Forrester, 'is too important a matter to be left to the theologians.'[1] A theology of reconstruction necessarily requires an encounter between theologians and proponents of other disciplines. If it is, however, no more than an encounter between experts it cannot give expression to the pathos, insights and creativity that come from those whose poverty and marginality have denied them expert theoretical learning, while empowering them with a level of experience for which no amount of academic learning can substitute.

The essential challenge facing socially engaged theologians in the immediate future is how to assist in the creation of a framework within which this broad interdisciplinary work can happen. To do so theology is obliged to at once take the challenges and insights of other disciplines seriously, while making its own contribution to this process in a language that makes sense to, and is understood by, other disciplines. As suggested earlier in this study, the interface between theology and law stands at the centre of the interdisciplinary encounter, providing a framework within which the debate on human rights, economics and culture building is to be pursued.

Inter-faith dialogue

Because theology is required to build a nation within which people of different faiths share, on the basis of the separation of religion and state, the inter-faith dimension of theology and social renewal needs increasingly to concern Christians as much as it is required to concern people of other faiths. In so doing Christians (and others) are driven to rediscover the essentials of their own faith, leaving aside the many accretions which have been imposed on their faith as a result of it being used as a tool of conquest and imperial domination. Without inter-faith dialogue, grounded in the separation of religion and state, the chance of cultural tolerance and mutual trust is simply not a possibility in a pluralistic state.

---

[1] Duncan B. Forrester, *Beliefs, Values and Policies: Conviction Politics in a Secular Age* (Oxford: Clarendon Press, 1889), p. 17.

Open-ended

This kind of theology involves ongoing reflection, re-evaluation and self-critique. Its major concern is not to make pronouncements which are securely defined or nailed down for the security of generations to come. It is open-ended, ready to secure compromises which provide the best solutions at the time to complex problems, while always insisting that any such solution is open to critique, new challenges and continuing transformation. This, ultimately, is perhaps the most significant contribution which theology can make to the process of social renewal. It involves an ethic that is both immediately relevant to society's needs and yet committed to transcending the limitations of the immediate time and place. The demands of the gospel are (as already suggested) such that theologically understood, social renewal must be a continuing revolution within which the concerns of the poor are continually employed as a lever to transform the structures of society to the greatest benefit of the least advantaged.

Constructive

A theology committed to continuing social renewal must be constructive in its critique of the existing structures. It is proposal oriented, seeking realistic solutions, sharing in the nation-building process. It is to be the servant of the poor in promoting their particular interests, while seeking the common good of all people. It is required to be a source of creative and imaginative solutions, seeking to translate into constructive proposals the implicit and latent ideals of the gospel.

A corporate process

In brief, a theology of reconstruction requires contributions from different disciplines and many different sources. The anger and enthusiasm of those who have suffered most from the injustices of society is usually greeted with suspicion (and sometimes disdain) by theoreticians and scholars. The implication being that those removed from the cut and thrust of struggle are able to be more dispassionate and therefore better agents of social renewal. This assumption is questioned as a liberating theology of reconstruction. The anger of those who suffer most often carries within it a creativity, imposed on it by sheer necessity, which needs to be incorporated into a theology given to social reconstruction.

This is a theology which gives expression to the corporate mind of those who, through sharing in a corporate struggle for liberation and social renewal, have gained fresh insights in reaching towards a new contextually specific solution to the most stubborn problems confronting society. It is a theology which necessarily needs to be a communal exercise that incorporates the perceptions of those who it has a special obligation to serve (the poor and oppressed), while being committed to the well-being of people in society.

Participatory and democratic

A consequence of a corporate approach to theology is a radical affirmation of democratic participation, both in the struggle for social renewal and in the mental constructs that help shape the new society that is waiting to be born. As such, whoever does the writing is to be open to the insights, stories and instinctive solutions of those who have suffered most in the old society and who have most to gain from a fundamentally different kind of society. It is often difficult for the exploited and impoverished in any society to articulate their understanding of social problems, their ethical goals and projected political solutions (to the satisfaction of the power brokers in society). To the extent that their views are ignored, however, to that extent is the process of social analysis and reconstruction undemocratic. As such the limited insights and prejudices of the powerful and dominant players in society are left unchallenged.

Those excluded from the dominant structures of society are often also freed from the dominant ideas of society which militate against social change. They (alone) are sometimes able to dream new dreams and see visions which are not controlled by the society that needs to be transformed. Required to serve the interests of the poor and oppressed, the theology of the church is to emerge out of this non-dominant sphere which includes the poor and marginalised in society. It is a theology which also needs to empower the poor. To the extent that it fails to do so it is illegitimate. It constitutes yet a further brand of opium.

VALUES AND ACTION

A theology of reconstruction is a corporate theology, given to democratic participation, expressive of interdisciplinary and inter-faith dialogue in its social analysis and theoretical structures. It offers no final answer to the complex problems with which society is confronted. As such it is open-ended, driven by an eschatological vision which demands more than a particular society offers at any given time. In brief, a theology of reconstruction is both *contextually responsible*, seeking to define the next logical step society is required to take at a given point in time, and *socially transcendent* in the sense of challenging society to reach forward to the social goals which form part of the social vision incorporated in the biblical metaphor of the reign of God.

This is a theology which, as indicated in the Introduction to this study, takes the sentiment expressed in the debate of several decades ago on 'middle axioms' seriously. Accepting the limitations of this debate for contemporary ethics, it is a debate that needs to be reopened in the light of the contemporary challenges which face the church. Recent studies on this debate by Dennis McCann, Ronald Preston and Duncan Forrester go a long way to locating the parameters within which this can happen.[2]

For present purposes it is sufficient to confine comments to several short observations:

1 James Gustafson's reference to middle axioms as 'anchors and compasses' constitutes an important dimension of the debate

---

[2] Dennis McCann, 'A Second Look at Middle Axioms', *The Annual of the Society of Christian Ethics*, 1981; Ronald H. Preston, *Church and Society in the Late Twentieth Century: The Economic and Political Task* (London: SCM Press, 1983); Forrester, *Beliefs, Values and Policies*.

around middle axioms.[3] Middle axioms involve a contextual attempt to define the social context of the gospel within a given situation. They are part of the process of discerning the signs of the times, an emphasis readily discerned by Oldham, Bennett and others when the middle-axiom debate enjoyed more prominence than it does today. Contemporary contextual theological debate cannot but take this insight seriously.

2 To read the signs of the times is closely related to the need to seize the moment as affirming God's time – the *kairos* – in contemporary history. In so doing it involves articulating 'what is implicit in the gospel as it bears on life'.[4] Critical of the middle-axiom debate at the time, Paul Lehmann correctly identified the danger of middle axioms being no more than a middle term between abstract ethical principles and action in a specific situation.[5] Paul Ramsey, in turn, fears an (endless) series of middle axioms between universal ethical principles, one level of middle axioms and another, and finally a specific plan of action.[6] This concern is what ultimately drives the middle-axiom debate in the direction of contextual theology. In Lehmann's understanding, these concerns compel ethical debate in the direction of a *koinonia* ethic, which involves discerning ethical behaviour in relation to what makes and keeps life human in a given situation at a given time in the history of a people.

Relocated within the framework of this concern, the middle-axiom debate can be seen as an attempt to state what the gospel requires at a given time in a given place, without ignoring its ultimate ethical demands on humankind. Thus conceived, it integrates the contextual and transcendental demands of the gospel. Without denying the higher demands of the gospel, it is concerned to suggest what these ideals require us to do when a certain set of circumstances prevail in a given situation.

3 To the extent that the middle-axiom debate is no more than a

[3] James Gustafson, 'Christian Ethics in America', *Christian Ethics and the Community* (Philadelphia: Pilgrim Press, 1979).   [4] Preston, *Church and Society*, p. 148.
[5] Paul Lehmann, *Ethics in a Christian Context* (New York: Harper and Row, 1963), p. 152.
[6] Paul Ramsey, *Basic Christian Ethics* (New York: Charles Scribner's Sons, 1950).

deductive approach to ethics within which there is an attempt to move down the ladder of abstraction in articulating yet a further set of principles, the reaffirmation of this heritage has little to contribute to an ethic appropriate for a society under reconstruction. In Forrester's words 'the collapse of consensus' concerning what the gospel requires of us, raises serious questions in contemporary society about middle axioms as originally employed by Oldham and others.[7] Given the hermeneutical, ethical and contextual pluralism within contemporary Christianity, and more essentially within societies like South Africa and Eastern Europe which are thrust into the cauldron of social renewal, the possibility of consensus around any ethical norms is at very best a complex process. It is perhaps this more than anything that has contributed to the mood of disenchantment with the middle-axiom debate.

Forrester suggests that an alternative approach to consensus among Christians in ethical debate is to be found in the Christian story rather than a theoretical system. While ethical systems, principles and axioms are time-bound, lacking the dynamic required for a contextual ethic, the biblical story provides a provocative, challenging incentive to meet the changing demands of each new age.

The prime Christian contribution to social ethics is in the indicative rather than the imperative mood . . . It is Christian belief about the kind of place the world is, about the depth of human sinfulness and the possibilities of divine grace, about judgement and hope, incarnation and salvation, God's concern for all and his care for each, about human freedom and divine purpose – it is beliefs such as these which make the difference, and provide the context within which the intractable realities of social and political life can be tackled with wisdom and integrity.[8]

It is this story, which constitutes a continuing struggle for justice and liberation under the call of God, that prompts Forrester to suggest with Barth that reflection on the Christian story

---

[7] Forrester, *Beliefs, Values and Policies*, p. 22.
[8] Habgood, *Church and Nation in a Secular Age*. Quoted in Forrester, *Beliefs, Values and Policies*, p. 28.

(theology) *is* ethics. Forrester is at the same time concerned that a closer link be established between theology and public policy. To promote ethical principles without application is both irresponsible and unintelligible. 'Principles', he insists, 'need to be tested, reconsidered, and modified in the light of the experience of trying to make them operational.'[9] It is at this encounter between theory and practice that a theology of reconstruction is located.

If middle axioms are seen as universal principles, in the sense of being applicable beyond a given time and place, the very notion would best be discarded. To the extent that the concept is employed as a *contextual* device to state the Christian imperative, discerned along the lines already defined in the earlier part of this chapter, it constitutes an important ethical facility in a theology of constructive reconstruction. Concerned to engage the church in policy formation and reconstruction, the early proponents of middle axioms (Oldham, William Temple, John Bennett and others) were by implication beginning to reach in the direction of a contextual ethic – formed not only by the Christian heritage, but also the prevailing social context. Story, tradition and biblical teaching are important. Ultimately, however, if the church is to share creatively in the reconstruction process it is obliged to translate this heritage into concrete proposals. It is required to say something 'new'. More than this, it is required to be part of a new creation, a new social order and the birth of new social, political and economic structures. Goals, principles and guidelines are not enough.

This requires the church to support certain specific political and economic proposals and not to support others. It may, where circumstances demand this, be required to make proposals of its own. In so doing it may well make some serious mistakes. These may or may not be corrected by the democratic process, leaving the church in any age (like any other social institution) to be judged by history. The biblical record states it will also be judged by God. This same record suggests that perhaps the most serious failure which the church can commit is not to be wrong in deciding which social initiative supports the

---

[9] Forrester, *Beliefs, Values and Policies*, p. 33.

common good, but to fail to support any initiative out of fear of being wrong. Such action suggests social indifference (a case of passing by on the other side of the road as the Samaritan lay bleeding). It might further suggest an archaic (medieval) residual sense of dogmatic pride which suggests it dare never be wrong, out of fear of being seen as less than a divine creation!

To stand aloof from the challenges of reconstruction, refusing to risk failure, could prove to be the most serious error the church can make in the reconstruction process. Risking itself, and going into the future without the luxury of certainty is part of the Sarahaic and Abrahamic journey to which the church is called. Other groups, political parties and individuals who are serious about reconstruction cannot escape the possibility of making mistakes. The church dare not regard itself as less vulnerable or more privileged.

Select bibliography

Ackerman, Bruce. *Social Justice in the Liberal State* (New Haven: Yale University Press, 1980).
Reconstructing American Law (Cambridge, Mass. Harvard University Press, 1984).
Ackermann, Denise. 'Women, Human Rights and Religion – A Dissonant Triad.' An unpublished Conference Paper.
Ackermann, Robert John. *Religion as Critique* (Amherst: University of Massachusetts Press, 1985).
Adams, James Luther. *Voluntary Associations (Socio-Cultural Analyses and Theological Interpretation).* (Chicago: Exploration Press, 1986).
Alperovitz, Gar. 'Building a Living Democracy', *Sojourners*, July 1990.
Altman, Andrew. *Critical Legal Studies: A Liberal Critique* (Princeton: Princeton University Press, 1990).
Arendt, Hannah. *On Revolution* (New York: Viking Press, 1965).
Austin, John. *The Province of Jurisprudence Determined* (New York: Noonday Press, 1954).
Ball, Milner S. *The Promise of American Law: A Theological Humanistic View of Legal Process* (Athens: The University of Georgia Press, 1981).
Lying Down Together: Law, Metaphor and Theology (Madison: University of Wisconsin Press, 1985).
'Stories of Origin and Constitutional Possibilities', *Michigan Law Review*, August, 1989.
Baran, Paul, A. and Sweeney, Paul M. *Monopoly Capital: An Essay on the American Economic and Social Order* (New York: Monthly Review Press, 1966).
Barnett, Richard J. and Muller, Ronald E. *Global Reach: The Power of the Multinational Corporations* (New York: Simon and Schuster, 1974).
Barry, Brian. *The Liberal Theory of Justice: A Critical Examination of the Principle Doctrines in a Theory of Justice by John Rawls*, (Oxford: Oxford University Press, 1973).

Benn, Stanley J. 'Sovereignty', in *Encyclopedia of Philosophy* (New York: Macmillan Company and the Free Press, 1967).

Bennett, John. *Christian Ethics and Social Policy* (New York: Charles Scribner's Sons, 1946).

Bentham, Jeremy, *An Introduction to the Principles of Morals and Legislation* (Garden City, New York: Anchor Books, 1973).

Berger, Raoul. 'Doctor Bonham's Case; Statutory Construction or Constitutional Theory?' *University of Pennsylvania Law Review*, 117, February 1969.

Berman, Harold. 'Religious Foundations of Law in the West: An Historical Perspective', in *Journal of Law and Religion*, 1:1, Summer 1983.

   Law and Revolution: The Formation of the Western Legal Tradition (Cambridge, Mass: Harvard University Press, 1983).

   The Interaction of Law and Religion (Nashville: Abingdon Press, 1974).

Bickel, Alexander M. *The Morality of Consent* (New Haven: Yale University Press, 1975).

Boeker, Hans Jochen. *Law and the Administration of Justice in the Old Testament and Ancient East* (Minneapolis: Augsburg, 1980).

Buchanan, Allen E. *Marx and Justice: The Radical Critique of Liberalism.* (Totowa, New Jersey: Rowman and Littlefield, 1982).

Chafee, Jr, Zechariah. *How Human Rights Got into the Constitution* (Boston: University Press, 1952).

Cobbah, Josiah A.M. 'African Values and the Human Rights Debate: An African Perspective', *Human Rights Quarterly*, 9:3, 1987.

Cohen, G.A. 'Nozick on Appropriation', in *New Left Review*, 150, 1985.

Cohen, H.E. *Recent Theories of Sovereignty* (Chicago: Chicago University Press, 1937).

Collins, Hugh *Marxism and Law* (Oxford: Oxford University Press, 1984).

Comblin, Jose. *The Church and the National Security State* (Maryknoll: Orbis Books, 1979.

Corbett, M.M. 'Human Rights: The Road Ahead', in *Human Rights: The Cape Town Conference*, edited by Forsyth C.F. and Schiller J.E. (Cape Town: Juta and Company, 1979).

Cort, John C. *Christian Socialism* (Maryknoll: Orbis Books, 1988).

Corwin, E.S. *Liberty Against Government: The Rise, Flowering and Decline of a Famous Judicial Concept.* (Baton Rouge: Louisiana State University Press, 1948).

Cosgrave, Richard A. *The Rule of Law: Albert Venn Dicey, Victorian Jurist* (Chapel Hill: University of North Carolina Press, 1980).

Cranston, Maurice. *What Are Human Rights?* (New York: Basic Books, 1962).

Cuomo, Mario. 'Religious Belief and Public Morality', an address delivered at the University of Notre Dame on 13 September 1989. Published in *Origins*, 14:15, September 1984.

Dahl, R.A. *A Preface to Economic Democracy* (Berkeley: University of California Press, 1985).

Daly, Herman H. and Cobb, John B., Jr. *For the Common Good: Redirecting the Economy Toward Community, the Environment and a Sustainable Future* (New York: Beacon Press, 1989).

Daniels, Norman (ed.) *Reading Rawls* (New York: Basic Books, n.d.).

De Klerk, Mike. 'Addressing Land Hunger: Choices for Supplying the Land', in Schrire, R.A. (ed.), *Critical Choices: Beyond the State and the Market* (Cape Town: Oxford University Press, 1991).

Dick, A.E. Howard. *The Road from Runnymede: Magna Carta and Constitutionalism in America* (Charlottesville: The University Press of Virginia, 1968).

Donnelly, Jack. 'Human Rights and Human Dignity: An Analytic Critique of Non-Western Conceptions of Human Rights', *American Political Science Review*, 76, June 1982.

Dorrien, Gary J. 'Economic Democracy: Common Goal For Liberation Movements', *Christianity and Crisis*, 50:12, 10 September 1990.

Duchrow, Ulrich. *Global Economy: A Confessional Issue for the Churches* (Geneva: WCC Press, 1986).

Dugard, John. *Human Rights and the South African Legal Order* (Princeton: Princeton University Press, 1978).

Dworkin, Ronald. 'Seven Critics', *Georgia Law Review*, 11, 1977.
Taking Rights Seriously (Cambridge, Mass: Harvard University Press, 1977).
A Matter of Principle (Cambridge, Mass: Harvard University Press, 1985).
Law's Empire (Cambridge, Mass: Harvard University Press, 1986).

Ehrlich, Eugen. *Fundamental Principles of the Society of Law* (New York: Arno Press, 1975).

Elsten, Jon and Karl Ove Moene. *Alternative to Capitalism* (Cambridge: Cambridge University Press, 1989).

Feinberg, Joel. *Social Philosophy* (Engelwood Cliffs: Prentice-Hall, 1973).

Finnis, J.M. *Natural Law and Natural Rights* (New York: Oxford University Press, 1980).

Forrester, Duncan B. *Beliefs, Values and Policies: Conviction Politics in a Secular Age* (Oxford: Clarendon Press, 1989).

Forsyth, C.F. and Schiller, J.E. (ed.) *Human Rights: The Cape Town Conference* (Cape Town: Juta and Company, 1979).

Foster, Don (with contributions from Davis Dennis and Sandler Dianne). *Detention and Torture in South Africa: Psychological, Legal and Historical Studies* (Cape Town: David Philip. New York: St Martin's Press, 1987).

Frank, Jerome N. *Law and the Modern Mind* (New York: Brentano Books, 1930).

Friedman, Milton. *Capitalism and Freedom* (Chicago: University of Chicago Press, 1962).

Frug, Gerald E. 'The City as a Legal Concept', *Harvard Law Review*, 93, April 1980.

Fuller, Lon L. 'Positivism and the Fidelity of Law – A Reply to Professor Hart', *Harvard Law Review*, 71, 1957–8.

Gierke, Otto (ed.) *Natural Law* (Boston: Beacon Press, 1957).

Gray, Alexander. *The Development of Economic Doctrine: An Introductory Survey* (London: Longman, 1980).

Habermas, Jürgen. *Legitimation Crisis* (Boston Press, 1971).

Hahlo, H.R. and Kahn Ellison (eds.), *The Union of South Africa: The Development of Its Laws and Constitution*. Volume 5 in Keeton George W. (gen. ed.) *The British Commonwealth: The Development of Its Laws and Constitution*. (London: Stevens and Sons. Cape Town: Juta and Company, 1960).

Harrelson, Walter. *The Ten Commandments and Human Rights* (Philadelphia: Fortress Press, 1980).

Harris, J.W. *Legal Philosophies* (London: Butterworths, 1980).

Hart, H.L.A. 'Are There Any Natural Rights?', *Philosophical Review*, 64, 1955.

'Positivism and the Separation of Law and Morals', *Harvard Law Review*, 71, 1957–8.

The Concept of Law (New York: Oxford University Press, 1965).

Henkin, Louis. *The Rights of Man Today* (New York: The Center for the Study of Human Rights, Columbia University, 1988).

The Age of Rights (New York: Oxford University Press, 1965).

Hennelly, Alfred and Langan, John. *Human Rights in the Americas: The Struggle for Consensus* (Washington DC: Georgetown University Press, 1982).

Hinchman, Lewis P. 'The Origins of Human Rights: A Hegelian Perspective', *Western Political Quarterly*, 37, March 1984.

Hinkelammert, Franz J. *The Ideological Weapons of Death* (Maryknoll: Orbis Books, 1986).

Hollenbach, David. *Claims in Conflict: Retrieving and Renewing the Catholic Human Rights Tradition*. (New York, Paulist Press, 1979).

Howard, Rhoda. 'Evaluating Human Rights in Africa: Some Problems of Implicit Comparisons', *Human Rights Quarterly*, 6, May 1984.

Jackson, Bernard. 'The Ceremonial and the Judicial Biblical Law as Sign and Symbol', *Journal for the Study of the Old Testament*, 30, 1984.

Jenkins, Iredell. 'From Natural to Legal to Human Rights', in Pollack, Erwin H. (ed.), *Human Rights* (Buffalo: Jay Stewart, 1971).

Jennings, Ivor. *The Law and the Constitution* (London: University of London Press, 1956).

John XIII. *Pacem in Terris*, Nos 9–27 in Joseph Gremillion (ed.), *The Gospel of Peace and Justice: Catholic Social Teaching Since Pope John* (Maryknoll: Orbis Books, 1976).

John Paul II in Mexico: His Collected Speeches (London: Collins, 1979).

John Paul II. 'Opening Address at Pueblo', in Eagleson, John and Scharper, Philip (eds.), *Pueblo and Beyond* (Maryknoll: Orbis Books, 1979).

Reconciliation and Penance (Reconciliatio et Paenitentis) (Washington DC: US Catholic Conference, 1984).

Centesimus Annus (Vatican City: Libreria Editrice Vaticana, 1991).

Kahn, Ellison. *The New Constitution: Being a Supplement to South Africa: The Development of Its Laws and Constitution* (London: Stevens and Sons. Cape Town: Juta and Co, 1962).

Kelman, Mark. *A Guide to Critical Legal Studies* (Cambridge: Harvard University Press, 1987).

Kelsen, Hans. *General Theory of Law and State* (Cambridge: Harvard University Press, 1945).

Kent, Edward Allen. 'Taking Human Rights Seriously', in Tammy, Martin and Irani, K.D. (eds.), *Rationality in Thought and Action* (New York: Greenwood Press, 1986).

Klein, R. *Israel in Exile* (Minneapolis: Fortress, 1979).

Kolakowski, Leszek and Hampshire, Stuart. *The Socialist Idea* (London: Weidenfeld and Nicolson, 1974).

Langan, John. 'Personal Responsibility and Common Good in John Paul II.' A paper delivered at Claremont Graduate School, Claremont, California, 2–3 February 1990.

Lash, Nicholas. *A Matter of Hope: A Theologian's Reflections on the Thought of Karl Marx* (Notre Dame: University of Notre Dame Press, 1981).

Lasky, Melvin J. *Utopia and Revolution* (Chicago and London: University of Chicago Press, 1976).

Lategan, Bernard. Kinghorn, Johann, du Plessis, Lourens. de Villers, Etienne. *The Option for Inclusive Democracy: A Theological–Ethical Study of Appropriate Social Values for South Africa* (Stellenbosch: Centre for Hermeneutics, Stellenbosch University, 1987).

Le Roux, Pieter. 'The Case for a Social Democratic Compromise', in Nattrass, N. and Ardington, E. (eds.), *The Political Economy of*

South Africa (Cape Town: Oxford University Press, 1990).

Leatt, James. 'Neither Adam Smith nor Karl Marx', in Albeldas Michel and Fischer, Alan (eds.), *A Question of Survival: Conversations with Key South Africans* (Johannesburg: Jonathan Ball Publishers, 1987).

Lebacqz, Karen. *Six Theories of Justice: Perspectives From Philosophical and Theological Ethics* (Minneapolis: Augsburg Press, 1986).

Justice in an Unjust World: Foundations for a Christian Approach to Justice (Minneapolis: Augsburg, 1987).

Lehmann, Paul. *The Transfiguration of Politics* (New York: Harper and Row, 1975).

Lewin, Julius. *Politics and Law in South Africa* (London: Merlin Press, 1963).

Lissner, Jorgen and Sovik, Aren (eds.), *A Lutheran Reader on Human Rights* (Geneva: Lutheran World Federation, 1978).

Lochman, Jan Milic. 'Human Rights from a Christian Perspective', in Miller, Allen O. (ed.), *'A Christian Declaration on Human Rights: Theological Studies of World Alliance of Reformed Churches'*,(Grand Rapids: Eerdmans, 1977).

Lutheran World Federation, *Theological Perspectives on Human Rights*, (Geneva: Lutheran World Federation, 1977).

M'Timkulu, D. *Africa in Transition: The Challenge and the Christian Response* (Geneva: AACC and WCC, 1962).

Malthus, Thomas. *An Essay in the Principle of Population* (New York: A.M. Kelley, 1965).

Mandela, Nelson. 'Black man in a White Court – First Court Statement', in *The Struggle is My Life* (London: International Defence and Aid Fund, 1986).

Mathews, Anthony. *Freedom, State Security and the Rule of Law: Dilemmas of the Apartheid Society.* (Cape Town: Juta and Co. 1986).

Law, Order and Liberty in South Africa (Berkeley: University of California Press, 1972).

Meeks, Douglas M. *God the Economist. The Doctrine of God and Political Economy* (Minneapolis: Fortress Press, 1973).

Miller, Allen O. (ed.), *A Christian Declaration on Human Rights* (Grand Rapids: Eerdmans, 1977).

Miller, William Lee. *The First Liberty: Religion and the American Republic* (New York: Paragon House Publishers, 1988).

Molteno, Donald B. 'The Rhodesian Crisis and the Courts', in *The Comparative and International Law Journal of Southern Africa*, 2:2, July 1969.

Moll, Peter, Nattrass, Nico and Loots, Lieb (eds.), *Redistribution: How can it Work in South Africa?* (Cape Town: David Philips, 1991).

Moltmann, Jürgen. 'The Original Study Paper: A Theological Basis of Human Rights and of the Liberation of Human Beings', in Miller Allen O. (ed.), *A Christian Declaration on Human Rights* (Grand Rapids: Eerdmans, 1977).

On Human Dignity: Political Theology and Ethics (Philadelphia: Fortress Press, 1984).

Muller, Alois and Greinacher, Norbert. *The Church and the Rights of Man* (New York: Seabury Press, 1979).

Murchland, Bernard. *The Dream of Christian Socialism: An Essay on its European Origins* (Washington: American Enterprise Institute for Public Policy Research, 1982).

Neuhaus, Richard John (ed.), *Law and the Ordering of Our Life Together* (Grand Rapids: Eerdmans, 1989).

Niebuhr, H. Richard. *Christ and Culture* (New York: Harper Torchbooks, 1951).

Niebuhr, Reinhold. *The Children of Light and the Children of Darkness* (New York: Scribner's 1944).

Nove, Alec. *The Economics of Feasible Socialism* (London: Allen and Unwin, 1983).

Nozick, Robert. *Anarchy, State and Utopia* (New York: Basic Books, 1974).

Ojo, Olusola and Sesay, Amadu. 'The OAU and Human Rights: Prospects for the 1980s and Beyond', *Human Rights Quarterly*, 8:1, 1986.

Olafson, Frederick A. 'Two Views of Pluralism: Liberal and Catholic', *Yale Review* 51, 1962.

Olafson, Frederick A. (ed.), *Society, Law and Morality* (Engelwood Cliffs: Prentice Hall, 1961).

Pashukanis, E.B. *Selected Writings on Marxism and the Law* (New York: Academic Press, 1980).

Paul VI. *On the Development of Peoples (Populorum Progressio)* (Washington DC: United States Catholic Conference, 1967).

Phillips, Anthony. *Ancient Israel's Criminal Law* (Oxford: Blackwell, 1970).

Phillips, Derek L. *Toward a Just Social Order* (Princeton: Princeton University Press, 1986).

Pinkard, Terry. *Democratic Liberalism and Social Union* (Philadelphia: Temple University Press, 1987).

Polanyi, Karl. *The Great Transformation: The Political and Economic Origins of our Time* (Boston: Beacon Press, 1967).

The Livelihood of Man, edited by Pearson, Harry W. (New York: Academic Press, 1977).

Pollack, Erwin H. (ed.) *Human Rights* (Buffalo: Jay Steward, 1971).

Pontifical Commission 'Justitia et Pax', *The Church and Human Rights* (Vatican City, 1975).

Poulantzas, Nicos. 'Towards a Democratic Socialism', in D. Held (ed.) *States and Society* (Oxford University Press, 1990).

Preston, Ronald H. *Church and Society in the Late Twentieth Century: The Economic and Political Task* (London: SCM Press, 1983).

Raitt, T. *A Theology of Exile* (Minneapolis: Augsburg, 1977).

Raphael, D.D. (ed.) *Political Theory and the Rights of Man* (Bloomington: Indiana University Press, 1967).

Rawls, John. *A Theory of Justice* (Cambridge, Mass: Harvard University Press, 1971).

Redhead, Steve. 'Marxist Theory, the Rule of Law and Socialism', in Beirne, Piers and Quinney, Richard (ed.), *Marxism and Law* (New York: John Wiley and Sons, 1982).

Robertson, Mike. *Human Rights for South Africans* (Cape Town: Oxford University Press, 1991).

Roll, Eric. *A History of Economic Thought* (London: Faber and Faber, 1987).

Rosecrance, Richard. *The Rise of the Trading State: Commerce and Conquest in the Modern World* (New York: Basic Books, 1987).

Ross, W.D. *The Right and the Good* (Oxford: Clarendon Press, 1930).

Sachs, Albie. 'Towards a Bill of Rights for a Democratic South Africa', *The Hastings International and Comparative Law Review*, 12, Winter 1989.

'A Bill of Rights for South Africa: Areas of Agreement and Disagreement', *Columbia Human Rights Law Review*, 21:1, Fall 1989.

Protecting Human Rights in a New South Africa (Cape Town: Oxford University Press, 1990).

Sibley, Mulford Q. 'Religion and Law: Some Thoughts on Their Intersections', *Journal of Law and Religion*, 11:1, 1984.

Schrire, R.A. *Critical Choices: Beyond the State and Market* (Cape Town: Oxford University Press, 1991).

Schumpeter, J.A. *Capitalism, Socialism and Democracy* (New York: Harper and Row, 1962).

Sennett, R. and Cobb, J. *The Hidden Injuries of Class* (New York: Knopf, 1973).

Sharlet, R. 'Pashukanis and the Withering Away of Law in the USSR', in Fitzpatrick S. (ed.), *Cultural Revolution in Russia 1928–1931* (Bloomington: Indiana University Press, 1978).

Shroyer, Trent. *The Critique of Domination: The Origins and Development of Critical Theory* (New York: Brazilier, 1973).

Sieghart, Paul. *The International Law of Human Rights* (Oxford: Clarendon Press, 1983).

Simkins, Charles. *Reconstructing South African Liberalism* (Johannesburg: South African Institute of Race Relations, 1987).

Slovo, Joe. *Has Socialism Failed?* (London: Inkululeko Publications, 1990).

Stackhouse, Max. *Creeds, Society and Human Rights* (Grand Rapids: Eerdmans, 1984).

Public Theology and Political Economy (Grand Rapids: Eerdmans, 1987).

Strauss, Leo. *Natural Rights and History* (Chicago: University of Chicago Press, 1953).

Sweeney, Paul M. *Modern Capitalism and Other Essays* (New York: Monthly Review Press, 1972).

Sweezy, Paul. 'Karl Marx and the Industial Revolution', in *Modern Capitalism and Other Essays* (New York: Monthly Review Press, 1972).

The Pontifical Commission 'Justitia et Pax', *The Church and Human Rights* (Vatican City, 1975); John Paul II, *On Social Concern (Sollicitudo rei Socialis)* (Washington DC: US Catholic Conference, 1988).

Theological Studies Department of the Federation of Protestant Churches in the German Democratic Republic. 'Theological Aspects of Human Rights', *WCC Exchange*, 6 (December, 1977).

Thomas, M.M. *Christian Participation in Nation-Building: The Summing Up of a Corporate Study on Rapid Social Change* (Bangalore: National Christian Council of India and Christian Institute for the Study of Religion and Society, 1960).

Thompson, E.P. *Whigs and Hunters: The Origin of the Black Act* (New York: Pantheon Books, 1975).

The Poverty of Theory and Other Essays. (London: Merlin Publishers, 1978).

Thompson, L.M. *The Unification of South Africa: 1902–1910* (Oxford: The Clarendon Press, 1960).

Tillich, Paul. *The Socialist Decision* (New York: Harper and Row, 1977).

Tödt, Heinz-Eduard. 'Theological Reflections on the Foundations of Human Rights', *Lutheran World*, 24:1, 1977.

Unger, Roberto. *Knowledge and Politics* (New York: Free Press, 1975). See discussion in Altman.

The Critical Legal Studies Movement (Cambridge: Harvard University Press, 1986).

Social Theory: Its Situation and Its Task (Cambridge: Cambridge University Press, 1987).

False Necessity: Anti Necessitarian Social Theory in the Service of Radical

Democracy (Cambridge: Cambridge University Press, 1987).

United Church of Christ in the United States of America, 'A Pronouncement on Human Rights', in Alfred Hennelly, S.J. and Langan, John. (eds.), *Human Rights in the Americas: The Struggle for Consensus* (Washington DC: Georgetown University Press, 1982).

United Nations, *A Compilation of International Instruments* (New York: United Nations Organisation, 1988).

US Catholic Bishops, *Economic Justice for All: Pastoral Letter on Catholic Social Teaching and the US Economy* (Washington DC: National Conference of Catholic Bishops, 1986).

Van der Vyver, J.D. 'Depriving Westminster of Its Moral Constraints: A Survey of Constitutional Developments in South Africa', in *Harvard Civil Rights–Civil Liberties Law Review*, 20:2, Summer, 1985.

'Group and Human Rights', *South African Law Journal*, 106, 1989.

Villa-Vicencio, Charles. 'Theology, Law and State Legitimacy', in *Journal of Law and Religion*, 5:2, 1987.

Civil Disobedience and Beyond: Law Resistance and Religion in South Africa (Grand Rapids: Eerdmans. Cape Town: David Philip, 1990.

Visser 't Hooft, W.A. and Oldham, J.H. *The Church and Its Function in Society* (Chicago: Willet, Clarke and Co. 1937).

Vogel, Howard J. 'A Survey and Commentary on the New Literature in Law and Religion', *Journal of Religion and Law*, 1:1, 1983.

Von Hayek, Friedrich A. *The Road to Serfdom* (Chicago: Chicago University Press, 1980).

Von Mises, Ludwig. *The Ultimate Foundation of Economic Science: An Essay on Method* (Princeton: D. Van Nostrand Co., 1962).

The Free and Prosperous Commonwealth: An Exposition of the Ideas of Classical Liberalism (Princeton: D. Van Nostrand Co., 1962).

Wai, Dunstan M. 'Human Rights in Sub-Saharan Africa', in Pollis, Adamantia and Schwab, Peter (eds.), *Human Rights: Cultural and Ideological Perspectives* (New York: Praeger, 1979).

Wallerstein, Immanuel. *The Modern World System* (New York: Academic Press, 1980, 3 vols. (Historical Capitalism* (London: Verso, 1983; Charles Scribner's Sons, 1958).

Walzer, Michael. *Spheres of Justice* (New York: Basic Books, 1983).

Welch, Don. *Law and Morality* (Philadelphia: Fortress Press, 1987).

WCC, *Human Rights and Christian Responsibility*, vols 1–3 (Geneva: WCC-CCIA, 1975).

WCC, *Human Rights a Challenge to Theology* (Rome: CIIA/WCC and IDOC International, 1983).

Welsh, David. 'Constitutional Changes in South Africa', *African Affairs*, 83:331, April 1984.

West, Cornel. *The American Evasion of Philosophy: A Genealogy of Pragmatism* (Madison: The University of Wisconsin Press, 1989).

Wilson, Francis and Ramphele, Mamphela. *Uprooting Poverty: The South African Challenge* (Cape Town: David Philip, 1989).

Witte, John. 'The Study of Law and Religion: An Apologia and Agenda', *Ministry and Mission*, 14:4 (Fall 1988).

Wogaman, J. Philip. *The Great Economic Debate: An Ethical Analysis* (Philadelphia: Westminster Press, 1977).

Economics and Ethics: A Christian Inquiry (Philadelphia: Fortress Press, 1986).

Wolff, Robert P. *Understanding Rawls: A Reconstruction and Critique of a Theory of Justice* (Princeton: Princeton University Press, 1977).

Wood, James E. *et al. Church and State in Scripture, History and Constitutional Law* (Waco: Baylor University Press, 1958).

Wood, James E (ed.). *The First Freedom: Religion and the Bill of Rights* (Waco: Baylor University Press, 1990).

Index

296